VICTIMS OF VIOLENCE

A Liverpool housewife and mother, Joan Jonker became increasingly concerned about the rise in crime and the soft approach to punishing offenders. She believed that if people were taught right from wrong, they would not be able to offend.

Joan set up the charity Victims of Violence in 1976 and over the years she helped twelve thousand victims, raised thousands of pounds and opened the first shelters for victims in the country. The support she received was often so overwhelming that there were many people as concerned as she was. She was forthright and unafraid to speak out, for she was the one to witness at first hand broken bones and shattered spirits. She attracted media attention, public support and honours for her work, but her many trips to the House of Commons bore no fruit and to some she remained an irritation. This is her story of courage and compassion in the face of adversity.

VICTIMS OF VIOLENCE

Joan Jonker

First published 1986
by
Fontana Paperbacks
This Large Print edition published 2004
by arrangement with Headline Book Publishing
Limited

ISBN 0 7540 9529 0 ~~(Windsor Hardcover)~~
~~ISBN 0 7540 9417 0~~ (Paragon Softcover)

British Library Cataloguing in Publication Data available

Printed and bound in Great Britain by
Antony Rowe Ltd., Chippenham, Wiltshire

DEDICATION

I dedicate this book to my late husband, Tony, for allowing me the freedom to carry out my work with victims of crime and violence. And to the thousands of wonderful, generous people who have supported me over the last twenty-six years, from clubs, pubs, shops and voluntary organizations as well as the man and woman in the street. They are far too numerous to mention individually, but I shall be forever in their debt.

There are a few I must mention in particular, though, because without them the charity would never have survived. Sir William and Lady Butlin supported me from the start, becoming Patrons of the charity. And after Sir William's death, Sheila Butlin has been there for me, to help financially, to lend a sympathetic ear, and now as one of my dearest friends. Lorna Cooper and Bernice Styles too, whose selflessness and commitment deserve the highest praise for without them the Victims of Violence charity would not have survived from 1976–2002.

Also, I would like to thank Ralph and Jackie Mosoph for agreeing to tell me their story; it must have been so painful for them to relive their tragedy.

INTRODUCTION

1984

'But the worst thing that happened to me was two weeks ago, when they cut my dog's throat.'

I leaned forward, thinking I must have misunderstood. 'Did you say they cut your dog's throat?'

Mrs Wycombe nodded, too overcome to answer. Fighting back the tears, she said, 'The vet said they had hung it on the line with a piece of thin wire and it had cut the poor thing's throat. She also said they must have beaten it while it was hanging there because its jaw and legs were broken.'

I was horrified. 'How could anyone do that to an animal?'

She handed me a photograph of a small white poodle. 'That's him. I had him for twelve years and he was my friend. I used to talk to him because you get lonely when you live alone. Now he's gone and I do miss him.'

I had been given Mrs Wycombe's name by Eileen of the CID in one of the police stations I ring each day as part of a Victim Support Scheme. She had given me three names today, and Mrs Wycombe was my first call. 'I've been told you've been burgled four times?' I continued.

She sighed and nodded. 'Last night they came in here when I was asleep. I'm frightened now because I think it was someone local who killed my dog. They probably did it so they could get in easier without it barking.' She was silent for a while, then said, 'It must have been someone living nearby because I only let the dog out in the back garden.'

She was a lovely lady, her pure white hair combed into a bun on top of her head, neatly dressed, and I noticed how well kept her hands and nails were. In an effort to cheer her up, I said, 'You look lovely. I hope I look like you when I get to seventy-nine years of age.'

With a sad smile, she said, 'I try to look after myself, I still have some pride left.'

We chatted for a while and I found out that Mrs Wycombe was partially sighted, a semi-invalid who could only walk with the aid of two sticks. She had lived in the same house for over fifty years, but now she was afraid and wanted to get out. The cowards who had attacked her had taken all her pleasure in life away and she no longer felt safe here.

When I left to visit the other victims, I promised to call and see her again. I gave her my phone number so she could ring me any time she needed help or felt like talking to someone.

Then I called on the other two victims, one of burglary and one who had had her bag snatched. Both were elderly people who had been left shaken and afraid, and the woman who'd had her bag stolen had been left penniless. I gave her ten pounds to see her over until her next pension day, and she was so grateful I felt very emotional. There had to be something very wrong in a society that allowed thugs to go unpunished while their victim could starve for all those in authority cared. The do-gooders and penal reformers had a lot to answer for, to my mind. They maintained they knew best, but any working-class housewife and

2

mother who had raised children seemed to have more common sense than they did.

Driving home I couldn't get Ann Wycombe out of my mind. I felt so sad and depressed, I voiced my thoughts aloud. 'After eight years and six thousand victims, you'd think it wouldn't affect me any more.' Then I told myself that if the time ever came when I wasn't affected by the sight of an elderly person crying, that would be the time for me to pack in.

I had started a chain of thought, though. Was it really eight years since I'd sat in my friend's kitchen and she'd told me about Mr Smith? I had only called in for a cup of coffee and a natter, but it was a visit that was to change my whole life and make me look more closely at the society I lived in. I didn't like what I saw, and I feared for the future.

CHAPTER ONE

1976

'Have another before you go.' Jean had picked up the cups and carried them to the sink before I could stop her.

'It's nearly three o'clock,' I said. 'I want to be home in time to get the dinner ready.'

'Just a quick one,' Jean coaxed, 'it won't take five minutes.'

We were sitting in the kitchen of my friend's small terraced house, which had been modernized and extended. Friends for eighteen years, since she had come to work for me in the grocer's shop I had opened near her home, we much enjoyed each other's company because we had the same sense of humour and laughed at the same things. We weren't laughing now, though. 'Did you read in the *Echo* last night about the old man who was attacked in his house?' Jean asked me over her shoulder.

'Yes, I did,' I answered. 'Every night the paper is full of reports of attacks on elderly people, sometimes to steal as little as fifty pence.'

Jean was frowning as she passed me the coffee cup. 'This one only lives around the corner, and I believe he's a lovely old man.'

'Does he live on his own?'

When she nodded, I went on, 'There's something wrong with the sort of thugs who attack elderly people. Apart from being cowards, they must have no human feelings at all. And there's no point in making excuses for them. How can there

5

be an excuse for robbing the elderly?'

We were on my pet subject now. I felt very strongly about what was happening in our society— so strongly, in fact, that I was heavily involved with the Campaign for Law and Order, an organization that had been set up by people like myself who believed the increase in crime was due to offenders knowing that if they were caught they would be entitled, free of charge, to the services of a solicitor, one who had never seen the victim so couldn't really assess the seriousness of the offence. His only interest in the case would be getting his client off the hook. And there are many solicitors who are well known to the criminal fraternity for getting them off even when they know the offender is guilty. I have heard lads as young as fifteen saying, 'I'm going to see me brief, he'll get me off.' But who can get the victim off? Who can give them back the things that were stolen from them? Money, treasured mementos of a loved one, any pleasure they may have had in life, leaving only pain and heartache.

The offender will also have a probation officer assigned to him, to make sure his human rights are not infringed. No such luxury for the elderly man or woman who has been attacked and robbed in their own home and will never again feel safe.

'It's getting bad around here,' Jean said, running her fingers through her hair. 'Every day you hear of more people being burgled or mugged.'

'It's bound to get worse, it stands to reason,' I told her. 'Look at children's behaviour. If they think they can get away with being naughty then they'll carry on and be more and more badly behaved.' I drained my cup. 'I'll have to go or I'll never have the dinner ready.'

Jean walked to the door with me and watched as I crossed the narrow street to where my car was parked. I was putting the key in the lock when I called to her, 'Where does this elderly man live?'

'Just around the corner.' Jean pointed down the street. 'I think it's the house next to the sweet shop.'

'I wonder whether I should call and see if he needs any help?'

My friend pulled a face. 'I wouldn't! I wouldn't know what to say.'

I drove down the street to the busy main road. While I was waiting for a break in the traffic, my eyes searched for, and found, the sweet shop that Jean had mentioned. When the road was clear I pulled out and parked opposite the shop and adjacent house. I switched off the engine and sat looking at the tall, narrow terraced house. I thought of Jean's words about not knowing what to say, and wondered what the elderly man's reaction would be to a stranger knocking on his door after his terrifying experience.

I made up my mind quickly. There was only one way to find out if he needed help, and that was to ask him. So before I had time to change my mind, I locked the car door and crossed the wide road to stand outside his house. That was when my nerve deserted me. Would I frighten him? I certainly wouldn't want to do that. Through the shop window, I could see there were no customers in there at that moment, only a man stocking shelves. Perhaps he could give me some information, I thought, and pushed the shop door open.

'Excuse me,' I said nervously, 'I heard that the

7

man next door had been hurt in a robbery and wondered if he needed any help?'

The man looked at me suspiciously. 'Do you know him?'

'No, but my friend Jean Herrity, who lives in the next street, told me about him.' When he still didn't answer, I went on, 'Look, I know it sounds crazy but I really would like to help him if he needs it.'

The suspicious expression faded and the man said, 'His name's Albert Smith, and there's no harm in knocking on his door and asking.'

I thanked him and walked to the house next-door. Without giving myself time to get cold feet I lifted the heavy brass knocker and gave two knocks. Little did I know then that this visit was to change my whole life.

I heard footsteps walking down the hall and then the door was opened cautiously by an elderly lady. I said quickly, 'My name's Joan Jonker, love, and I've come to see if Mr Smith needs any help.'

The door was opened wider. 'Come in, dear.'

I waited until the front door was closed then followed her down a narrow hall decorated in the dark greens and browns which had been fashionable decades ago. The first thing I noticed when I entered the living room was the coal fire burning brightly in the huge old-fashioned black range.

She bent over a man sitting in a chair at the fireside. 'There's someone to see you, Albert.'

'Hello, Mr Smith,' I said softly. 'I'm from Maghull but my friend lives around the corner and she told me what happened. I've called to see if there's anything you need?'

The woman waved me to a chair facing him. He

8

was obviously very nervous and agitated, clasping and unclasping his hands. There were bruises round his eyes and on his forehead, and his eyes were watering so much he appeared to be constantly crying. He was neatly dressed, however, his shirt spotlessly clean and his hair combed into place.

Wiping his eyes with a large handkerchief, he said, 'I can't see properly, but I expect I'll be all right in a couple of days.'

'I'm surprised you can see at all after what they did to you.' The woman's voice was full of anger as she turned to me. 'Two of them had him on the floor, kicking him in the face.'

'What happened exactly?' I asked Mr Smith, but it was the woman who answered.

'We were watching television the night before last when we heard this terrible bang. Albert went into the hall to see what it was and the two men who'd booted the door in pushed him to the floor and started kicking him. I went out to see what the noise was, and when I saw these men kicking Albert in the face I just started screaming.'

Mr Smith took up the story. 'I didn't have a chance to do anything. I saw the men, then the next thing I knew I was on the floor and they were kicking me in the head and body.' As he spoke, he automatically shielded his face. 'All I could do was put my arms up to try and protect myself.'

As I listened, my stomach was churning with a mixture of anger and pity.

'My screaming must have frightened them,' the woman said. 'They'd burst the front door open so anyone passing would have heard me. They snatched my necklace, took the rings from my

9

finger and fled.'

'What happened then?' I asked.

'I don't really know,' she answered, 'everything was so confused and I was hysterical.'

'Someone must have heard the screams and called the police,' Mr Smith said.

'Have you seen a doctor?' I asked, noticing his continual wiping of his eyes.

'The police sent for an ambulance and the hospital wanted to keep me in for observation, but I wouldn't stay.'

The woman shook her head. 'He was worried about me being here on my own.'

'Do you live here, love?' I asked.

'Call me Ann,' she insisted. 'No, I live in London. Me and Albert's wife were friends from school days, and although she's been dead for many years I still come up once a year to see him.'

'It's a good job you were here,' I told her, shuddering at the thought of him being alone.

'God knows what would have happened to him if I hadn't been, they'd have killed him.'

I looked around the room, wondering what on earth the thieves had expected to steal. The furniture, though clean and well looked after, was of no great value. I didn't think it was worth more than a few pounds. That is to anyone but Albert, who probably cherished it for the memories it held.

Along the high mantelpiece there was a parade of old photographs, and I found myself staring at one of a young man in army uniform. 'Is that you, Mr Smith?'

I could hear the pride in his voice as he answered, 'Yes, that was in the First World War.'

'You were a very handsome lad,' I said. 'Can I

10

ask how old you are now?'

'I'm eighty-seven, and if I'd been any younger, those thugs wouldn't have got away with it.'

'How are you feeling now?'

It was Ann who answered me. 'I'm terrified! I don't think I'll ever get over it. I ought to go home, but I can't leave Albert in this state.'

'I'll be all right in a couple of days,' he insisted. 'Once these bruises go, I'll be able to see properly.'

I had a thought and asked, 'Have you had your front door made safe?'

Albert struggled to his feet. 'Come with me.'

As I followed the frail figure down the hall, I had a sudden, horrific picture in my mind of him huddled on the floor trying to protect himself. We reached the front door and Mr Smith picked up a stout piece of wood that was propped up against it. He handed it to me, saying, 'I'm keeping this here to protect myself if anyone tries to break in.'

I smiled at him as he replaced the wood. I wasn't going to tell this once proud soldier that he was too old and frail to protect himself against thugs without mercy or compassion.

When we got back to the kitchen, I asked Ann, 'Have you got enough food in?'

'Yes, and I can get his messages in. I'll stay for a few days until he's better.'

'I can run to the shops for you, if you like.'

Mr Smith shook his head. 'It's very kind of you to come and see me, but we'll manage.'

Impulsively, I bent down and kissed his cheek. 'Look after yourself. I'll call again some time and hope you'll be feeling better by then.'

At the front door, Ann said bitterly, 'I hope the men that did that to him get their just deserts.

11

Fancy doing that to a man of his age who has never hurt anyone in his life.'

Perhaps Ann's white hair and comfortable figure reminded me of my mother. I put my arm around her as if I knew her well. I felt so many emotions filling my heart: compassion, pity and, uppermost, anger. 'He's lucky to have a friend like you,' I told her.

She stood at the door waving as I drove away. I could feel the tears burning behind my eyelids. All the way home I went over the incident and always I came back to that horrific impression of Albert lying on the floor, watching those heavy boots coming towards his face.

*　　　*　　　*

I was late home that day, and had just put the potatoes on to boil when my son Philip came in. He is mentally handicapped, and goes each day to a training centre. The bus drops him off outside our house which saves me waiting at a bus stop for him. He was twenty-six then, the most placid, good-natured person I had ever met. When he was born and Tony and I were told he was handicapped, we thought it was the end of the world. Nobody told us, in fact nobody knew, how badly affected he would be, and Tony and I suffered many years of heartache and worry. There was in fact no need because Philip turned out to be so selfless, so loving, with such a marvellous sense of humour, that he brought a lot of love and happiness into our lives. We knew he would never lead a normal life and would always live with us, but now saw this as a bonus in our lives. We also had a younger son, Paul,

12

married to Pauline and living just a few miles up the road in Ormskirk.

When Tony came in from work he asked, as he usually does, what I had been doing with myself all day. It was only a few months since I had sold my three greengrocer's shops and I wasn't used to a lazy life. I think Tony thought I would soon get bored being at home, and was expecting to come home one night to find I'd opened another shop.

While we were eating our meal I told him about my visit to Albert Smith and Ann. He listened attentively while I told him all the details of what had happened to them, then shook his head, saying, 'It's terrible, love, but don't get yourself upset, there's nothing you can do.'

'It's about time somebody did something,' I replied, heatedly. 'Those thugs not only broke his front door, they broke his pride and his spirit.' I suddenly realized Philip was listening so I changed the subject. My son hated to see anyone hurt or upset and I didn't want to worry him. The incident wasn't mentioned again that night, but when I went to bed I just tossed and turned, unable to chase away the thoughts of Albert and Ann, probably too frightened to go to sleep after what they'd been through.

*　　　*　　　*

When I was still thinking of them a week later, I decided to visit them again and put my mind at rest.

Ann opened the door to me, and I said, 'Hello, love, it's Joan Jonker, I called last week.'

'Yes, I remember you, you're the lady from

13

Maghull.' She opened the door wider to let me pass. 'Come in, love, it's nice to see you.'

As I followed her to the living room, I said, 'You've got a good memory.'

'It wasn't difficult, there's been nobody else over the doorstep since you came.' ·

I greeted Albert with a kiss before turning back to Ann. 'Do you mean that nobody has been to see if Albert needed any help?'

She shook her head. 'There's been nobody since you last week.'

I couldn't believe it. What was happening to our society, was there no sympathy or compassion any more? I looked at Albert and saw the bruises had faded a little, but his eyes were still red and watery. 'How d'you feel now, Albert?'

'I'm less sore,' he told me, 'but I still can't see out of this eye.' He indicated his left one. 'The other is still blurred, too,' he added.

'I can't believe no one has been to see if you need help.' I shook my head. This was all wrong.

'That's why I'm still here,' Ann told me. 'I should be back home in London by now.'

Albert stood up to go to the kitchen and I noticed how he gripped the end of the table until he was near enough to the door to hold on to it for support.

'I'm worried about him,' Ann said softly when he was out of earshot. 'He can't see properly and I don't know how I can go home and leave him.'

'Doesn't he have any family?'

'He's got a son, but he goes out to work and has a family to care for. We haven't seen him since the night it happened and the police sent for him.'

'How old are you, Ann?' I asked gently.

14

'I'm eighty-three, and I've never felt my age until now. I feel really old and tired. I'll never be able to make the journey up here again.'

Albert came back into the room then and we talked for a while about the old days. 'When we were young,' Ann said, 'nobody had anything, but we helped each other. Today, everyone seems so selfish and greedy.'

Memories came flooding back of my own childhood. While considerably younger than these two lovely people, I could nevertheless remember the two-up-two-down terraced houses with the lavatory at the bottom of the yard. There were no lights down there, and all sorts of creepy-crawlies. Money was scarce in those days, but what our family lacked in material things my parents made up for with love and kindness. And, most important, everyone in the family was blessed with a good sense of humour. 'We'll never see the likes of those days again, I'm afraid,' I said as I got to my feet. 'Where we used to help each other, the thugs of today help themselves.'

*   *   *

When I visited Albert the following week he was alone. Ann had finally gone back to London. The house seemed empty without her, and Albert seemed ill at ease with me at first. Then he showed me into the front parlour and when I admired the room he seemed to relax and was pleased with my comments on the old-fashioned plant stand and the beautiful fire screen. He was meticulously tidy, and I felt like hugging him because in spite of his ordeal at the hands of men who would never match him for honesty, integrity and bravery, he had no intention of lowering his standards.

I asked how he was coping, and he told me he still couldn't see out of his left eye, but with the help of a walking stick he managed to get to the shops for his groceries and to put a bet on. 'I miss reading the papers,' he admitted. 'I like to have a bet every day, but I can't see the list of runners even with the help of a magnifying glass my son brought.'

'You should see a doctor,' I told him, though in fact I had grave doubts about his ever again having the sight of his left eye. 'He could give you some advice.'

'I'll be all right.' Albert appeared eager to get back to the kitchen to write out his bet, so I didn't stay long that day. But I thought about him a lot, and I think it was because he had affected me so much. Once a proud soldier fighting for his country, he'd been reduced to a state of powerlessness against thugs who would be too scared to face someone who might fight back. Albert had fought for a better world for these men, and they were destroying it.

The following week when I called on him, he took me straight through to the kitchen where newspapers were spread out on the table. 'I'm just doing my bet,' he told me, holding the magnifying glass over the racing section. I watched as he picked up a stub of pencil and, eyes two inches from the betting slip, slowly wrote out his bet. When he had finished he put the slip of paper in his jacket pocket and picked up the coat that was draped over a chair. As he slipped his arms in, he asked, 'Did you hear that a lady was mugged over the road yesterday?'

I shook my head. 'I hadn't heard, no. Is she elderly?'

'I only know her by sight,' he said. 'I'd say she was in her late-seventies.'

'Do you know where she lives?'

'I don't know the address, but I know the house. I'll point it out to you if you like.'

A few minutes later we stood at the end of Albert's block and he pointed to a house in a side street. 'The one with railings round, I think that's where she lives.'

'Do you want me to come to the shop with you?' I asked.

Proud as ever, he shook his head. 'No, I'll be all right, it's not far.'

I stood for a while watching him walk down the street, leaning heavily on his stick. His back was stooped, and he seemed much more vulnerable than he did in his home. When he turned the corner and was out of sight, I sighed and made my way to the house he'd pointed to.

After knocking on the door, I stood back and looked around. The houses here were about a hundred years old, and while some had been modernized, most were in need of repair. When I could hear no sound from inside the house, I knocked again. I waited for a while, then turned to leave at the same time as the door of the house next-door opened. A small elderly lady in a floral apron with a scarf tied round her head stepped down on to the pavement and called to me, 'There's no one there.'

I approached her, saying, 'I believe the lady who lives there has been attacked, and I was knocking to see how she was.'

'I was with her when it happened,' the woman told me. 'We were going to the church bingo when this man jumped out and stole Ethel's bag.'

'Was she hurt?' I asked.

'I don't know, they took her to hospital. Her son came last night to feed the cats and he told me she would be staying with them for a while.'

I noticed the frail little woman shivering. Thinking she was cold, I said, 'Go inside, love, you're shaking.'

'I've been like this since it happened. It was such a terrible shock. We were walking down the road, arm in arm, at a quarter to two in the afternoon, when this man jumps on Ethel's back. The next thing I knew she was on the ground and the man was running off with her bag. Ethel couldn't move, and I couldn't help her. Some women came along and they got someone to carry her to the church hall, then sent for the police and an ambulance.' Close to tears and very distressed, she went on, 'I can't get over it. I never went to bed last night, I sat on a chair all night.'

'Don't get upset,' I said, knowing as I spoke that my words were inadequate but I could think of nothing else to say. Putting my hand on her arm, I said, 'Go inside, love, it's cold for you standing out here.'

'I can give you the son's phone number, if you like,' she offered.

'Would he mind if I rang?'

'I shouldn't think so. He's a very nice man, and a marvellous son. Her first husband's boy, that's why their names are different.'

I took a piece of paper and a pencil from my bag

18

and wrote down the name and phone number she'd given me. Then I smiled at the little woman who was so eager to help. 'What's your name, love?'

'Victoria Gardiner.'

'Thank you, Mrs Gardiner, I'll ring Mr Rodgers tonight. Now you go inside where it's warm. I'll call and see you again.'

*　　　*　　　*

That night, when I rang Mr Rodgers, I explained how I had called at Ethel Attwood's house and her neighbour had given me his phone number. I asked how his mother was, and was told she was in a bad state. The doctors wanted to keep her in hospital, but she wouldn't stay and was being discharged into his care. I asked if he'd mind my visiting her, and he said of course not. He would be at work the following day, but his wife would be in with his mother if I wanted to call. I jotted down the address and told him I would be there the next day about eleven o'clock.

Mr and Mrs Rodgers lived in a semi-detached house in one of the middle-class areas of the city. I walked up the path, noticing the well-kept garden and the attractive modern windows. I rang the bell and as I waited it occurred to me that these people were probably wondering why a total stranger wanted to see Mrs Attwood. If they'd asked, I couldn't have answered because I didn't know myself.

Mrs Rodgers smiled to see me and stood back to let me enter. Then she led the way to the living room. 'She's in here.'

I came to an abrupt halt when I saw Mrs

Attwood, sitting in a chair, propped up with pillows. I gasped at the extent of her injuries. Her whole face was a mass of black, blue and yellow bruises, and there were cuts on her cheek and forehead. Her left arm, which was in a sling and cradled in front of her, was also covered in bruises and weeping sores. 'My God,' I said, feeling sick in my stomach. 'Someone did that to you!'

'He jumped on my back and I finished up on the ground with him on top of me.' Although her injuries must have been causing her pain, there was no self-pity in that voice, nor in the blue eyes that looked into mine.

'You haven't seen the half of it,' her daughter-in-law said as she raised the cardigan that was draped over Mrs Attwood's frail shoulders. 'Just look at this.'

My hand went to my mouth in horror as I saw the extent of the bruising and weeping sores. They covered the whole of one side of her body, angry black and blue marks with the skin scraped and cut in several places. And now the cardigan had been removed, I could see how frail the victim was. If she weighed more than six stone I'd be surprised.

'It's all down her legs, too,' Mrs Rodgers said, anger in her tone.

I sat down, not able to find words to express my feelings of horror and pity. 'And what did the brave man get after doing that to you?'

'All the money I had in the world,' came the answer. 'I had seventy-eight pounds in that bag, every penny I owned. It was to pay my electricity, rent, television licence, housekeeping, and a few pounds I had saved to go on a holiday with the pensioners' club.' There was bitterness in her voice

20

as she went on, 'I won't be able to go now, I've nothing left.'

There was a lump in my throat and I had to swallow hard to stop myself from crying. Mrs Attwood was the most pathetic figure I had ever seen in my life, and to think that these horrible injuries had been deliberately inflicted was horrifying. 'Why were you carrying so much money, love?'

'Well, it's difficult to know whether it's safer to leave it at home or take it out with you! Two young boys knocked at my door a couple of weeks ago, said their ball had gone over my backyard wall and would I get it for them. When I went through the house to look for it, they ran in the living room and stole my purse.'

I was thinking that if young boys of ten or eleven were robbing elderly people, then there wasn't much future for our society. 'What did the hospital say?'

'They wanted to keep me in, but I wouldn't stay.' Then she chuckled. 'You should have heard what the doctor called the man who attacked me! He said he certainly picked his mark with me.'

A pitiful sight she may look, I thought, but there's nothing pitiful about her spirit. She has more guts than the coward who attacked her. And at that moment I would have loved to have been able to look him in the eye and tell him so.

I had an idea. 'Would you mind if I came back and took your photograph?'

Mrs Attwood's free hand went up to pat her hair. 'Oh, I couldn't have my photograph taken looking like this.'

'That's just the point,' I told her. 'It's because

21

you look like this that I want the photograph. People should see what's happened to you. We read about these things, but never see the victim.'

Mrs Attwood slowly nodded. 'You're welcome to if that's what you want, and if you think it will help.'

*   *   *

I asked a friend to come with me the next day to take the photographs. Bill was very good with a camera and I needed someone who knew what they were doing. When he saw her injuries he was deeply shocked. He couldn't believe a man would do this to a frail elderly woman, only about four foot six in height. Mrs Attwood, who now insisted we all call her Ethel, was in good spirits, and as I had with Albert, I marvelled at her strength of character and resilience.

When Bill and I were leaving, I asked if I could call and see her again in a few days.

'Come to my home,' she said, 'I can't stay here any longer, my cats need me.'

'You're not going home yet,' her daughter-in-law said firmly, 'you're not able to look after yourself.'

Ethel showed her stubborn streak when she smiled and said, 'I'll be all right. Jack comes in twice a day, and I've got good neighbours.'

'I'll ring first to see where you are,' I promised as I kissed her goodbye.

I made arrangements to call at Bill's the following night to collect the photographs. His wife Sadie and I looked at them together. They showed in stark detail the full horror of Ethel's injuries, and accentuated her frailty to such an extent we were deeply affected.

'The person who did this should be ashamed to call himself a man,' Sadie said with feeling. 'I wouldn't insult an animal by saying he was one.'

After thanking Bill for his help and having a tussle with him because he wouldn't take any money off me for the photographs, I set off for home. Before I took my coat off I handed Tony the packet of photographs. I studied his face for his reaction. After a while he looked at me, shaking his head. 'How in the name of God could anyone do this?' Then he asked me what I intended doing with them.

'I don't know yet,' I said. 'I feel like showing them to the whole world, then perhaps they'll get off their bottoms and do something about what is going on. If someone in authority doesn't use their common sense before it's too late we'll be living in a lawless society where there are more crooks than decent people. In fact, the decent people will be outnumbered by the criminals and afraid to speak out. Anyway, I can't do anything, I'd be just a lone voice. But there's a meeting of the CLO in a few days, I'll show them the photographs and see what they think.'

The next few days passed quickly and soon I was in my car and on my way to the meeting which was held at a Bible college belonging to Charles Oxley, our chairman. Several of the members were there when I arrived and I showed them the photographs of Ethel. As we were taking our seats I told them what had happened to her, and to Albert Smith. They expressed horror and disgust, but it was obvious they were eager to get on with our business. I was dismayed, but realized they hadn't seen the victims. I could talk with as much fervour

23

as I liked, it would not have the same impact as actually seeing the injured people for themselves and hearing of their experiences from their own mouths.

The business before the committee that night was the organization of a mass lobby of the House of Commons. As organizer it was my job to liaise with other groups up and down the country who, like ourselves, were pressing the Government for stiffer punishments for offenders. I had already met my own MP, Graham Page, who had agreed to book a conference hall and invite a number of other MPs to address the meeting. To make the lobby a success we were hoping that at least five hundred people would participate, which meant a lot of organizing over a few months. After bringing the committee up to date on the arrangements so far, and explaining what still had to be done, we all took our diaries out to fix a date for our next meeting.

When this was completed, I tried once again to raise the subject of the local victims. While everyone expressed sympathy and concern, they felt that the committee should concentrate on the aims of the CLO and not diversify. While they were donning their coats I commented on how strange it was that the very people expressing concern over the increase in crime seemed reluctant to show the same concern for its victims. My argument seemed to fall on deaf ears, and I wasn't particularly happy about it. I had been completely outraged by what had happened to Albert and Ethel, and couldn't understand why others didn't feel as strongly.

CHAPTER TWO

My days were freer now than they had been for twenty years. I'd loved the three shops I'd owned because of the hustle and bustle, but most of all I'd loved the contact with people. The only reason I sold them was the daily six o'clock trip to the market each morning which, together with the lifting of heavy sacks of potatoes, vegetables and fruit, was beginning to wear me out—although I have to admit the market men were very gallant and came to my aid every morning. I didn't miss the heavy work entailed, but I did miss meeting people. Every job I'd had since leaving school had entailed my working with people. For many years, when my two children had started school, I'd worked as a door-to-door collector and really enjoyed that time and the laughter I'd shared with the customers. Now, after a few months without having to get out of bed at some unearthly hour, I felt at a loose end, as though there was something missing from my life. My involvement with CLO was worthwhile and something I believed in but it didn't give me much cause for laughter. And laughter is important to me because I'd been brought up in a family where warmth and laughter were part of our life.

A few days after the CLO meeting, I was listening to the nine o'clock news on the radio, and heard the newsreader speaking about an elderly woman who had been attacked and robbed. He mentioned the name of the street where the incident had happened: Mill Street in Toxteth. This

25

was the other side of the city from where I had always lived, and I wasn't familiar with it. So I took my *A–Z* out of the cupboard and turned the pages until I found Toxteth, and then Mill Street. I looked at the clock. It was nine-thirty and a long empty day lay ahead of me. The beds were made, dishes washed and rooms dusted and hoovered. All that needed doing before Tony and Philip came home were the preparations for dinner. These could be done in half an hour. After that, why not try and find the elderly lady who had been attacked?

A short time later I was backing the car off the drive, happy at the thought of having something to do. My life had a purpose once more. It was about twenty miles to Toxteth from where I lived, and I stopped many times to consult the *A–Z*. But finally I found Mill Street, and my heart dropped to find it was a busy main road with hundreds of houses, blocks of flats and shops. It was going to be an impossible task to find one woman in this road—I couldn't even see the end of it. I felt downhearted as I turned the situation over in my mind, then suddenly I asked myself what was the good of sitting there thinking about it. After coming this far, the least I could do was try.

I left the car at the start of Mill Street and walked towards the nearest block of flats. There were three doors on the ground floor and I knocked at the first. When there was no reply after a few seconds, I knocked on the next. There was no reply from there either, and my spirits were flagging. I did get an answer from the third, though: it was opened by an elderly man who shook his head when I asked if he knew thc lady who had

26

been attacked. He seemed very suspicious and couldn't get the door closed on me quickly enough. I didn't blame him. Anyone would have thought I was mad.

When the door closed behind him I looked at the flight of stairs leading to the next landing, but decided against going up them. It was so quiet and still in that block I began to feel rather nervous. So I walked back into the street where I hesitated. Should I try one of the next blocks, or should I take the car and try further up the street? I decided to have one more try this end, and walked to the next entrance. The first door I knocked on was opened by a smartly dressed, middle-aged woman who returned my smile and made me feel better. She listened to my reason for being there with interest but no surprise.

'I haven't heard about this particular attack,' she told me, 'though they're not unusual around here.'

I sighed. 'It's like looking for a needle in a haystack.'

The door opened wider and the woman stepped aside. 'Come in and have a cuppa.'

I was left in the living room while she put the kettle on, and was admiring the comfortable, well-furnished flat when there was a knock on the door. My hostess came through, put two cups of tea on the table and went to answer it. A few seconds later she came back accompanied by an older woman.

'This is a friend of mine,' she said, 'and if you're looking for a victim, Mrs O'Toole has been attacked five times.'

'You've been robbed five times?' My voice rose in surprise.

'Yes,' she said with a faint, tired smile. 'Five times they've had my bag.'

'My God! Why do they pick on you?'

'They don't just pick on me, they pick on anybody.'

'Aren't you afraid to go out?' I asked, wondering what the world was coming to.

'I've got to go out sometime,' she said, 'I can't spend my life between four walls. I wouldn't go out at night, though.' Turning to the lady whose flat we were in, she said, 'Mrs McDermott's house was broken into yesterday while she was out, and they left it in a terrible state. Every room had been ransacked.' Mrs O'Toole turned back to me. 'You're not safe on the street or in your own home these days.'

I looked at my watch, mindful of the distance I had to drive. It was too late to go anywhere else today or I wouldn't be home in time to have the dinner ready. 'If I come back tomorrow, would you take me to see Mrs McDermott?' I asked.

Mrs O'Toole nodded. 'I'll give you my address and you can pick me up from there. Mrs Mac doesn't live far from me.'

I had plenty of food for thought on the drive home. Five times a victim must surely be a record. I decided Mrs O'Toole was picked on because she walked very slowly and painfully due to severe arthritis, and was an easy target. But soon I was to find out that it didn't matter whether you were handicapped or not—if a thug wanted money he wasn't fussy who he took it from.

With Mrs O'Toole's help, over the next few weeks I was to meet many wonderful, kind and warm people. But I was also to meet dozens of

28

elderly victims of crime. One of them was a lady I shall call Ruth. She had been robbed four times before the last break-in when, as she sat watching television, she was confronted by a man who had broken in through her bedroom window. Although she didn't show any fear of the thief and actually fought with him to try and stop him stealing her money, the after-effects had been devastating. With rows of pill bottles lining the kitchen window sill, Ruth explained to me that her nerve had gone completely. She'd had bars fitted across the kitchen window because it was through this that thieves had twice entered. 'What's wrong with the parents of these people?' she asked. 'If my kids had money, I'd want to know where they got it from.'

Ruth had lost money and jewellery in the robberies, and it had affected her health very badly. She couldn't sit and enjoy watching television any more. She would always be listening for strange noises, and would never have peace of mind.

From Ruth's, Mrs O'Toole took me to see her friend Mrs McDermott, still devastated by the state in which thieves had left her home. 'I've tidied up now, but you should have seen the mess they left it in.' She was crying and wiping her eyes with the back of her hand. She was wearing a coat and had a scarf tied around her head. I thought she was ready to go out but when I asked her, she said, 'I just can't settle. I've lived in this house for forty years and always been happy here, but after this lot I don't feel safe any more.' She looked at her friend, 'They stole all my mother's jewellery.'

'The swines,' Mrs O'Toole said vehemently. 'They deserve a bloody good hiding, but they don't get it. You daren't say a word to the kids around here or they put your windows in. And it used to be lovely round here years ago, didn't it, Mrs Mac? We could go out and leave our front doors open. Now we can't even go for a game of bingo. Life isn't worth living any more.' She pointed to her friend. 'Mrs Mac's been mugged as well.'

'A few months ago,' she admitted. 'Some youths snatched my bag. That upset me, but this is worse.' She shivered. 'The fact that they've been in and touched my things.'

Thinking it might do her good to get out of the house for a while, I asked, 'Would you like to go out for a run in the car with us?'

'No, thanks, love, I'm waiting for the police.'

Saying goodbye to Mrs Mac, at her front door, I could feel the breeze blowing off the nearby river, and thought what a pleasant place this area would be if it weren't for the villains.

We made one more call that day, to a woman who had been robbed in the street and because she'd tried to hold on to her bag had been thrown to the ground and pulled along. Her arm had been broken and she'd been left lying there in agony until someone rang for the police. And the story she had to tell made my blood run cold for this lady knew the identity of the youth who had robbed her. He only lived a few doors away. He'd seen the police call at her house after the attack and that night a brick was thrown through her window as a warning. After that she refused to co-operate with the police out of fear, and they couldn't take the case any further because there were no other witnesses. Apparently this was quite common. Elderly people who were robbed or mugged were warned what would happen to them if they reported the crime to the police. And when you are in your late-seventies or eighties, you don't argue with a young thug.

I went out with Mrs O'Toole quite often in the next few weeks and became more familiar with the area. There were many streets of the old two-up-two-down terraced houses, and many more of new council houses and flats. Although the terraced houses were badly in need of repair, I knew I would prefer to live in one of them than in the monstrosities built in more recent years. At least there was some character to an old property, and you had neighbours you could actually see. The modern houses and blocks of flats were built in such a way that no front door faced another and you could go weeks without actually seeing a neighbour. In one fell swoop the clever planners had done away with neighbours and community spirit. Looking at these concrete prisons, I wondered where the planners themselves lived. Certainly not in the urban jungles they had created; more likely in detached houses somewhere in the country, surrounded by leafy trees and large gardens. They had a lot to answer for. They had torn whole communities apart; split neighbours who had known each other all their lives and had more common sense than any well-paid planner.

I knew crime was increasing, you only had to read the papers to know that. But until then I'd had no idea of the heartbreak and misery it caused. Now I was learning the true stories behind the crime statistics, and laying the blame squarely at the door of those who believed they knew what was best for other people. They were very wrong, but didn't have to pay for their own mistakes.

31

Others did.

*   *   *

I was finding my days very full now, and gaining satisfaction from the thought that, although I wasn't able to do anything practical to help crime victims, I was at least able to offer sympathy and show someone did care. My visits were really appreciated by the elderly people I befriended. My husband Tony was interested in what I had to tell him each evening, and although a quiet man, not given to excitable outbursts like me, was frequently disturbed to hear of the dreadful things that were happening.

One morning, a few days later, I was busy at the dining-room table writing out the names of people from across the country who were to take part in the CLO's mass lobby of Parliament. Suddenly my attention was caught by an item on the radio news. It concerned an elderly lady who had been injured when a youth tried to snatch her bag. She was eighty-nine years of age, and her address was given as Birken Walk, Kirkby. I knew Kirkby quite well; it was an overspill area built about twenty years previously to house the people moved out of the inner city by the redevelopment scheme. I had worked as a credit collector in the area for a few years so I was quite familiar with it. It was only a ten-minute drive by car, and on impulse I decided to make the journey.

Birken Walk was easy to find, and when I discovered there were only a few houses and flats in it, I knew I would have no difficulty finding the victim. This proved to be the case. Within minutes

I was directed to a house where the nephew of Sally Wilson, the victim, lived. Apparently everyone in the area knew Sally, and like her nephew they were horrified and angry that she had been the target of a thief. Unfortunately, no one knew her current whereabouts, though her nephew said she would probably be at her granddaughter's because they were very close. 'If she's anywhere,' he said, 'she'll be at Patsy's.' Then he gave me the phone number, saying he knew she wouldn't mind my ringing.

When I got home, I rang the number I had been given. Patsy confirmed that her grandmother was with her. I explained why I was ringing and enquired after Sally's health.

'My nin's in a terrible state,' I was told. 'If I could get my hands on the thug who did it, I would wring his neck.'

'Can I come and see her tomorrow?' I asked.

'Yes, of course you can!' Then Patsy gave me directions on how to get there. It was a short distance away.

As soon as she opened the door of her bungalow and gave me a friendly smile, I knew I was going to like her. An attractive woman in her early-thirties, she seemed to bubble over with good humour and friendliness.

'Come in, Joan, my nin's waiting for you.' As she was closing the front door, Patsy asked, 'Aren't you the lady who had those petitions on crime going round last year?'

When I nodded, she said, 'We all signed them at work.'

I followed her into the well-furnished room. It wasn't until she stepped aside that I could see the

33

elderly lady sitting propped up in a chair. It was like seeing Ethel Attwood all over again: her heavily bruised arm was supported in a sling, and her face too was covered in dark bruises down the left side. The only difference between Sally and Ethel was in the colour of their hair.

I looked down into a pair of bright blue twinkling eyes that were full of laughter, as if she could see the funny side of her appearance.

'Hello, sunshine,' I said as I bent to kiss her. 'What on earth happened to you?'

'You should see the other feller,' she chuckled.

It was then I fell in love with Sally, and realized why I had been so assiduous in seeking out her fellow victims of crime: Albert, Ethel, Mrs O'Toole and all the others. I felt drawn to these marvellous old people with more spirit and guts than so many subsequent generations. If only the rest of the world had lived up to their example, I thought sadly.

'I wish I *could* see the other feller, Sally, I know what I'd like to do to him.'

'I know what I'd do to him too,' said Pasty bitterly. 'They certainly know who to pick on, don't they?'

'What exactly happened?' I asked.

'I was coming back from my daughter's.' Sally turned to Patsy. 'Was it two days ago?' She waited for a nod, then went on. 'Three young fellers came up and one of them tried to grab my bag. The straps were wrapped around my wrist so he couldn't pull it away. He kept on tugging until he'd pulled me to the ground, and when the bag still wouldn't come loose he dragged me along the pavement.' All the time Sally was speaking she was

34

rubbing her shoulder, and I could see she was in pain. 'I would have given him the bag,' she said, 'but I couldn't let go. I started screaming and one of them kicked me. I don't know what happened after that, they must have run away.'

'You mean, he didn't get your bag?' I couldn't describe my feelings at that moment. 'He did this to you for nothing?'

'He didn't get a thing. Someone came along and they called the police and an ambulance.' Sally rubbed herself again. 'The doctor said my shoulder had been pulled out of its socket, but because of my age they couldn't do anything.'

When she stood up to show me how tall she was, the cardigan fell away from her shoulders to reveal heavy bruising there and on her back. I wondered angrily if the youths who had done this to Sally would feel proud of themselves if they could see how small and frail she really was: about four foot eight and weighing seven stone at the very most.

As she sat down, Sally laughed. 'The betting shop will be missing me, I have a bet every day. Their takings will be down.'

'You and your horses,' chided Patsy affectionately.

'Slow horses and fast men have been the ruin of me,' chuckled Sally, still brimful of humour. As I was laughing at the jokes, which were flowing freely, I happened to glance at Patsy to see her gazing at her nin with love and pride.

I was still smiling when I kissed Sally goodbye. 'Can I come back tomorrow and take your photograph, sunshine?'

'Of course you can, queen, I'd like to see you.'

Once out of Patsy's road, though, my smiles

turned to tears. I marvelled at the bravery of the lovely eighty-nine-year-old woman who could still laugh after what those thugs had done to her. I doubted I would be so brave, and was certain the culprits didn't know what bravery was. They were cowards, and a disgrace to society.

*   *   *

I didn't say anything to Tony about my visit to Sally until we had finished our meal and sat down to watch television. I started calmly enough but when I started to describe her appearance I became emotional and began to cry. Tony was studying my face carefully as he listened, and when I was finished sat in silence for a few seconds as though making up his mind on how to put his thoughts into words.

'Look, love,' he said firmly, 'if you're going to get distressed and be so affected, then you're going to have to stop visiting victims. You'll really make yourself ill if you take it to heart like this.'

'But you should see them,' I sobbed. 'They're so old and frail.'

'I know it's terrible, but there's nothing you can do,' Tony said gently. 'If you make yourself ill then you'll be no use to anyone.'

I knew my husband was right about that, so next day when I went back to take Sally's photograph I was determined to keep my feelings in check. I had thought things over carefully, and decided that I would continue to visit victims but would also try to make the public and politicians more aware of what was going on.

Sally was very amused that I wanted to take her

photograph. She watched as I moved from side to side, snapping her from every angle. I used up all the film, determined I would get at least one snap which would show Sally as I wanted people to see her. All too often my attempts at being a photographer in the past had shown the subject without a head!

I didn't stay long that afternoon because I wanted to get to the chemist's in time for the roll of film to be added to others being dispatched to the developers. With a bit of luck I would have the photographs back by late-afternoon the next day, and I'd keep my fingers crossed I hadn't made a mess of them. When I got to the chemist's shop, I warned the women behind the counter that they may find the snaps disturbing, and explained why.

When I called the next afternoon, I could tell by the assistant's face that my photographs were going to have the desired effect because horror was written all over it. She took them out of the wallet to show me and said, 'What is the world coming to if someone can do this to an elderly woman? They deserve to have it done to them, see how they like it.'

I went straight from the shop to Patsy's house and sat down to watch her reaction as she took the snaps out of the folder and studied them one by one. 'The swines,' she said, 'I wish I could get my hands on them.'

When she passed them over to Sally, both she and I laughed at the expression on her wrinkled face. 'My God, I don't look very glamorous, do I? I'll never get a feller looking like that. Just look at the state of me hair.'

I asked Sally if she would mind me showing the

photographs to other people and she gave her permission readily. 'If it'll help, queen, then I don't mind. You do what you think best.'

That night I rang Jack Rodgers to ask if he would object to my asking his mother if I could show her photographs too. 'My mother's gone home,' he told me. 'We tried to get her to stay but she wanted to get home to her cats and there was nothing we could do to stop her.'

'Have you any objection, Jack?' I asked.

'Certainly not,' he assured me, 'and I'm sure my mother won't.'

He was right, too, because when I called on her the next day, Ethel had no objection whatsoever. Propped up in her chair, cushions around her, she seemed genuinely glad to see me. She studied the snaps of her and Sally, then said, 'We make a fine pair, don't we?'

'I think you're both wonderful. You are both very brave, and have got more guts than the people who attacked you.' I looked around the room and saw the two cats curled up under the table. 'How are you managing on your own?'

'I can't do anything for myself,' she admitted, 'but Jack comes in every morning before he goes to work, then at lunchtime, and again at night.'

'You've got a marvellous son,' I told her, 'you are very lucky.'

'The best son a mother could have,' she said proudly.

'Are you still in pain?'

Ethel nodded. 'In my arm and shoulder, and my hips and legs. I can hardly lift my arm, and can't walk without help.'

'Isn't there compensation you can claim?' I

asked. 'I'm sure I've heard that you can claim from somewhere if you're injured.'

'The police told Jack to send away for a form and gave him the address to write to.' After a pause Ethel went on, 'I could do with some money. Every penny I had for my bills was in the bag that was stolen.'

'Won't Social Security help?' I asked.

'My home help rang up, and there's someone coming to see me today. I hope they give me enough to pay my rent and the five pounds I had to borrow for food.'

While I was talking to Ethel, I wondered if Albert Smith and Sally knew about the compensation scheme. I'd mention it to them next time I paid them a visit.

Ethel still had the photographs in her hand, and her eyes went from one of herself to one of Sally. 'Don't we look a right mess?' she asked sadly.

'I think you are both lovely, and very brave.'

'I didn't have any option, did I?' Ethel's laugh was hollow. 'If I'd known what was going to happen I would have run like mad.'

When I was leaving I told her I would ring her the next day to see how she got on with the visitor from Social Security.

'Ring or come any time you want, Joan, you'll always be welcome.'

The words told me how lonely Ethel was, now she was confined to the house and unable to care for herself. The coward who had stolen her money would have spent it by now, on drink or drugs, and more likely than not she wouldn't have been his first victim. He'd have found other elderly targets to steal from to keep the money jangling in his pocket, and wouldn't have given a second thought to what he'd done to Ethel and the others he'd robbed. He wouldn't dream of getting himself a job and earning an honest living, like the vast majority of people in this country have to. Everyone has a choice: honest or dishonest. Those who choose to be honest should not have to be afraid to walk the streets or sit in their homes fearful of every noise. Those who choose to be a criminal should be made aware that every crime carries a punishment. Unfortunately we haven't had a Government since the war strong enough to ignore the do-gooders and penal reformers, and listen instead to the innocent victims. Their weakness is ultimately as much to blame for what happened to the likes of Albert, Ethel and Sally, as the criminals' greed and inhumanity.

*   *   *

At home again, still highly indignant about everything I'd seen, I rang the *Liverpool Echo* and asked for the news desk. They already knew of me through my campaigning with CLO, but this time I told them about the victims I had visited. I didn't mention any names because I thought that would be wrong, and potentially dangerous to the victims who lived alone. In stronger terms than I had ever before used I told the reporter how elderly victims of crime were left injured, afraid and penniless. I went on to tell him exactly what I considered should happen to offenders who used violence for their own gain—be it political, sexual or financial. In full flood now, I said I was sick of listening to trendy sociologists making excuses for people who

40

break the law. There is never any excuse, and the sooner the thugs were made to understand this, the sooner decent people would be able to live their lives without fear and feel free to walk the streets in safety. I attacked in particular the MPs who promised so much when they were asking people to vote for them, then refused to listen to the voice of the people once they were elected. And when I'd finished I felt a whole lot better for getting some of the frustration off my chest.

The following evening the *Echo* carried the story, giving my views in full. I won't say it made me happy, because I would have had to be very naive not to know that my comments would make me a lot of enemies, but I felt relieved, as though a burden had been lifted. It was my society, I had to live in it, and I had as much right to say what I believed as anyone else.

The next morning, Saturday, I went to keep an appointment with my MP, Graham Page. I had a lot of respect for Mr Page, a gentle, friendly, understanding man. I told him of the victims I had met, the injustices I had seen. We shared many of the same views, both believing in capital and corporal punishment for certain crimes, and when he saw my photographs of the injuries inflicted on Ethel and Sally, he suggested he try for a Private Members Bill advocating the reintroduction of corporal punishment. He wasn't very hopeful, though, saying even if he were successful it was not certain that enough MPs would be in favour to carry the vote.

'Why is there no help for victims?' I asked him.

'Because I'm afraid that for years the penal reformers have been fighting for the rights of the offender while no one has been fighting for the innocent victim.'

We went on to discuss the mass lobby, and when I told him we were expecting over five hundred people to attend Mr Page said there was only one hall which would accommodate such a number. 'Leave it to me, Joan,' he advised. 'With a gathering of this size, there's a lot of work involved. I'll find out what day the hall will be available, notify the police about the number of people expected to take part, then contact you with the date. It won't be until after the summer recess now, though, I'm afraid.'

I didn't prolong the interview because I knew there was a queue of constituents waiting to see him, but I was more than satisfied with our meeting.

When I got home, though, Tony didn't look as happy as I felt. Apparently the phone had been ringing all the time I had been out and he was fed up with asking the callers to ring back. To confirm his words the phone rang before he'd finished speaking and I answered the first of twenty calls that day. All were from people who appreciated the views I had expressed in the local paper the night before, and all were offering help should I need it. Other people too were concerned about the way society was heading, and were fearful for the future. After tea I decided that in fairness to Tony I should take the phone off the hook before we sat down to watch television for the evening. But first I wanted to ring Ethel to see how she had fared with Social Security.

'I don't know yet,' she told me. 'The woman took down all the particulars of the money stolen and the bills I have, and she said she would send me a cheque as soon as she got back to the office. I won't get it until Monday now.'

'Have you got food in for the weekend?' I asked.

'Yes, Jack has seen to that for me.'

After saying goodbye to Ethel, the phone came off the hook and I sat down to relax with Tony. He was a fantastic husband, quiet and gentle, and I loved him dearly. He was also very indulgent and I felt I was taking advantage of that. I kept expecting him to complain about my activities, but apart from the odd 'tut-tut' when the phone calls became too much, he never did.

'How about an early holiday?' I suggested. 'Could you take a week of your holidays in June, or late in May?'

He moved his head from side to side as if to say he probably could. 'Where are you thinking of going?'

'You know my friend Frances? Well, her brother Ray lives in Jersey, and he and his wife told her we could go there if we like.'

'I wouldn't want to stay with strangers,' Tony said. 'I'd feel under an obligation.'

'Both Ray and his wife Ruth work all day so we'd be on our own,' I coaxed. 'We wouldn't be tied to them all the time.'

He gave in. 'If you want to, it's up to you.'

First thing next morning I rang Ruth to make sure her invitation was genuine, and was pleased when she said they would look forward to it. So we chose a date. Then Tony and I discussed whether to fly or take the car and go by boat. Knowing my fear of flying, my lovely husband said I would look forward to the holiday more if I didn't have the

43

flight on my mind all the time. So we decided to take the car and I promised to book the passage the next day.

Funny that I could face a thug and tell him what I thought of him, but was terrified at the mere thought of getting on a plane. I had flown to Holland a couple of times to see Tony's family, but just the sight of a maintenance man with a screwdriver in his hand at the airport was enough to give me the jitters. Once on the plane I refused to look out of the window or even speak, and going to the toilet was a definite no-no. In fact, I was a real misery until I stepped on to the ground and put a smile back on my face.

CHAPTER THREE

On the following Monday my first phone call was from Radio Merseyside, to ask if I would go to the studio the next day for an interview. I had never been in a broadcasting studio before, and was a little apprehensive. But I realized there was no point in campaigning if I was going to turn down this chance of publicity, so I agreed to be at the studio at two o'clock the following afternoon.

When I opened my diary to enter the appointment, I noticed there was a CLO meeting the following night which I had forgotten about. Life was getting to be quite hectic. Fortunately I had always been the type to prepare things in advance, so meals and housework were never left till the last minute. I now found that having a routine was a great help, otherwise Tony and Philip would have come home each night to an untidy house and no smell of dinner to meet them when they walked through the door. My husband had been very patient with me up till now, I didn't want to stretch that patience too far.

Tuesday morning dawned and I decided that rather than hang about the house getting more nervous over the impending radio interview, I would pay short visits to Albert and Sally. I wanted to find out whether they knew about the Criminal Injuries Compensation they were entitled to apply for. I called at Patsy's first because it was on my way into the city, but neither she nor Sally had been told, or knew of, the Criminal Injuries Compensation Board. I promised to make further enquiries and let them know. Then I went on to Albert's to hear that the police had told his son about the compensation scheme, and he had already written off for an application form.

From Albert's I drove to a street near a taxi rank, and after locking my car took a taxi to the Radio Merseyside studio. My nerves were giving out on me by this time, and I was not looking forward to the interview at all. During a restless night I had planned all the things I wanted to talk about, including the most recent crime figures which had been sent to me by a friend in Yorkshire. Now, though, as I entered the studio, my head emptied of all the things I had rehearsed. My mind went a complete blank and my tummy felt as though there were hundreds of butterflies flying around inside. The producer introduced me to Philip Pinnington, the presenter, and told me the interview would last about five minutes. Philip said they would be asking for my views on

45

various subjects, including capital and corporal punishment.

Sitting at a table opposite him, waiting for the programme to start, I tried to think what I was going to say but just couldn't concentrate. When I was asked to speak a few words into the mike so they could check my voice levels, I managed to croak something about the weather. In a state of sheer panic I heard Philip saying into the microphone, 'In the studio with me is Mrs Joan Jonker, well known for her views on law and order. It is those views we are going to discuss now. Good afternoon, Mrs Jonker.'

'Hello,' I squeaked.

The first few questions I only managed to answer briefly. But gradually, because Philip Pinnington was so calm, I began to relax and was able to marshal my thoughts into some semblance of order. I was able to explain, when asked why I hold the views I do, that I believe a victim of crime should have the right to see justice done. That I believe the frightening increase in crime today is due to the fact that offenders are not punished realistically or in such a way as to be deterred from committing further crimes. My main argument is that the offender has a choice. If he doesn't want to be punished, then he shouldn't commit the crime. Those who live within the law have the right to be protected from those who choose to break it.

I knew the interview was going well because the producer, after the proposed five minutes, popped his head round the door and whispered that Philip should carry on. After twenty minutes, he brought the interview to a close with a question that shook me at first.

'Do you not think that people might regard you as a middle-class activist?' he asked.

I stared at him for a few seconds, then replied, 'Will you answer me a question? What exactly is middle-class?' I was in my stride now, and before he had time to answer I went on. 'I was born in a two-up-two-down house in a very working-class area. When I was young we were poor. I left school at fourteen with no qualifications except plain common sense, drilled into me by good teachers. I've worked hard all my life and now live in a semi in the suburbs. Does that make me middle-class?' When Philip didn't answer immediately, I went on, 'In fact, I am very proud of being working-class.' Then before he had time to reply to anything I'd said, a thought struck me. 'Do *you* think I'm a middle-class activist?'

'No, I don't,' he answered, 'but our listeners might.'

'Only if you put the idea into their heads,' I told him.

Both Philip and the producer were pleased and said the interview had gone very well. I was not convinced. On the way home I thought of loads of things I should have said. But by then I didn't have a microphone in front of me, or hundreds of thousands of people listening.

*   *   *

At the CLO meeting that evening I brought out the photographs of Sally and passed them around. I could hear the tutting and clicking of tongues, denoting the disgust everyone felt. But having been handed the snaps back, I was again told that our

47

meeting was for the purpose of discussing CLO business and not victims of crime. I argued heatedly that the victims should in fact figure prominently in our discussions as to my mind they were more important than anything we would be discussing that night.

'I can't go out every day and see victims of crime, then not be allowed to talk about them at our meetings,' I argued. 'These people need help, and I want to help them.'

With the backing of our secretary, Olive Fairman, I persuaded Mr Oxley to listen. All the other members left, but Mr Oxley stayed to hear my suggestions on how I thought we could help. I told him of the victims I'd seen, many of them living on the poverty line, and the help I thought they should have been given. And I described, with feeling, the gratitude showed by these people for the very little I had done for them. I also explained that the ones I had seen were only the tip of the iceberg. There must be hundreds more, up and down the country, left alone after similar ordeals with no one to talk to, no one to hold their hand. I felt so passionate about it, Mr Oxley was converted and agreed we should do something to help. He then came up with an idea which pleased and excited me. He suggested placing an advertisement in the *Liverpool Echo*, asking any victim who needed help to contact us. Three phone numbers would be given, Olive's, mine and Mr Oxley's—in case we were flooded with calls. Mr Oxley was a very clever man but noted for sometimes forgetting things, rather like the absent-minded professor, so I asked him to write himself a reminder about the plan on a piece of paper and enter it in his diary.

With a half smile, he promised he wouldn't forget and the advert would be in the *Echo* in three days' time, at the very latest.

The next morning I rang the local police station and asked for the address of the Criminal Injuries Compensation Board. As soon as I'd put the phone down from that call I wrote asking for a supply of application forms. The next thing on my list was to ring Ethel to see how she had fared with the DHSS.

'Oh, I got a cheque all right,' she told me, 'for the grand sum of three pounds. That's all I got!' She sounded very bitter. 'It won't even pay back the five pounds I borrowed.'

'But what about your rent and all your other bills?' I asked. 'Won't they help with those?'

'I told the woman all about them,' she said, 'but that's all they sent—three pounds.'

I could understand her feeling bitter. Like all the elderly people I had met, she had her pride and had never owed anyone in her life. And now she would have to struggle for many months, going without necessities, to make up the money that was stolen from her weekly pension. 'Are you sure it was Social Security who sent the visitor?' I asked.

'I think so. My home help rang them.'

I found out later that week that it wasn't the DHSS who had sent the three pounds. They had obviously not been notified. The lady who had called to see Ethel had been a home help supervisor, and in the circumstances the three pounds she'd sent had been a generous donation.

Fortunately, Ethel had her son to help her out financially, and I knew she wouldn't go short of food or heating. But I started to wonder what would have happened if she hadn't had him to help

49

her. There must be many elderly people in the same circumstances with no one to turn to, and most would certainly be forced to go without food or heating if they were short of money.

This was proved to me the next day when I called, as promised, to see Mrs O'Toole. We had arranged that she would take me to see some other victims she knew in her area. We saw six that day, two who had been attacked and robbed in the street and four whose homes had been burgled. I asked each one how they had managed for money, and each said they'd had to cut down on everything. Some borrowed from relatives or friends, some couldn't pay their rent. This meant that the following week, when they'd repaid what they owed, they'd be struggling again. These were all people whose only income was their state pension. They had no money in the bank, had never had a bank account in their lives, and had no private pension.

I was very angry that day. Angry with the people who had robbed these poor defenceless pensioners, and angry with politicians of every party who'd closed their eyes to what was going on in their constituencies. I don't belong to any particular political party, never have done. In fact, I don't have much time for any of them although I've often wished we had someone in charge of the country with the strength of Winston Churchill. Now *there* was a leader who would certainly not have allowed elderly people who had fought in the war to be attacked in their own country and no help be forthcoming. He would have listened, unlike those who had followed him. Well, I was only a very ordinary housewife and mother, without any claim to fame, but I made up my mind that somehow, somewhere, someone would listen.

* * *

For the next two nights I scoured the evening paper for the advertisement that Mr Oxley had promised, but was disappointed. However, on the third day I received a phone call in response to the advert before I'd even seen it. The call was from a man who told me his mother, a cripple, had been robbed of her life savings. I took his name, address and phone number, and promised to ring before calling to see his mother.

As soon as Tony came through the door, I grabbed the paper from under his arm and turned the pages quickly until I found the advert. It stated merely that victims of crime who wished to could contact us on one of the three numbers given.

Expecting a busy night, I quickly washed the dishes after our meal and sat down to wait for another call. It didn't come. The man who'd rung earlier was the only one to contact me.

I waited until ten o'clock then rang Olive. Like me, she had expected numerous calls but had received none. I then rang Mr Oxley. He had received one call from a man who told of his crippled father being badly injured during a robbery. We discussed what we should do about the two calls, and Mr Oxley suggested we visit the victims together, on Sunday afternoon. He said he would also like to visit Albert and Ethel. I rang Olive back to bring her up-to-date with the news, and she said she would like to come with us on Sunday.

51

The following afternoon I was just putting the pans on the stove to prepare our meal when the phone rang.

'Did you put that advert in the *Echo* last night?' a man's voice asked.

'Yes,' I replied.

'My son was murdered . . .' The voice tailed off.

I waited for a few seconds. 'Hello, are you there?'

'Yes, I'm here.'

'What's your name, please?' I didn't know what else to say.

'My name's Sam Kingsley, and the man who murdered my son only got eighteen months in jail.'

'Eighteen months for killing a man?' I swallowed hard.

'That's right, eighteen months.' His voice faltered.

'Mr Kingsley, would you like to meet me? It's very difficult to discuss this over the phone. If you'll give me your phone number I'll contact our chairman and make arrangements for the three of us to meet.' When there was no reply I went on quietly, 'You could tell us your story then and we'll help all we can.'

'There's no one can help us.' Mr Kingsley sounded distraught. 'Our son's dead and no one can bring him back.'

I finally persuaded Sam to give me his phone number and promised to ring him back later that night. Then I dialled Mr Oxley's number.

After listening to my account of what Sam

Kingsley had said, Mr Oxley surprised me by saying, 'I've had a phone call from the father of a murdered boy, too. His name is Mr Aldis, and I've made arrangements for him to come here next week. But I'll be here tomorrow night if you'd like to bring Mr Kingsley then.'

Mr Oxley was principal of two private schools, one of which, Tower College, was where he and his family lived. I said I would contact Sam Kingsley and, if it was agreeable to him, I would take him to Tower College the following night at seven-thirty.

*   *   *

When Sam Kingsley knocked at my door the next night, I thought at first he was drunk. His hair was dishevelled and his eyes had a glazed look. I suggested we went in my car, but Sam gave me a look that I was not going to argue with, and I began to feel uneasy.

On the twenty-minute drive to Mr Oxley's, I tried to talk to him about what had happened to his son, but his words were disjointed. He was obsessed, naturally, with the ridiculously light sentence the murderer had received, and I could sense the bitterness he felt.

When Mr Oxley showed us into his drawing room, Sam sat on the chintz-covered settee while Mr Oxley and I sat facing him. I asked him to tell us what had happened, and as he told his story I realized Sam wasn't drunk as I'd first thought, but doped with tranquillizers. It was only after many questions and interruptions that his story became clear. His son Alan, who was twenty-three, was to have been best man at his friend's wedding. The night before he'd arranged to sleep at the bridegroom's flat, and when he left home on a Friday night he was laughing as he told his parents he'd see them at the church tomorrow when they went along for the service although they were not guests at the wedding.

There were many people at the church when Sam and Joan arrived and took their seats. Time went by with still no sign of the groom or best man. Eventually, when it was obvious that something had gone wrong, Sam and Joan followed the congregation out of the church where they were told the wedding was off. Thinking their son would ring them to say what had gone wrong, they made their way home. Even when Alan hadn't rung by the time they went to bed, neither Sam nor Joan was worried—they were curious, but not concerned.

The police woke them later that night to say that Alan was in hospital, critically wounded, and Sam threw some clothes on and dashed to the hospital. He was too late, though. Alan was dead by the time he arrived.

By now Sam seemed to have lost control of his emotions. Shifting about on the settee, he reminded me of a trapped animal.

Mr Oxley was obviously concerned about Sam's mental state when he said, 'If it's too distressing for you, don't tell us any more.'

'No, I want to tell you. My wife and I are doped to the eyeballs twenty-four hours a day,' Sam raved, 'but nobody cares what happens to us. My wife sits crying all the time. She's on tablets and won't go out or see anyone.'

He ran his fingers through his hair, then went on

to tell us what had happened. 'The uncle of the groom went with the rest of the guests to the reception, which the bride's family decided to go ahead with because it had all been booked and paid for. Apparently the uncle drank all afternoon, then at night went out drinking again. At the trial they said he was drunk and didn't know what he was doing, but he walked for a mile from the pub to his home, took a dagger off the wall, then walked the distance to the groom's flat. He started shouting and kicking the door, causing neighbours to come out to see what the commotion was about. The groom, whose flat was on the first floor, was going to go down and talk to the man, but Alan said it would only make matters worse. He then offered to go himself and quieten the uncle down. Witnesses saw Alan put his hands on the man's shoulders and try to calm him. The next moment they saw Alan slump to the ground.

'The groom saw from his window what had happened and ran downstairs. The front door was lying inside the hall, torn off its hinges by the uncle just before Alan got down the stairs. He had been determined to get to the groom who had cancelled the wedding only minutes before the bride left her house for the church because he was no longer sure he wanted to marry the girl. By the time he got down the stairs his uncle, a Mr Walder, had run away, and his best friend Alan was lying in a pool of blood.'

'What happened at the trial?' I asked.

'Trial? What trial?' Sam spat the words out. 'Walder had been charged with murder, the witnesses were in court, even the door he'd burst off its hinges was there. It was all straightforward, or so I thought, but everything changed just before the trial started. Nobody told me or the wife anything, but apparently the charge was reduced to manslaughter and he pleaded guilty before the trial started. No witnesses were called, nothing.'

Mr Oxley and I were silent, waiting for Sam to continue. I had never seen anyone so disturbed, and felt very concerned. I also felt heartbroken for the man's loss, thanking God I wasn't in his shoes. 'Sam,' I said gently, 'you are a very sick man. Have you been to see your doctor?'

'My wife and I are both under the doctor. He gives us pills.' He laughed bitterly. 'We've lost a son, and he gives us pills. How can they help? Nothing will help while that man is alive. I will never rest until he is dead, too, like my son.'

Alarmed now, I said, 'You mustn't talk like that, Sam. What good would it do if you killed him and ended up in jail yourself? You've got your wife to think of.'

'She agrees with me. Neither of us will rest until he's dead.' And Sam meant it, too.

'We'd better be going.' I was thinking of my husband when I stood up. It wasn't fair of me to leave him on his own so often. 'Are you all right to drive, Sam? I don't think you're in a fit state, really.'

'I'll be all right,' he assured me. 'The effect of the tranquillizers is wearing off, that's why I'm like this. You've no need to worry, I'll get you home safe.'

Mr Oxley shook his hand. 'We'll keep in touch, Mr Kingsley, and I'm sure we'll meet again in the near future. In the meanwhile, if you think we can help, you know where we are.'

On the way home, I asked Sam if I could call and see his wife.

'She won't see you,' he told me. 'If anyone comes she just runs upstairs, crying.'

'Let me try,' I asked. 'Even if she won't see me, at least I'll have tried.'

Sam gave me his address but once again said he was certain she wouldn't see me. But I felt I had to try.

*　　　*　　　*

I was nervous when I knocked on Sam's door the next day. I had never met the family of a murder victim before, and wasn't quite sure I could cope.

The door opened a couple of inches, and I could just see a woman's tear-stained face. I gulped then said, 'Joan, my name is Joan, too. Joan Jonker. I met your husband yesterday.'

'Sam isn't in.' Her voice was so low I could scarcely hear it.

'I came to see you,' I said gently. 'Please let me in, Joan. If you want to cry, then let me cry with you.'

The door opened wider and I walked through.

Joan should have been a very pretty woman, small with fair hair, but her face was red and blotched with crying and her blue eyes told of the pain and despair she suffered.

'Sam told me what happened, Joan. It must be like living a nightmare for you both.' I knew I would have to talk to her about the tragedy, and rightly or wrongly believed it would help. It is dangerous to bottle things up at the best of times, but for people like Sam and Joan, who were filled

57

with bitterness and hatred, it was vital to release some of that bitterness before it sent them over the edge.

After a while Joan began to unwind and talked about Alan and what had happened to him. My heart went out to her because I could imagine how I would feel if anyone killed one of my sons in this way. She told me about their other son, two years younger than Alan, and how it had affected his life. 'We sit and talk about it,' she told me. 'He knows Sam wants to kill Walder but doesn't have much to say, he's gone very quiet.'

'Joan, Sam is a sick man, you must know that. You've got to help him. Just think what it would do to your other son if Sam did kill this man. His brother murdered and his father in jail. You can't let that happen, it wouldn't be fair on your son. He's only young and has his life to live.' All the time I was speaking I was telling myself how easy it was for me to sit telling her what to do, I wasn't the one suffering.

Sam came in then, and we went over the story once again. Then I asked, 'Did no one come to see if you needed any help?'

'Nobody came near us,' he said. 'I used to go and stand outside Walder's house and I saw a social worker going in and out there. *They* could get help, but not us. We've both been in hospital, in the psychiatric ward, out of our minds, but nobody cares. One day I stopped the social worker as she came out of Walder's and asked why no one had been to see my wife. She promised to call and see Joan.' Sam stopped and looked across at his wife. 'She did come, didn't she?'

Joan was looking better now, and I knew it was

helping her to talk about it. 'Oh, she came all right,' she said. 'She'd only been in the house a few minutes when I happened to say "that murderer", and she said, "Don't call him a murderer, call him Mr Walder. And don't forget, he's locked up in prison without sex."'

I nearly exploded. 'She said what?'

'She said he was in prison without sex.' Joan turned to her husband. 'Didn't she Sam?'

'My God,' I said, 'what sort of a woman is she? She sounds the last person who should be a social worker! She must be sick in the head to talk like that to you.'

'Sam ordered her out of the house.'

'Ordered her out—I would have thrown her out,' I told them. I was so angry that a so-called social worker, whose job it was to help and understand, had been asked by Sam for help for his wife and then shown she had more pity for the man who had killed his son than she had for them. She was only concerned that the man who had caused their grief and heartbreak wasn't able to have sex in prison. I was so disgusted I thought it best for me to leave because I didn't want my anger to affect the others.

I was glad I had called, though, because Joan looked better for talking about it. She and Sam were a lovely couple who didn't deserve what they were going through. As I kissed Joan goodbye, I told her I would call again in a few days but would ring first to make sure she was in.

*   *   *

A few days later I went up to Tower College to meet Mr and Mrs Aldis. The murder of their son,

Lewis, had affected them as deeply as it had the Kingsleys, but they showed it in a different way. A very quiet couple, they didn't shout their anger and grief but the emotions were written on their faces for all to see. I have never in my life seen a face reflect sadness the way Mr Aldis's did, nor eyes that seemed so haunted.

Lewis had been stabbed to death by his girlfriend's ex-boyfriend. They were in her flat when the killer burst in and went for the girl with a knife. Lewis had thrown himself in front of her, and in saving her life was killed himself. Apparently, the girl had stopped seeing the man when she found out he had been in jail for acts of violence. He wouldn't accept her rejection, and it was Lewis who was the victim of his revenge. In their quiet, gentle way, the Aldises described how they could still see their son's face everywhere they looked. He seemed to be with them all the time, in their home and in the street. Listening to them, with a massive lump in my throat, I remembered Joan Kingsley too saying her son was everywhere in the house. She could see his face, smiling as he was the last time she saw him.

I told the Aldises about Sam and Joan, and asked if they'd like to meet them. I had an idea it might help if they could talk to someone who had suffered the same tragedy—someone who understood what it was like having to live with such pain and despair. Only someone who had suffered in the same way could hope to understand what it was like. While my heart went out to them, and while I could sympathize and cry with them, how could I possibly know the depth of their feelings?

There was another man at Mr Oxley's that night,

60

Raymond Pearson, a councillor from Yorkshire. He had been in touch with us regarding our CLO work, and was interested in starting a branch in his area. He listened while I suggested arranging a meeting between the Kingsleys and the Aldises, then said he knew the family of a murdered girl who would be interested in meeting the other two families. It seemed a good idea and we arranged to bring the three families together at Tower College in three weeks' time.

In the meantime I continued to visit victims every day. If I hadn't heard of any new ones, I would revisit the old ones. Albert Smith was a loner, I discovered, used to being on his own since his wife had died many years ago and not at ease with strangers. Sensing this, I would make my visits brief, staying only for long enough to make sure he was all right.

Ethel Attwood, on the other hand, was just the opposite. She loved me to call and tell her all about what I'd been doing. Her next-door neighbour, the one who had been with her when she was attacked, used to come in too and we would have a cup of tea sitting around the coal fire. Ethel loved to talk about the old days when she used to go ballroom dancing, or to the afternoon tea dances at Reece's. She had obviously led a full, happy life, and I believed this was standing her in good stead now. People of her age hadn't had it easy years ago, they'd had to struggle to make ends meet, and it had made them stronger, both physically and mentally.

'You must have been quite a girl in those days,' I teased one day when she was reminiscing and looking rather sad. I knew she had been married

61

twice, both husbands good men who had died at fairly young ages.

'Yes,' she sighed, 'they were hard days, but we were happy.'

'Would you like to come out with me one day?' I spoke out as the idea came into my mind, looking from Ethel to Mrs Gardiner.

Ethel brightened up, a gleam in her eyes. 'Oh, that would be lovely!'

Mrs Gardiner smiled. 'I'd love to.'

'Right,' I said, nodding my head, 'I'll see what I can do.'

'We'll hold you to it, you know,' laughed Ethel.

'You won't have to do that, sunshine, I won't let you down. I have made you a promise, and I never break a promise.' By hook or by crook they would get their day out. How, where and when I'd have to work out.

*   *   *

It was as I was driving home that I thought of a way to keep my promise. I'd have to ask Charles Oxley for his help but even as this thought was running through my mind, another idea was forming. It involved hiring a coach so that many more victims could enjoy the luxury of a day out. How marvellous if that could be arranged, a day by the sea or in the country for people who had little pleasure in their lives after becoming the victims of mindless thugs. A coach that could take fifty of them would be wonderful . . .

But I couldn't organize it on my own, I couldn't afford to. It was costing me money every day for petrol and the bunches of flowers or boxes of chocolates I was buying to cheer up the victims I was visiting. It was my own small way of showing them that they hadn't been forgotten, that there were people who cared. Over the next few days my enthusiasm for a coach trip didn't diminish, it gained strength.

CHAPTER FOUR

The day the supply of application forms came from the Criminal Injuries Compensation Board I rang Patsy to tell her I would be round to help her nin fill one in. When I arrived I found Sally in very high spirits. I smiled as I said, 'You're very happy, aren't you?'

'Well, girl, it's no good being miserable, is it?' she said philosophically. 'Nobody wants someone who's crying all the time.'

With a welcome cup of coffee in front of me, I sat at the table with Sally and Patsy. It took a long time to fill the form in because there were four pages of questions. It was the first time I had ever seen a form like this, and I found it quite complicated. I remember thinking how difficult it would be for an elderly person if they had to fill it in on their own. I could well imagine them being put off sufficiently to throw the form to one side and not bother.

When it was completed to the very best of our abilities, I told Sally, 'I'll post it for you, but as soon as you get a reply, will you let me know? I believe it takes a long time, though, so don't worry if you don't hear for a few months.'

'I can't use the phone, girl, but I'll get Patsy to ring you.' She gave one of her cheeky chuckles. 'I can't be doing with these new-fangled contraptions.'

'Be handy to put your bets on,' I pointed out.

'I'd rather go to the betting shop.' She grinned. 'That's where I get all my jokes from.'

'How would you like to come with me and some friends on a day out?' I asked. 'Perhaps on a coach trip.'

'That'd be nice, girl.' Again that famous chuckle. 'I might meet a feller.'

I laughed. 'You'll not get up to any mischief while you're with me.'

*   *   *

Sunday afternoon saw Mr Oxley, Olive and myself knocking on Albert Smith's door. I had told him we were coming, and he must have been watching for us because the door was opened before I took my hand from the knocker. We were shown into the front parlour where I made the introductions. At six foot four Charles Oxley towered over Albert as they shook hands. The old man was immaculate in his white shirt, brown tie and beige cardigan. When I asked how he was, he said he would be all right if he could just see out of his left eye. He was reticent at first, but soon relaxed and warmed up when Mr Oxley asked him to relate what had happened. He even took Mr Oxley into the hall to show him the piece of wood which he still had propped against the wall by the front door in case of intruders.

When we were leaving, I gave Albert one of the boxes of chocolates Mr Oxley had been thoughtful enough to bring with him. Albert was delighted, and once again I thought how easy it was to make these people happy.

Our next call was round the corner to Ethel's. She was sitting pretty in her best clothes waiting for our arrival. There was no embarrassment from Ethel, who loved company and was enjoying our visit so much she would have kept us there as long as possible. But we had another two calls to make and couldn't stay too long. When I gave her a box of chocolates her face lit up with pleasure and appreciation, and I said a silent thank you to Charles Oxley for his kindness and thoughtfulness.

We sat in the car as Mr Oxley looked through his *A–Z* for our next address. While he held his finger on the page he needed, he and Olive discussed the two victims they had seen so far. I could tell by their expressions that they had been moved as they'd listened to Albert and Ethel, and now they voiced their horror and dismay. It wasn't only the attacks and the injuries that upset them, it was the appearance of the two victims. Their age, frailty and courage brought home to my two colleagues exactly why I had been so insistent in my demands that we should help victims in any way we could.

The next name on the list for visiting was a victim I had never met. A son had rung to say that his father, Stephen, who was a cripple, had been injured in a burglary. He had said we should use the back door as the front had now been nailed up. We found the flat easily as the son had given clear directions. We walked up the path through the back garden and I rapped on the door.

'Come in,' a gruff voice called, 'the door isn't locked.'

When we entered the small room and I looked at the man in the wheelchair I felt I had been dealt a body blow. I knew the man we were visiting was a cripple, but I wasn't prepared for this. Both of Stephen's legs had been amputated. This was all I noticed for the first few seconds, then, as he told us to sit down, I noticed that his hands and arms were misshapen with arthritis. My colleagues and I were quiet as we sat down. I could tell that they were as shocked as I was. Pulling myself together, I managed a smile as I said, 'Hello, Stephen, my name's Joan Jonker and these are my friends, Charles Oxley and Olive Fairman.'

Stephen smiled. 'My son said you were coming.' His voice had a slight Irish accent.

He was a man of seventy-two, with a thick mop of hair neatly combed back showing a large wound on the side of his head. The wound, which was covered with a scab, was about three inches long and two inches wide.

Mr Oxley leaned forward. 'Your son said you had been attacked, but he didn't give any details. Do you feel up to telling us what happened?'

Stephen reached towards the sideboard for a packet of cigarettes. Opening the packet, his hands were shaking so badly that I stood up, placed a cigarette in his mouth for him and lit it with his lighter.

Stephen's story was like a TV horror movie. We were shocked into silence as he told us how, a few weeks ago, he had been woken in the middle of the night when the mattress he was sleeping on was moved. He opened his eyes to see a youth bending over him, hands scrabbling first under the mattress, then the pillow. The terrified man could see another youth going through the drawers and cupboards of the dresser. Struggling to raise himself, he asked what they were doing. The youth near the bed raised his hand and Stephen could see that it gripped what looked like a cobblestone. And when he went on to say what happened next, I could feel my blood running cold.

'Where's your money, you legless bastard?' the youth growled.

'You'll not find any money here,' Stephen told him. He saw the hand holding the stone coming down towards him, then a blinding pain before becoming semi-conscious, and another blow before losing consciousness completely. There was silence in the room as we could all picture the scene in our minds, wondering at the cruelty of youths who would do this to a man they obviously knew couldn't fight back.

Then Mr Oxley broke the silence. 'How could you see them if it was dark?'

Stephen pointed to the window. 'I never draw the curtains at night,' he told us. 'The light from the street lamp outside the flat shines in, and I could see plainly.' We waited as he tried to compose himself. Reliving such an horrendous attack must be dreadful for him, I thought, my heart full of pity and my head full of anger. When Stephen did speak again, it was in a quiet voice. 'When I came around it was daylight and I was covered in blood. The bedclothes were soaked and there was blood splattered all over the walls.'

I shivered with horror. 'What did you do to get help, Stephen?'

'I tried to pull myself to the edge of the bed so I could reach the wheelchair. I was in agony and it took me ages. But eventually I got the chair, rolled into it from the bed and managed to ring the police.'

Mr Oxley's face was white. 'The boys who did it knew you were a cripple?'

'I know the father of one of them,' Stephen said simply. 'The police caught him right away.'

'What did they steal?' I asked.

'Seven pounds and my watch.'

I exchanged glances with Mr Oxley and Olive. We were in shock, filled with disbelief that any human being could sink so low as viciously to attack and rob a man as helpless as Stephen. What cowards they must be that they deliberately picked on a man they knew to be a cripple and unable to fight back. A man they should help and show compassion to, for God knows he had enough problems to cope with.

'Do you have many visitors, Stephen?' I asked, in an effort to cheer him up.

'I have a home help, and a lady from Age Concern. In fact, she came the morning it happened. I was told she fainted when she saw all the blood.'

'How d'you feel now?' Mr Oxley asked. 'Are you still in pain?'

'I have terrible pains in my head,' Stephen said. 'I don't go to bed at night because I'm too frightened. I just put my pillow on the sideboard and sleep like that. Not that I sleep much. Every sound I hear makes me jump.'

'Can I come and see you again?' I asked. 'Just to see how you are and keep you company for an hour or so.'

'You will be very welcome,' he told me.

'Then I'll call in on Tuesday, shall I? About eleven o'clock.'

We made our farewells, and I couldn't stop myself kissing Stephen's cheek. From the smile on his face, he enjoyed the human contact.

*   *   *

We sat in the car around the corner from Stephen's flat, and there we let our feelings of disgust and anger erupt.

'Don't look at me or I'll start crying,' Olive said, a catch in her voice. 'I have never seen anything so sad in all my life.'

'What cowards those youths must be to pick on Stephen,' Mr Oxley said. 'You wouldn't believe anyone could be so cruel.'

Olive, like myself, was near to tears. Although she'd been a nurse when she was younger, and had seen a lot of pain and suffering, she had never before encountered suffering that had been deliberately inflicted in the pursuit of gain. She was also upset that Stephen had so little in the way of material comforts. A hospital bed, a sideboard, a settee and armchair, a two-bar electric fire and television were all he possessed. Mr Oxley was used to seeing poverty, as he spent a lot of time and energy helping those less fortunate than himself, so he wasn't as upset by Stephen's circumstances as Olive and I. What he was upset by, and very angry over, was the cruelty of the attack on someone so completely helpless and vulnerable.

'They knew he was a cripple yet they hit him with a brick. And all for seven pounds.' Mr Oxley couldn't comprehend how anyone could be so

69

wicked. He turned on the ignition and as the car purred into life, said softly, 'They could easily have killed him, and all for a measly seven pounds.'

*   *   *

The next door we knocked at was opened by a man who had contacted me about his mother, Mrs Seldon. He led us into a front room where she sat before the fire in a comfortable easy chair. He introduced us, and explained that his mother was so crippled with arthritis she couldn't move without help. We were invited to sit down, then he left us, going to finish the chore he was doing when we arrived.

Mrs Seldon's story was that two men had forced their way into her house, threatened her with violence if she made a noise, then frightened her into telling them where she kept her money. It was quite a considerable sum—her life's savings.

While she was talking, I noticed how clean and comfortable the room was. There was a small table at the side of her chair, and on it stood the telephone, a box of tissues, a glass with water in and a great number of pill bottles.

It didn't take long, however, to realize that Mrs Seldon was not a sweet old lady. She was a bad-tempered, moaning woman. She complained about everything and everyone. Even making allowances for her painful, crippling complaint, we couldn't help comparing her with the other victims we had seen, particularly Stephen who had far more to complain about but still managed to be pleasant, friendly and grateful. Mrs Seldon it seemed would never be satisfied. Her poor son was criticized very strongly, and we all felt embarrassed because we knew he could hear what his mother was saying.

'If he'd been here,' she said in a loud voice, nodding her head in the direction of the door, 'it wouldn't have happened.'

Her son came to stand in the doorway. 'I can't be here all the time, Mother,' he said in a quiet, tired voice. 'I have a job to go to and a family to look after. I come as often as I can, and do as much as I can.'

He turned and walked back to the kitchen with her complaining voice following him. 'I'm your mother, you should look after me better. You should have been here, and then it wouldn't have happened.'

I could understand the woman's anger against the men who had made her sit by while they searched for, and found, her life's savings. It must have been a terrifying ordeal for her. But I could not understand her anger against her son. It was obvious from the clean, comfortable room that she was well looked after. Apart from daily visits from her son, she also had a home help. But it clearly wasn't enough for her. In fact, even if her son left his home and family to come and live with her, she *still* wouldn't be satisfied but would think he was just doing his duty. And she would make the poor man's life a living hell.

Not wanting to prolong her son's embarrassment, as soon as we had finished drinking the tea he had kindly made for us, we took our leave. And this time I did not say I would call again.

At the front door, Mr Seldon tried to apologize

71

for his mother's bad temper and lack of manners, but I cut him short. 'Mr Seldon, you don't have to explain anything to us. It's obvious your mother is very well looked after and that you do your best. She doesn't know it, but she is very lucky to have a son like you.'

'She doesn't think I should spend any time with my family. I've cooked her dinner today and now I want to go home for my own, but she's moaned so much I feel guilty leaving her.'

'I would say your mother plays on that guilt, Mr Seldon, and she'll wear you out if you let her. She has everything to hand here, and a telephone she only has to reach for in the case of an emergency.' He looked so weary and miserable, I said, 'Go home and have your dinner with your family, they're entitled to your company as much as your mother is.'

When we were sitting in the car, Mr Oxley said, 'Oh, dear, what a difficult lady.'

For the first time that day I roared with laughter. That had to be the understatement of the year. 'Not all victims are pleasant, you know. You can't love them all.'

*　　　*　　　*

When I rang Charles Oxley a few nights later to discuss the meeting of the families of murder victims, which had been arranged for the following week, I found we now had the names of seven families who wanted to come. 'I have never heard of a meeting like this taking place before,' I said, 'it really is a one off. I wonder if we should invite a reporter to listen to their stories? If any of them don't want any publicity, then they needn't get involved. But I know Sam Kingsley would like his story made public, I think it would ease his mind a lot if he knew the public realized the injustice his family have suffered.'

'I don't think any of the families would mind,' Mr Oxley said. 'Otherwise they wouldn't have got in touch with us. Anyway, I'll contact the Press Association, I'm sure they'll be very interested.' We were about to bid each other goodnight, when he said, 'Oh, I had a call from a girl who told me her mother had been attacked and robbed. Would you give her a call when you get a chance, Mrs Jonker?'

I was grinning at the other end of the line as he gave me her name and address. I'd known Mr Oxley and the other members of CLO for a long time now, and everyone used first names— except Mr Oxley! As principal of two private schools, he was used to being strict and commanding obedience. He was exceptionally tall, straight-backed, and very clever. A very religious man, he didn't smoke, didn't touch alcohol, and not even the mildest swear word crossed his lips. He was also rather pedantic. Everything had to be perfect because that was how he lived his life. I doubt if he would ever tell a lie, even a small white one, because to do so, would be wrong in his eyes.

So we seemed an unlikely pair to be involved in anything together. I'd left school at fourteen with no qualifications except common sense and a sense of humour I'd inherited from my parents which had always stood me in good stead. But while we were poles apart in most respects, I have always considered Charles Oxley to be one of the finest men it has been my privilege to know. I may have

73

been in awe of him, but I was never afraid to tell him when I thought he was wrong. Like the time he asked me to write a letter to someone—I can't remember who now, but that isn't important. I duly wrote the letter and took it along to show him before posting it. As he opened the letter, he automatically took out a pen from the pocket of his waistcoat. It was as though he was about to mark a pupil's composition, and the pen was to correct any spelling errors. And I'm afraid it got my back up. 'Don't you dare, Mr Oxley!'

He looked at me, a perplexed expression on his face. 'I beg your pardon?'

'You look as though you're checking my letter for spelling mistakes and I feel like one of your pupils. In fact, there are no mistakes. My written English is probably as good as yours.' Then, at the look of surprise on his face, I added, 'As long as there are no big words.'

The surprise turned into a smile and the pen was replaced in the pocket of his waistcoat. 'I sometimes forget I'm not in the classroom,' he admitted.

Anyway, that was some time ago. Right now I had a new victim's name and address in front of me. 'I'll try and get along there tomorrow, Mr Oxley. Goodnight.'

*　　　*　　　*

My life was settling into a routine these days, almost as though visiting victims was a regular job. Every morning, after rushing through the household chores, I would back the car off the drive and head for the inner-city areas. I was

74

finding new victims every day, from the local paper or radio, or from the grapevine of victims I already knew and visited. I was covering every area of the city and my *A–Z* was invaluable in helping me find my way around.

The morning after my conversation with Mr Oxley, I leafed through the street maps and found the address he had given me. I decided to make it my first call, and half an hour after leaving the house I was walking up Mrs Delahunty's path. The door was opened by a small woman with brown hair who appeared to be in her late-forties. There was no smile of welcome on her face and, when I explained who I was and why I'd called, she just turned around without a word and walked back along the hall, leaving the front door open. I hesitated for just a few seconds, then, shrugging my shoulders, I followed her inside and closed the door behind me. When I entered the room she was sitting with her head bowed and made no move to acknowledge my presence.

I sat in a chair facing her. 'Your daughter rang a colleague of mine—Mr Oxley.'

'I don't know why she rang,' came the soft reply.

'She told him you had been attacked and robbed, and I'm here to see if there's any way in which I can help?'

Her only answer was a shake of the head.

'D'you want to tell me about it?' I asked. 'It sometimes help to talk.'

Practically dragging every word from her, I finally got the story. She had gone out one morning a few weeks before to call on an elderly lady who lived around the corner.

Apparently she went there every morning at nine

o'clock to light the old lady's fire. That morning she'd gone out as usual, and as she reached the corner of her road a man asked her if she knew the time. She lifted her arm to see her watch and, as she did so, the man grabbed for her bag. Because her arm was raised he couldn't pull it clear, and to Mrs Delahunty's horror she saw a knife appear in his hand. Her mind and body froze as the knife came towards her and she felt the cold steel against her cheek. The next minute she was wheeled around and pushed into a concrete post. As she put out her hand for support, the attacker grabbed the bag and ran away. By this time the blood was pouring down her cheek on to her coat, and she looked around, dazed, for someone to help. The street was deserted, so Mrs Delahunty staggered back to her house and rang for her daughter who asked for time off work and hurried home. The police and ambulance were called and Mrs Delahunty was taken to hospital.

There was no life in her voice as she told me this, and I didn't need to be a doctor to know that here was a very depressed woman. She couldn't muster any animation or interest, even when I asked about her family. She was a widow—her husband had died when the youngest daughter was only eighteen months old, and she had been left to bring up six children. The attack came when she was already weary of bringing up a large family on a widow's pension, and I think it was the last straw. She needed a shoulder to cry on, and there wasn't one. A couple of her children were now working and capable of understanding, but she didn't want to cry on their shoulder, it wouldn't be fair.

'What's your Christian name?' I asked. 'Mrs

Delahunty is a long name to keep calling you.'

'Stasia,' came the reply. 'It's short for Anastasia.'

'Golly,' I said, 'that's a very grand name. Anastasia Delahunty.'

She had been sitting sideways on to me. Now she turned to face me, and I could see the cut running down from her eye to her chin. She touched her cheek. 'The doctor decided not to put stitches in the wound because they would leave a nasty scar. She said it would heal up in time.'

'Would you like to come out for a run in the car with me?'

'I'm not going out.' She sounded very determined.

No amount of coaxing would bring any change of heart from her, so I stood up to leave. 'I'll ring you in the morning, shall I?'

Her only answer was a shrug of the shoulders, and I was left to let myself out of the house. But I worried about her all day, even when I was visiting new victims. I sympathized with the sadness in her life. Next morning when I got out of bed she was still in my thoughts, so when I thought it a reasonable hour for her to be up and about, I rang her. The conversation was mostly one-sided as Stasia didn't seem to want to talk. Her whispering voice sounded full of misery and despair. Once again I asked if she would like to come out for a run with me, and once again I was told she wasn't going out. I said she couldn't carry on like that, that it wasn't good for her children, but all she said was she didn't care.

I went about my calls that day feeling uneasy. Before making my way home, I called in on Stasia. There was something badly wrong with her, I felt sure, and I wouldn't be able to live with myself if something awful happened and I hadn't done my very best to help.

She seemed surprised when she opened the door to me, but once again walked away into the house and left me to make my own way in. I tried the bright and breezy approach first to see if it would bring her out of her shell, but had no luck.

'Stasia, what's the matter with you?' I said very gently. 'Why won't you talk to me?'

I think it was the sympathy she heard in my voice which broke the ice. Suddenly the last ten years of worry and strain came pouring out. She sobbed her heart out as she told me of the struggle she'd had trying to be both mother and father to her children. How there'd always been a shortage of money for essentials, and how much she missed her husband.

I felt like crying with her, but thought this would be the wrong thing to do. So I listened in silence until she'd finished. 'How long are you going to sit around being depressed, Stasia?' I asked then. 'You're young enough to make a new life for yourself. You've got to buck up and start living again.'

'What for?' she asked. 'I don't care what happens to me.'

'You should care what happens to your children,' I said. 'They must be worried, seeing you sit there depressed all the time.'

'They're good kids,' she admitted, 'but I just feel there's nothing to live for.'

I kept my thoughts and feelings to myself because I feared Stasia was suicidal and couldn't force my views on her, couldn't make her snap out of herself; only she could do that. 'I'll call in tomorrow, shall I?'

The answer I got wasn't very encouraging. 'Please yourself.'

Nevertheless, I couldn't get her out of my mind and rang her again the next morning. After five minutes of trying to involve her in conversation, I really felt afraid for her. She wasn't rational, and I feared she might do something stupid. I put the phone down wondering what to do, then quickly made up my mind.

Half-an-hour later I was knocking on Stasia's door. When she opened it I just marched past her into the living room. 'Get your coat, you're coming with me.'

'I'm not going out,' she said, surprised by my attitude.

'Oh, yes, you are,' I told her. 'It's about time you got off your bottom. Now get your coat on, or do I have to drag you down the path?'

One arm was only half in the sleeve of her coat as I bundled her down the path and into the car. Without a word I drove off, and we didn't speak until I stopped the car outside of the flat where Stephen lived. 'Come on,' I told a startled Stasia.

When Stephen saw me walking up the path, he waved and shouted for us to come in. I let Stasia go in ahead of me then, without looking at her, crossed the room and bent to kiss Stephen. 'This is a friend of mine, her name is Stasia.'

As I watched her walk over to shake hands with Stephen, I wondered whether I should have warned her about him being a cripple. I had intended to shock her out of her depression, but now I wondered whether I had been right to do so.

Stephen, of course, was oblivious to any

undercurrent. He was always happy to have visitors, and chatted away happily. I kept glancing at Stasia, who didn't join in the conversation, and could see her eyes were fixed on Stephen. Gradually I brought the conversation round to what had happened to him by asking if he'd heard from the police whether the two youths who'd attacked him had been arrested. And then I casually told him that Stasia too had been a victim. We chatted for a further half-hour, then because I had more calls to make I stood up and said I'd have to be on my way. 'I'll be in again next week, Stephen,' I said as I kissed him goodbye. 'But you've got my phone number if you need me.'

He nodded. 'Yes, I've got it on a piece of paper on that side table. I've got Mr Oxley's as well. Thank you for coming, Joan, it's nice to have someone to talk to, I don't get many visitors.'

Then I stood back and watched as Stasia kissed his cheek and asked, 'Can I come and see you some time, Stephen?'

'Of course you can, and welcome.' Stephen didn't ask much of life, just his television, cigarettes, and a trip to the pub when his son came down to wheel him there. Little did he realize that seeing him was the turning point for Stasia.

When we got to the bottom of his path, we both waved before I closed the gate behind us. Once out of sight, I turned to Stasia. 'I know you have problems . . .'

Her eyes moist with unshed tears, she shook her head. 'I thought I had, but they're nothing compared to his.'

Walking back to the car, I breathed a sigh of relief. I had taken a chance bringing Stasia to meet

Stephen, hoping the sight of him would shock her out of her lethargy. It could very well have gone wrong. But, thank God, it had worked.

CHAPTER FIVE

Any doubts I may have had about the wisdom of bringing together the families of murder victims faded as soon as the meeting started. They immediately made friends and chatted without reserve. I knew I would never understand them as they understood each other because I hadn't suffered as they had. My child hadn't been suddenly and brutally taken from me, and I didn't have the nightmare of knowing that child had died in fear and agony.

The reporters had turned out in numbers, but before they were allowed to question the parents we had some tea and sandwiches to give everyone time to relax and get acquainted. I was very interested in Sam Kingsley's reaction to Ann West, mother of Lesley Ann Downey, a victim of the Moors Murderers. He seemed to be drawn to her and, as he kissed her cheek, I heard him say, 'What happened to my son was bad, but not nearly as bad as what happened to your little girl.'

After a while we sat the families in a row in front of the reporters, and each in turn told their own story. Three of the families present had daughters who had been murdered by the same man. Their accounts were horrific—one of the young girls had been brutally decapitated and her body buried at the side of a canal. I wondered if I could have kept

81

my sanity if that had happened to one of my children.

The man who had murdered the three girls was living with a woman at the time he committed the first murder. He'd told her about it and even, one day, showed her where the body was buried. The woman didn't go to the police, she kept quiet. After murder number two, she actually washed the blood from his clothes and knew exactly what he had done. Even after hearing of the murder of his third victim, Sharon Mosoph, she didn't go to the police. In fact, when they came looking for the man, she hid him behind an old fireplace that had been boarded over.

After Sharon was killed her body was thrown into the canal. The man the papers named The Beast was walking home after disposing of the body when he remembered that the police could identify a person from their teeth marks. As he had left bite marks all over Sharon's body, he turned around and made his way back to the canal.

It was a cold night and the water was almost frozen so it was only with great difficulty that he dragged the body towards the side of the canal. With a six-inch nail, he hacked away at the body in an attempt to remove the teeth marks. One of Sharon's nipples had been completely ripped off.

There was complete silence as the three families told their stories. The only sounds to break the silence were gasps of horror and disbelief. The reporters didn't speak as their pens flew over their note pads.

Jackie Harrington told of her lovely young sister who had been murdered. A man had been charged, but instead of bringing relief that he'd been caught, the trial proved a nightmare for the family. The defence barrister claimed that Jackie's sister had enjoyed sex with many men. This was so far from the truth that her family were shattered. The dead girl was quiet, pretty, popular but reserved— certainly not the kind the defence was making out. How does a dead girl defend herself, though? She can't, and that's why the defence was able to make some of the mud stick. Jackie was heartbroken; because her parents were in such deep shock they refused even to go out. From my experience I would say that there are some lawyers who will fight to get their clients off even when they know they're guilty. I wonder how they can live with themselves—I couldn't.

We all knew Ann West's story—I think every person in the country knew the horror of the Moors Murders and the acts of brutality and depravity perpetrated by Myra Hindley and Ian Brady. Ann told of her agony every time Lord Longford renewed his campaign to have Hindley released. She also promised that her threat to kill Hindley would be kept if it were humanly possible.

'I said I would kill her,' Ann told a hushed room, 'and I mean it. If I die, or am too ill to carry out my threat, then my sons will do it. That evil woman should not be allowed to live.'

The stories Sam Kingsley and Bill Aldis had to tell were familiar to me, but I still felt sad at the heartbreak and suffering in their accounts. As Bill Aldis told of how he and his wife had moved away from their house of memories to a small cottage in North Wales, and how each morning he would go down to the bottom of their long back garden to talk with his dead son, I didn't even try to keep my tears back.

Geoffrey Levy of the *Daily Express* was there, and he asked the families what they hoped would come from this unique meeting. Although their words were different, they all said they hoped it would be the start of a campaign to fight for justice for victims of crime, and also that they would like to help other families who were in the same position as themselves. I could see the meeting had been of value to them, not only as a platform on which to air their views but also to relieve them of some of the bitterness they had bottled up inside. Knowing that the reporters, who had been very understanding and sympathetic, would write up their stories seemed to have lifted a burden from their shoulders. Because until now nobody had really wanted to know. Although nothing else might come of the meeting, I still thought it had been worthwhile for the families.

*   *   *

All the national papers carried the story, with pictures, the following day, and one of the results was a phone call from David Davies of BBC TV Manchester. He asked if I would come into the studio that night to talk about the families of murder victims. When I asked if I could bring a member of one family with me, he readily agreed.

I put the phone down and sat puzzling over who I could ask. Then I settled on Jackie Harrington, thinking it would help her and her parents if the truth were told about her murdered sister. But when I rang Jackie she refused point blank.

'Oh, my God,' she said, 'I couldn't go on telly,

84

I'd be terrified!'

It took a lot of persuasion to get her to change her mind. In fact, it was only because she thought it would help her parents that she agreed.

'But suppose I dry up and can't get a word out?' she asked.

'If that happens,' I told her, 'just remember your sister. You would be doing it to clear her name. In one minute you can tell the whole of the country— not just a few people in your street, but millions— that your sister was a lovely girl who didn't deserve to die.' I didn't tell her that I was already shaking like a leaf myself at the prospect of going on television. It was no good two of us worrying for the next couple of hours.

As it turned out there was no need for either of us to worry. Because David Davies was so gentle, he made the interview less of a nightmare than Jackie had expected. Afterwards she was overjoyed that she had been able to tell people exactly what her sister was like. And this confirmed what I had been thinking since meeting Albert, the first victim. If they weren't ignored, but listened to and sympathized with, many victims would feel less bitter. It seemed to them that no one cared, all the consideration and understanding went to the offender. How could things be changed so justice was more even-handed? The only way I knew was to keep on shouting until someone listened. And it was going to take a lot of shouting.

*   *   *

At last our holiday time had arrived and Tony and I were really looking forward to having a break. My

85

mum and dad were minding Philip so there were just the two of us. On the drive down to the ferry we were in high spirits, and adding to our pleasure was the beautiful weather. The signs were good for a lovely, well-earned holiday.

It had been arranged that my friend's brother would meet us off the overnight ferry at St Helier. As soon as our car rolled off the boat I could see him standing next to his car. I had never met Ray but his sister had shown me a photograph so I had no hesitation in waving to him. Tony wound his window down when Ray came over to us, and after exchanging greetings it was decided we would follow his car to their home. He warned us to be careful of the narrow roads and the many dangerous corners.

I knew Ruth and Ray worked for Sir William Butlin, but I didn't know their house was on the Butlin estate. One of a pair of semis, it had a large front garden with an archway to one side leading to the Butlin residence. There wasn't time for getting acquainted with our hosts because they were due to go to work so, after making us a pot of tea and some toast, they left Tony and me to help ourselves to some breakfast before unpacking our cases.

Being a typical woman, and very nosy, I went out into the garden and was immediately drawn to the archway leading to Sir William's house. The gardens were absolutely magnificent, and the long driveway from the ornate gates to the house was very impressive. I could only see the house side on, but the general effect was enough to make me sigh with envy.

That night Ruth said we had been booked into one of Sir William's hotels for a meal. But first of

86

all she wanted to be brought up-to-date with news from the area where she used to live. That didn't take long because I knew very little, and eventually I told her how I had been working with victims. 'It's not a job, as such,' I told her, 'I don't have to do it, it's voluntary, but it's in my blood now and it's something I want to do.'

For the next two days Tony and I explored the island, and we really loved it. There were so many interesting places to go, and so many beautiful beaches to laze on. Then when Ruth and Ray had finished work, we would go out for an evening meal and a few drinks. It was a lovely, relaxing and lazy holiday. Just what Tony and I needed.

It was on the Tuesday night, while we were having a nightcap, that Ruth asked casually, 'These victims you say you visit, how many are you talking about?'

I thought for a while before answering. 'You know, I can't remember offhand how many I've seen.' I tried going round the areas in my head, counting, but it was impossible. So I reached for my handbag. 'Have you got a piece of paper and I'll try and write them down?'

When I totted the number up, I was surprised to find they totalled fifty. I handed the paper over to her. 'There's fifty names there, though there are probably some I've forgotten. But honestly, Ruth, if you could just see how old and frail they are, you'd have to be made of stone not to be affected.'

Tony yawned and stretched his arms. 'It must be all the fresh air, but I'm bushed. It won't take me long to drop off tonight.'

I will never know who dropped off first because the next morning I couldn't even remember putting my head on the pillow, and it was nine o'clock before we got out of bed, which is very unusual for me since I usually get up with the lark. After getting washed and dressed, Tony and I sat in the garden reading the morning papers which Ray had thoughtfully left for us, until Ruth came dashing around the corner of the house.

'Get dressed up in your best clothes,' she said, excitedly. 'Sir William wants to see you.' She saw the startled look on our faces and grinned. 'Come on, get yourselves tidied up.'

'What does he want to see us for?' I started to ask. Then, 'You're pulling our legs.'

'I told Lady Butlin about the victims of crime you've seen, and she told Sir William.' Ruth was serious now. 'He was interested and wants to know more.'

I flew upstairs, laziness gone, and in record time I had changed my dress and made my hair and face presentable. When I got downstairs I found Ruth waiting impatiently. As we neared the house, I was able to see, for the first time, the beautiful building that was home to the Butlin family. We weren't allowed to dawdle because Sir William was expecting us and we were taken to a door just past the main entrance. In answer to Ruth's knock it was opened by a slim woman in black slacks, a black jumper, and a scarf tied gypsy-fashion on her head. Ruth introduced us, and I was struck immediately by her friendly, welcoming smile. After shaking hands, Lady Butlin said she would take us right through to Sir William's study where he was waiting for us.

Everything was happening so quickly that I didn't have time to feel at all nervous. The study door was opened, I followed Lady Butlin through, and Tony brought up the rear. My first impression as I walked into the room was that there were a lot of people there. But when I glimpsed someone who looked like myself, I realized the walls were lined with mirrors. And there was Sir William, hand outstretched and a huge smile on his face.

After waving us to chairs, he started saying, 'Well, young lady, I've been hearing a lot about you. Tell me what you do to help people?'

I told him briefly, outlining some of the cases where an elderly person had been hurt, left in distress and sometimes penniless. I explained that I worked mostly in the working-class areas of Liverpool, and the people I met had only their pension to live on. I always get very emotional when talking about victims and the injustices suffered by them, and this time was no exception. 'In real terms, there's very little I can do,' I explained. 'I give a few pounds to help out when I can, but obviously I'm very limited in that respect. The only thing I can do is to visit, hold their hands, cry and sympathize with them. Actually, I think that is the best way to help because they can see someone cares and they appreciate my visits. Mostly they live on their own and have no family to help them. A bunch of flowers or a packet of cigarettes works wonders when a person is distressed and thinks nobody cares. They are only little things, but it's the best I can do. I give hugs, kisses, lend a sympathetic ear, and they are much appreciated.'

'Well, I would like to help,' Sir William said. 'I want to give you some money so that you can do more.'

'I can't take money from you, Sir William,' I protested. 'You don't even know me!'

He seemed surprised by this reaction. 'I'm a pretty shrewd judge of character,' he said, 'and I don't think I could go far wrong with you.'

I shook my head. 'That is the nicest compliment anyone has ever paid me,' I told him, 'but I can't take money off you.'

'Where do you get the money from to do what you do?' he asked.

'I use my own,' I told him.

'But you're only an ordinary housewife,' he said, 'you can't keep doing that!'

I laughed. 'It's a case of putting my money where my mouth is.'

'You can't do that,' he insisted. 'I've often read about the terrible things that are happening to old people, and been horrified. Now, through you, I can help.'

'I'm very sorry, Sir William, you are very kind and I do appreciate it but, you see, I have always been very careful with money, and if I were to take any from you I would leave myself open to criticism. People would say I was profiting from my work.'

Sir William had a cheeky grin, and his eyes were shining with humour. 'This is the first time anyone has refused to take money from me.'

'I'm sorry,' I said, and really meant it because it was obvious he wanted to help.

'Why don't you register as a charity?' he said suddenly, a thought that had never entered my head. 'Then I could be of use.'

Lady Butlin leaned forward. 'That's a marvellous idea, Joan. It isn't a difficult procedure,

90

and Bill will help you.'

I suddenly began to feel excited. 'It would be marvellous, but I wouldn't know how to go about registering.'

'I'll do everything I can,' Sir William said. 'It doesn't take long to register. Come to London one day, soon after your holiday, and I'll have my accountant there. He'll advise you on anything you need to know.'

'I'll ring Charles Oxley today,' I said, 'and ask if he'll come with me.' I then went on to explain the reason for this. 'If you are going to give us money, you have the right to know what sort of people we are.'

Sir William shrugged his shoulders. 'You can do that if you wish, of course, but you are the one I am helping.'

We shook hands, and Lady Butlin escorted us out of the study and into the kitchen. 'Have a cuppa with me?'

I watched as she moved around the gleaming kitchen, putting the kettle on and setting the cups out. She talked as though we had known each other for years, friendly and easygoing. It would be hard not to be relaxed in her company. While we were chatting over a cup of tea, I found that Lady Butlin had been away from her home town of Liverpool for over twenty years, but she certainly hadn't lost the quick wit that Liverpudlians are noted for. We were laughing at one of her jokes when Sir William came through to see what the laughter was about. Soon he was demonstrating his own keen sense of fun, and while listening to him I realized he was much more than the Billy Butlin, holiday-camp king, that everyone knew. He was kind, generous, friendly, and compassionate. A man you could turn to in times of trouble.

*   *   *

Like all good things, the holiday in Jersey came to an end. Tony and I both enjoyed ourselves because we were with each other all day and every day, which was rare for us. I was sad at leaving, but at the same time looking forward to visiting London with Charles Oxley to discuss our application for charitable status. I was happy that at last someone was interested and prepared to help, because with that help I could do so much more to relieve the suffering of elderly victims. So when I went round to the big house to say farewell, and was shaking Sir William's hand, I bent forward on impulse and kissed his cheek. Even if we were, for some reason, never to get any money from him, I would always be grateful that he was prepared to trust me.

Three days after getting home from holiday, I found myself sitting next to Mr Oxley on the train bound for London. In my bag I had photographs of some of the victims which I wanted to show Sir William so he would know exactly the type of people I was helping. On the back of each photo I wrote the name and age of the person—between seventy-eight and eighty-nine. Their injuries and the looks of despair on their faces would melt a heart of stone.

I also took advantage of the journey down to London to pluck up courage and tell Mr Oxley of my idea of a coach trip for some of the victims. I didn't have to press very hard. He had seen them for himself, and without hesitation said it was an

92

excellent idea and offered to pay all expenses himself. My spirits rose—things were moving now, and we would be helping in a definite and constructive way. Mr Oxley said for me to go ahead and book a fifty-seater coach, which delighted me. How wonderful to give pleasure to fifty people who had been badly treated by thugs and then by those in authority who didn't seem to care. These were people who had worked hard all their lives; now they lived in fear of cowards who preferred stealing and maiming to earning an honest living. At least now, with the help of Mr Oxley I could offer the victims a day free from fear.

I was still feeling light-hearted when, later, we were shown into Sir William's office. After greeting him and Lady Butlin with a kiss, I introduced Charles Oxley, and was myself introduced to Peter Hetherington, Sir William's accountant. Tea was provided, and we then got down to discussing our application to the Charity Commission. Peter Hetherington, at Sir William's suggestion, offered to do the necessary work for us, but Mr Oxley said he knew the procedure and would make the application himself. We agreed that we would have to have a name for the charity and, after several suggestions, decided upon Victims of Violence.

Sir William was eager to give us money right away, but when I expressed my doubts about this Peter Hetherington agreed that it would be better to wait until we were registered as a charity. I felt so much at home with the Butlins that it seemed I'd known them for years. I was certain of one thing: I had gained two very good friends.

Back in Liverpool's Lime Street station later that night, Mr Oxley and I chatted briefly before going our separate ways. He promised to apply immediately to the Charity Commission, while I agreed to book the coach and get in touch with the fifty victims I thought would most benefit from a day out in the company of like-minded people.

* * *

I was tired by the time I got home that night. It had been a long day, but a good one for me and the elderly people I would soon be able to help as I thought they should be helped. Tony made me a cup of coffee and sat down to listen to my account of what had happened. I had barely begun when the phone rang. 'Oh, no,' I groaned, pushing myself up from the couch. 'I hope whoever it is doesn't keep me long.'

The caller was Ann West, mother of Lesley Ann Downey. She was both excited and nervous. 'I've had a call from Brass Tacks, asking if I would like to take part in a programme they are recording on Wednesday night. They've asked me to take three people to sit on a panel, and I wondered if you would come?'

'What's the programme about? Did they say?'

'Well, you know Lord Longford is campaigning to have Myra Hindley paroled? The programme's about that.'

Ann spoke very quietly and I could barely hear her. 'Who else is on the programme?'

'I don't know,' she answered. 'But Lord Longford will definitely be on, and I know Brian Truman is the presenter, but that's all.' I could hear her sigh before she went on, 'I'm frightened that I will get upset, and anyway I can't explain myself properly. You know how to put things over, that's why I'd like you to come.'

'Ann, I'm not that good, and I think I'd be terrified on a major programme like Brass Tacks. I only wish I were that good, but I might just let you down.'

'You won't let me down, I know you won't. And d'you know anyone else who would come?' she asked. 'I need someone who could hold their own with Lord Longford, because I don't think I'll be able to say anything myself, I'll be too nervous.'

'Shall I ask Charles Oxley?' I said.

There was relief in her voice when she said, 'Oh, if you would, Joan, please. I don't know anyone else to ask, only a woman called Win Pilkington who has been very good to me since Lesley Ann was murdered. She came to see me after it happened, and she's been helping me ever since.'

'I'll ring Mr Oxley and call you back as soon as I've spoken to him.'

I replaced the receiver, then picked it up immediately and dialled Tower College. Mr Oxley answered the phone himself, and when I told him the reason for my call he didn't hesitate to say he would gladly take part in the programme. Ann had given me the time we had to be at the studio so I arranged to meet Mr Oxley there. Then I rang her back and told her I would call at her house and have a cup of tea with her before going on to the studio. I thought it might help to relax her, and take her mind off the forthcoming ordeal.

But when I got to Ann's house on the Wednesday night she was a nervous wreck. In the taxi to the studio, she shook the whole time. We were shown to the hospitality room where tables

95

were set out with sandwiches and drinks. We were told by one of the researchers that there would be two panels, Ann's and Lord Longford's, a police inspector would be interviewed and there would be a phone-in near the end. Apart from that, they would take things as they came. Easy for her to talk.

My heart was pounding as we were led through to the studio, and it didn't help that the audience was to be in darkness. It seemed quite a large audience by the noise, but formed of only vague shapes and shadows. The studio floor where the tables were set out was just the opposite, with huge lights burning down relentlessly. When Charles Oxley, Win Pilkington and I were led to a table, I took an end chair and was about to sit down when I realized Ann West had been separated from us and was sitting on her own at a table about six yards away. Surely, I thought, they are not so insensitive as to leave her alone when the subject of the programme is the murder of three children, one of them hers. She looked absolutely lost, and even from that distance I could sense her fear.

'They're not going to leave her there, are they?' I asked the woman sitting next to me.

'They must be,' Win Pilkington answered. 'It seems a bit heartless.'

I looked over at Ann, twisting a white handkerchief in her hands. She looked so sad I turned my head to see if I could see a member of the programme team, but my attention was diverted when Lord Longford and his panel entered and took their seats at a table on the far side of the room. I had vaguely wondered when we were in the hospitality room why there was no sign of Lord Longford. Now I realized that we had been deliberately kept apart.

My eyes went from Lord Longford to the woman sitting next to him, and for a minute I thought my eyes were deceiving me for it was the notorious Janie Jones! What on earth was she doing on the programme? Then I remembered reading that Lord Longford had campaigned energetically for her release from prison and had been successful. Next to Janie Jones was a woman who was later introduced as Dr Sarah Trevelyan.

Brian Truman opened the programme by telling us we were to be shown, on a monitor, all the details of the Moors Murders. Then the two panels would be asked their views on whether Myra Hindley should be released from prison. He went on to explain to us, the studio audience and the watching millions, that the studio had tried without success to trace the families of the two boys who were murdered. They had apparently vanished without trace, and the only parent present was Ann West, the mother of little Lesley Ann.

There was an almost unnatural hush as the details of the case which had horrified and angered the whole nation unfolded on that small screen. We heard how Myra Hindley lured the two young boys into her car and how later they were brutally murdered. We heard of the atrocities inflicted on little Lesley Ann, heard her recorded cries to be allowed to go home to her mam. How she pleaded with them not to take her clothes off again, how she was forced to pose naked while Brady took photographs of her, and how she was gagged to keep her quiet. I kept glancing across to where Ann West sat, and she was such a pitiful sight I felt like standing up and asking why they were putting her through this torture.

My thoughts were interrupted by Brian Truman asking Lord Longford to give his reasons for thinking Myra Hindley should be released from prison. My attention was riveted to Lord Longford as he told us Myra Hindley had changed, that she was now a reformed character and had actually embraced his faith. I couldn't believe what I was hearing. Of course Hindley would embrace his faith if she thought he would get her out of prison. She was wicked, evil and clever enough to know when she was dealing with a do-gooder. Not once did he refer to the film that we in the studio, and the watching public on their screens, had just seen. Not once did he show compassion or sympathy for the sad figure of Ann West who for fourteen years had suffered the agonies of knowing her little girl died in fear. Not once did he mention the other victims of Hindley and Brady. I have always thought they were evil, but if I was asked who I thought the most evil it would be Hindley, for most women are born with maternal instincts and would protect a child from harm. She didn't, she actually encouraged Brady to commit the dreadful things he did to little, innocent Lesley Ann.

I had been feeling nervous and apprehensive about how I would conduct myself when eventually I was asked for my views, but when Janie Jones stood up to tell us how she had befriended Myra Hindley in jail, and how she was sure that if we could meet her we would see what a really nice girl she was, my blood started to boil. I didn't even hear what Dr Sarah Trevelyan was saying, except that it was in the same vein as her two colleagues. In fact, it was almost as though the three had been programmed prior to the show.

It was fortunate that Brian Truman came to me first for my views for by now I was too angry to be nervous. Without thinking about where I was, I blurted out, 'Have those three people really been watching the same programme as we have on that small screen? Have they really been listening to the horrors suffered by three young innocent children?' I couldn't have stopped myself then even if I'd wanted to. 'As for Janie Jones,' I pointed a finger, 'why is she here? At the end of her trial the judge said she was the most wicked woman in the country, and she'd still be in prison if Lord Longford hadn't fought so hard for her release. What makes her think decent people would be interested in what she has to say?' I watched Janie Jones fling her hair back and raise her eyebrows at Lord Longford, as if to say what right did I have to criticize her. 'I don't think the three opposition panellists are normal people with normal reactions.'

I was so incensed that I didn't hear half of what Charles Oxley or Win Pilkington said next, except they were more controlled in their speech than I had been. All I could think was, how dare Lord Longford bring along an ex-convict to say Hindley was a nice girl, when the mother of one of that 'nice girl's' victims was present? Not one of the opposition panel even mentioned feeling sorry for Ann.

The next person to speak was a retired police officer who had been involved with the arrest, and subsequent trial, of Brady and Hindley. Although not a strong speaker, he did put across clearly the revulsion of the policemen involved in the case.

Now all the speakers had given their views, the phone lines were open to members of the watching public who wished to air their views. The first few calls were all from people who were strongly against the release of Hindley. The next one was from a woman who said she was a Roman Catholic, like Lord Longford, and that she had at one time been a nun. Her opinion was that the Moors Murderers should not have been allowed to live. Brian Truman asked Lord Longford if he would like to speak to the woman, but he shook his head vigorously and muttered something no one could understand. It was clear that if you didn't agree with him, then he wasn't going to waste time talking to you.

The next call was a shock to everyone, and suddenly the atmosphere in the studio was charged with expectation. The caller was the father of John Kilbride, one of the murdered boys. He spoke in a low, strange voice that made me think he was drunk or distraught. With the audience hanging on to his every word, he described how he had left his home town in a vain effort to forget what had happened. He had been watching the programme and felt he had to speak out. His life, he said in a voice thick with emotion, had been shattered by the murder of his son, and he vowed, in public, in front of millions of viewers, that if Myra Hindley were ever released he would kill her. He was crying as he spoke, and when I looked at Ann West she too was crying. When my gaze went to Lord Longford and Janie Jones to see how Mr Kilbride's words had affected them, it was to find expressions on their faces which said they found the whole thing distasteful. But I think the expression on mine got through to Janie Jones at least because she quickly looked away.

After the programme Charles Oxley said he would make his way home, but I went with Ann West to the hospitality room for some refreshment. As we entered the room the first person I saw was Janie Jones, chatting to some people. She happened to catch sight of me and spun on her heel and left the room, never to be seen again. I went to the table to help myself to some food then glanced around for Ann. I was surprised to see Lord Longford talking to her, and crossed the room to join them. As I got closer, I heard him say, 'Will you come with me to visit Myra? I know you would like her if you met her.'

As Ann shook her head, I thought, is this man completely insensitive? and backed away, not wanting to be in his company.

Later on, I was talking to Brian Truman when Lord Longford walked over to the buffet table. I reached into my handbag and brought out Ethel Attwood's photograph which I passed to Brian. I heard his gasp of horror and saw the disgust on his face before I took it back from him and walked over to Lord Longford. Placing the photograph in front of his eyes, I asked, 'What do you think should happen to the person who did this?'

He glanced at it briefly and handed it back as though it was burning his hand. 'Where does she live?'

'I could tell you, but if I did I'd have to tell you about thousands more,' I said. 'The thousands of frail, elderly people who are attacked and injured on our streets, and left without any money for food

101

and heating.'

It was obvious he wasn't in the least interested in victims, but I was determined to prise some sort of reaction from him. By this time Brian Truman had come to stand beside me and was clearly listening. 'Why don't you help victims?' I asked. 'They are the ones being punished, and yet they have committed no crime.'

'Many of the offenders need help,' he answered, 'and keeping them in prison doesn't help.'

When he saw me looking at him in dismay, he came out with a remark that will stay with me all my life. 'We can't bring Lesley Ann back, so why keep Myra in jail?'

I stared at him with incredulity. For once in my life I was bereft of the power of speech. I turned to Brian Truman and saw that he too was stunned.

There was no way I could reason with a man who ignored what he didn't want to know. 'Lord Longford,' I managed to say calmly, 'you are not real.' And I turned and walked away.

*   *   *

That night I couldn't get off to sleep. I could hear Tony's gentle breathing beside me and I envied him. My mind was too active for sleep. I kept going over the remarks made by Lord Longford's panel on the Brass Tacks programme. How could those people talk of Myra Hindley being a reformed character who should be allowed out of jail? Never once did they mention the children killed by her and her evil accomplice, or the horrific manner in which they died. Nor did they mention the fear that must have been in those young hearts and on the innocent faces as they pleaded to be allowed to go home to their mothers. Or that as they were pleading Brady was carrying out his acts of wickedness while Hindley looked on and even assisted him. The very thought is enough to send any parent out of their mind.

I turned on my side, trying to clear my head so sleep would come, but it was impossible because I was too emotional. I was remembering all the families I had met with a child who'd been murdered, and how deeply I had felt for them. But with the best will in the world I could never put myself in their shoes and suffer the heartache, sadness and anger they felt. No one could, except someone who had gone through the same nightmare.

I remember before I became involved with victims of violence how I would often see reports in the daily papers of another murder, and shake my head in despair while turning the page over and going on to another piece of news. Everyone in the country was probably doing the same because no one told them the full story. How the heartache and raw emotion, plus the desire to know why someone would deliberately kill their much-loved child, was enough to send a family over the edge of sanity. It all happened so quickly, with no time for them to stop it, and was so final. No one could bring their child back, no one could tell them why, and except for close family and friends nobody seemed to care. I thought everyone should know the true story behind the newspaper headlines, but how to do that? I knew many families of murder victims, but for most of them going over all the details publicly would hurt too much.

I glanced at the alarm clock on the bedside cabinet and groaned. It was two o'clock and I was still too restless to sleep. In my mind's eye I went over all the families I had met, and the one who stood out as most likely to want to tell his story was Ralph Mosoph whose seventeen-year-old daughter Sharon had been brutally murdered. I had spoken to him a few weeks before and had sensed he'd harnessed his grief with anger. He wanted to talk about his daughter, wanted to tell everyone of his family's loss and need for justice. I believed it would be good for him to relieve his pent-up feelings by writing down his thoughts, and the hurt and grief of his family. Once I had convinced myself that Ralph would be willing to tell the world his story, I snuggled up to Tony and emptied my mind of everything except the need for sleep.

I rang Ralph the following day and explained what I had in mind, and why. I asked if he would be willing to put his thoughts into words. He was not only willing but appeared to be keen to do it. He thought it would help to ease the hurt bottled up inside of him.

'Ralph, can I ask you if you would start writing from the time your family got out of bed on the morning of Sharon's murder? I know it's a lot to ask, but it would help the readers if they knew what she looked like and what sort of personality she had. They could visualize her while they were reading.'

'I'll start today, Joan, it will give me something to do instead of sitting here, hurting inside and feeling helpless and hopeless. I'll borrow a typewriter off one of the family and give you a ring when I've finished. It'll take a while, though, because I can't type.'

Four weeks later I received the typewritten pages and was surprised by how professional they looked for someone who couldn't type. There were one or two slight alterations needed, and I rang Ralph to ask if it was all right with him if I did these. He sounded calmer over the phone, more in control of his emotions, and said writing it all down from beginning to end had been harrowing but had at least helped release some of his bitterness. The hurt would never leave him, but he had to learn to live with it if he was to keep his sanity.

The following account tells of the agony, heartbreak, anguish and despair of just one of the many families who have a loved one murdered. Not because they had done anything wrong, but because they innocently came into contact with evil.

CHAPTER SIX

As Ralph Mosoph stood by the kitchen sink peeling potatoes for the cottage pie he was making for the family's evening meal, his thoughts were miles away. He was going over the events of the last few weeks, since he'd been told, a week after his thirty-ninth birthday, that he was suffering from angina and hypertension. He'd been off work since then, but rather than hang around all day doing nothing, he did little chores to help his wife, Jackie, who was out at work all day. Like today, he was making the cottage pie so it would be ready to put on the table when she came home, and they could sit down and enjoy it with their five children. When he was working, it was all rush for Jackie; having to dash in from work and prepare a quick meal for them. Now, in his mind's eye, he could visualize a lovely, golden-brown cottage pie, ready to put on the table when she came in.

'Dad?' The voice floating down the stairs was that of his seventeen-year-old daughter, Sharon. 'Are any of the kids home from school yet?'

Ralph walked to the bottom of the stairs. 'Not yet! Why?'

'I need some hair clips from the shops.'

'I'll tell Maxine as soon as she comes in. She won't be long.' Ralph walked back into the living room and sat down. Automatically he reached for the packet of cigarettes while at the same time reminding himself that the doctor had warned him he must stop smoking. Striking a match, he promised himself he would stop next week.

The door was pushed open and the youngest of the family, seven-year-old Mark, walked in. 'Hi, Dad! Can I have a jam butty? I'm starving'

'Only one,' Ralph warned. 'Your dinner won't be long.'

Mark grabbed the sandwich with eager hands and Ralph smiled as he turned to the wall cupboard to get a box of tablets. He heard the door opening behind him, and looking over his shoulder saw Maxine and Paul playfully pushing each other into the room. Maxine was ten and Paul eleven, high-spirited children who were now going to disrupt the peace and quiet of the Mosoph household.

'Maxine, will you go upstairs and see what our Sharon wants?' Ralph asked. 'I think she needs you to go to the shops for her.'

'Okay, Dad!' Maxine answered cheerfully, before dashing into the hall and bounding up the stairs two at a time. Within minutes she was back again, her face alight with excitement.

'Our Sharon's hair looks great, Dad! It's got streaks in it! She needs more clips, and she wants a packet of crisps so I'm going to the shops for her. I won't be long.'

Ralph walked to the window to watch Maxine flying down the path. 'Doesn't that kid ever walk?' he thought aloud. 'Every time I see her, she's flying like a bat out of hell.'

Just then a friend's car pulled up outside and Ralph's stepson Lester stepped out. At seventeen he was the same age as Sharon. Ralph and Jackie had both been married before, and had started their married life with Ralph's daughter Sharon and Jackie's son Lester. Then their own three children had come along, and they were now a close, devoted family.

Lester put his head round the door.

'Where's our Sharon, Dad? I'm going out early tonight and want to ask her if she'll press my clothes for me.'

Ralph jerked his head 'She's been up there all afternoon—God knows what she's doing! If you're going upstairs, tell her the dinner's nearly ready.'

As he heard Lester running up the stairs, Ralph chuckled. 'He'll be lucky if he gets her to do anything for him tonight! It's her big night!'

Sharon was going for a night out at the local Pack Horse Hotel, and was so excited you'd think she was going to the Ritz. It was a sales promotion night, organized by the furniture factory where she worked, and she'd bought herself a new dress for the occasion.

The front door nearly burst off its hinges as Maxine dashed back through. She made straight for the stairs, and Ralph shook his head as he walked into the hall just in time to see her disappearing into Sharon's room.

'Don't you stay up there! Your dinner's ready.'

Paul was watching television when Ralph walked into the living room. 'Come on, son, set the table. Your mam will be in soon.'

'Okay, Dad.' Paul moved to the sideboard to get the cutlery out of a drawer without taking his eyes off the TV set, terrified he'd miss something exciting. He used his hands to feel where to put the knives and forks on the table then went back to sit on the couch and watch in comfort the latest thrilling episode of the children's programme.

When he heard a car pulling up outside, Ralph walked to the window and saw Jackie locking the car door. It was Lester's car, but because he hadn't passed his test yet, and couldn't drive it himself, he let his mam use it for work. Jackie checked that all the doors were locked and was walking up the path when Ralph opened the front door for her.

'Hello, love, everything all right?' A small, slim woman, Jackie looked too young to be the mother of a seventeen-year-old son, particularly in the jeans and jacket which were her working clothes. 'Mmm—something smells nice, what are you cooking?'

'Cottage pie—everyone's favourite.' Ralph laughed as he went towards the kitchen. 'We never have any complaints when cottage pie's on the menu.' He turned round to ask, 'Did you see Mark in the street?'

'Yes, he's playing with Timmy next-door, I'll go and shout him.'

Five minutes later all the family were seated round the table and Ralph proudly produced his masterpiece. Unlike other nights when he had to coax the children to eat all their meal, the cottage pie was devoured in minutes.

'It takes hours to make and minutes to eat,' he said good-humouredly as the children scrambled from the table. Lester dashed upstairs to make sure he claimed the bathroom before Sharon, and she disappeared to her bedroom to spend yet more time on her hair. The younger children were making for the street to play with their friends when Ralph called, 'Hey, Paul, don't forget it's your turn to wash the dishes.'

He pulled a face but made no objection to the chore which worked on a rota basis with every member of the family taking their turn.

Ralph and Jackie were watching television when Sharon came downstairs in all her finery. She had only worked in this job a few weeks but she liked it and the people she worked with. Tonight she wanted to make a good impression.

'How do I look?'

'You look lovely,' Jackie said sincerely. 'You should click tonight—what do you think, Ralph?'

'You look great.' He laughed as Sharon spun round to show off her new dress. It was black with silver lurex threads running through the material, and a red silk rose was pinned to the left shoulder. Sharon was a pretty, vivacious girl, with a bubbly sense of humour and a ready smile. She suited her affectionate nickname of Titch, as she was small and dainty.

'How do you like my hairstyle?' she asked, touching her long dark hair which tonight was streaked with fair tips and curled under in a pageboy style.

'It looks really nice.' Ralph and Jackie spoke together, both proud and happy that their daughter looked so attractive.

'Why don't you come with me?' Sharon coaxed. 'You could sit downstairs in the pub until we have finished our sales project, then I could join you and we could have a drink together. It would do you good—you don't go out enough.'

'No, thanks, love,' Ralph said. 'Even if we wanted to, there's no one to mind the kids. You go with your mates and enjoy yourself.'

'Okay.' Sharon smiled as she put her cardigan on. 'I'll see you later.' She let herself out of the front door. As she walked down the street, she met Maxine talking to one of her friends.

'Don't forget you owe me a cream egg for going on that message for you,' Maxine reminded her.

'I won't forget.' Sharon smiled at her younger sister. 'I'll see you later.'

'Your hair looks smashing,' Maxine called after her.

Sharon turned her head. 'Thanks,' she said, before continuing on her way, really looking forward to this night out and knowing she looked good in her new dress and hairdo.

*　　　*　　　*

Ralph and Jackie watched television, enjoying the luxury of having the house to themselves for a short

110

time. It was when Coronation Street finished that Jackie made a move. 'I'd better get the kids in, it's nearly bedtime.' She noticed Ralph lighting up a cigarette. 'I thought the doctor said you had to pack in smoking.'

He sighed. 'If I gave up everything the doctor told me to, life wouldn't be worth living. I'm not supposed to smoke, drink or get excited. There's not much I *can* do.'

Jackie, who didn't smoke or drink, wasn't very sympathetic. 'I can think of better things to spend my money on.'

By nine o'clock Maxine, Paul and Mark were in bed and their school clothes laid out for the next day. There was a good film on television after the news so Jackie made a pot of tea and some toast to enjoy while they watched it. Although she stayed awake until the end, Ralph dropped off to sleep halfway through and was surprised when he was wakened by Jackie shaking his shoulder. 'Come on, love, you've slept all through the film. It's nearly midnight and we should be in bed.'

He was first in bed and Jackie was just about to switch the light off when the phone at the side of the bed rang. She jumped visibly. 'Who the hell is ringing at this time of night?' she said as she picked the receiver up.

'Hi.' The voice was Sharon's.

'Hello, love, how did it go?' Jackie laughed. 'Did you click?' She got on very well with her stepdaughter and they shared all their secrets.

'It was all right,' Sharon answered. 'I'll tell you about it tomorrow. Will you ask my dad which bus I can get home?'

Jackie looked across the bed to Ralph. 'She

111

wants to know which bus to get.'

'She'll have to get a number ninety-eight all-night bus.' He heard his wife passing the information on to Sharon, adding, 'Don't be too late, it's midnight now.'

'I won't, I'm going for the bus now and I'll tell you all the news tomorrow—'bye.'

Sharon sounded so happy that as Jackie climbed into bed, she said, 'I bet she's clicked.'

*   *   *

Ralph was woken the next morning by sounds of activity coming from Lester's room. His stepson had to be out early that day as he was going to Scotland for the firm he worked for. His job entailed travelling to different parts of the country in a lorry containing a variety of goods for sale. These were displayed and sold at various hotels which had been booked for the day.

Ralph looked at the clock. 'Half-seven,' he muttered, 'I'd better get up.' It felt cold and he shivered as he sat on the side of the bed putting his slippers on. It was even colder in the bathroom as he washed and shaved, and he didn't envy Lester the long drive to Scotland. It would have been nice to have gone downstairs and made a cup of tea, but Ralph knew if he didn't make use of the bathroom now, before the rest of the family stirred, he wouldn't get a chance for hours.

Downstairs in the kitchen he decided to make porridge for breakfast, to warm the children up before they went to school. He was spooning it into bowls when Jackie came into the kitchen looking angry. 'I'll have something to say to that Sharon

112

when I see her,' she said. 'She hasn't been home all night.'

Ralph's heart skipped a beat. 'How do you know she hasn't been home all night?'

'Because I heard Lester come in, in the early hours of the morning, and I went along to Sharon's room to see if she was all right. She wasn't in bed!' Jackie sounded angry.

'Why the hell didn't you wake me?' Ralph demanded. 'For all we know she might be lying in a ditch somewhere.'

'Don't be silly, she's probably slept at a mate's house because it was so late.'

They were eating their breakfast with the three youngest children and Ralph was quiet for a while. Then he said, 'Don't forget that eighteen-year-old girl who died a few months ago—Wendy Slater. Her body was found on derelict land near her home and she'd been brutally murdered. They haven't found the person who did it yet.'

Jackie noticed that the children were listening to the conversation with anxious faces. 'Come on, you lot, it's time for school.' She waited until they had left, then reached for her coat. 'I'm going to call at the store on my way to work and give Sharon a piece of my mind. She knows she shouldn't stay out without letting us know.'

Ralph followed her to the front door. 'Why would she ring us to ask about buses if she was going to stay at a friend's?'

'I don't know,' Jackie said crossly, 'but I'm going to find out.' She was about to walk through the door when she turned back suddenly. 'I'd better take her overall with me—she's not allowed to work without it.' Stuffing Sharon's overall into her

113

bag, Jackie walked down the path. 'I'll see you later, love.'

Ralph waited until his wife drove away, and then walked back into the kitchen. He switched the radio on to try to take his mind off Sharon, but it didn't help. His heart was thumping wildly and his tummy turning over. He'd be glad when the day was over and she came home from work. Only then would he stop worrying.

*   *   *

Jackie turned off the main road into the street where Sharon worked. To reach the furniture store she had to cross a bridge over the canal, and it was as she was crossing this that she gave a cry and hit the brake hard with her foot. There were police everywhere—on the bridge and down beside the canal. Jackie went cold with fear as she remembered what Ralph had said about the girl who was murdered. Pulling the handbrake on and flinging the car door open at the same time, she prayed, 'Dear God, no.'

Leaving the car door wide open, Jackie hurried over to the nearest policeman. 'What's happened?' she asked.

'You can't stay there, madam,' the officer said. 'Move along, please.'

'But my daughter hasn't been home all night,' Jackie cried. 'I'm just going to see if she's in work.'

'What's all this about your daughter?' The voice came from behind Jackie and she turned to see a plain-clothes officer coming towards her.

'My daughter Sharon didn't come home all night. I'm going to see if she's in work,' Jackie

114

repeated.

The detective cupped her elbow and walked her back to her car. 'What was your daughter wearing?'

Her heart thumping, Jackie told him, 'A black and silver lurex dress, and she was carrying a black handbag.' She turned round to view the police activity, nervously clutching the pocket of her jacket. 'Look, what's going on? Why are all these police here?'

The detective didn't answer her question. Instead he asked, 'Do you mind if I come with you to where your daughter works?'

'She only works there.' Jackie pointed to the store near the bottom of the canal bridge, and slipped into the driving seat while the detective walked round to the passenger side. Shaking like a leaf, she drove to the store car park. Then the detective suddenly asked, 'What sort of shoes was your daughter wearing?'

'Black cut-out shoes.' Then she blurted out, 'She's in that canal, isn't she?'

'No,' the detective said quickly, 'we don't know yet who it is.'

They entered the store together and as they passed one of the assistants, Jackie asked, 'Did our Sharon go home with you last night?'

The girl looked surprised. 'No, she left us. Said she was walking up to catch the bus.'

Jackie screamed, 'Oh, my God, she's in the canal! Our Sharon's in the canal.'

The detective took her arm and gently but firmly led her through the store to the manager's office. After sitting her in a chair, he turned to one of the office girls.

'Look after Mrs Mosoph, will you, please?'

Jackie could hear him talking in low tones to the manager, and then they both left the office together. She was sobbing uncontrollably, unable to take in what was happening to her. In ten short minutes her whole world had collapsed. Then she remembered Ralph. 'Oh, my God, this will kill him,' she cried softly. 'The kids are his whole life, he'll never stand up to this.'

There was no doubt now in Jackie's mind that Sharon was dead. She had known from the second she saw those policemen by the canal that something terrible had happened to her stepdaughter. She didn't need to be told, she could feel it with every part of her mind and body.

The detective came back into the office alone. 'Mrs Mosoph, would you come to the police station with me, please?' He gave no explanation, but he didn't need to. Jackie knew, without being told, that the manager of the store had identified the body as Sharon's.

'I want to phone my sister-in-law first,' she sobbed, 'and whatever you do, don't send anyone to our house. My husband has a bad heart and there'll have to be a doctor there when he's told.'

Alice was married to Ralph's brother, George. When Jackie rang to explain what had happened, Alice couldn't believe what she was hearing. Sharon dead—she just couldn't believe it. 'Have they told you it's our Sharon?' she asked.

Jackie was sobbing so much, she couldn't explain what had happened. 'Will you ask George to go round to our house as soon as he can?' she cried. 'I don't want Ralph on his own when the police call.' After putting the phone down, she followed the detective out to the car where two other policemen were waiting to accompany them to the police station.

* * *

It was like a nightmare, sitting in a police car with the three officers who were taking her to the police station. They were going to question her about Sharon who was dead. Jackie felt she couldn't take any more—not on her own. She leaned forward in her seat. 'Will you take me to my sister-in-law's works first? I want to ask her to come with me.'

After asking directions, the driver took them to the factory where Ada worked. As Jackie made to get out of the car, the detective put his hand on her arm. 'I'll go in for her—you stay here.'

He was gone for about ten minutes, returning with Ralph's youngest sister, Ada, who looked puzzled and surprised. The detective opened the car door. As Ada stepped in, her first words were, 'What's wrong, Jackie—what do the police want with you?'

When Jackie, shaking with sobs, told her, 'Our Sharon's dead,' Ada was shocked into silence. She sat through the journey with her arm round her sister-in-law, trying to comfort her the best way she could.

When they reached the police station they were led to an interview room. Jackie was shivering from head to toe but although it was a cold day the weather wasn't the cause. It was fear. Stark, cold fear. She answered the detective's questions in a voice that didn't seem to belong to her. Automatically, like a robot, she told of Sharon's friends, her habits, where she went in the evenings,

117

her hobbies, and where she'd gone the night before. If Jackie hadn't been in a state of shock, she would probably have queried the reason for some of the more intimate questions but her mind wasn't working normally.

When the detective had the answers he needed for the time being, a cup of tea was brought in for Jackie and Ada. As they were drinking their tea, the detective said, 'We can't ask you to identify the body yet, Mrs Mosoph, we're not quite ready.'

Jackie's hand started to shake so violently the tea spilled over on to her coat. She hadn't thought she would be expected to identify Sharon and the prospect filled her with dread. 'I won't do it,' she said to Ada. 'Surely to God, they wouldn't expect me to.'

For six hours Jackie and Ada sat in that interview room. The police kept coming in with more questions until Jackie felt her head was going to burst. Sometimes, when answering a question, she would think, What do they want to know that for? It's got nothing to do with Sharon being dead. It was only much later, when she was able to think clearly, that Jackie understood that the police had to ask a lot of questions if they were to build up a picture of what had happened.

It had been an hour since they'd finished the last question session and Jackie was wondering when they were going to let her go home to Ralph and the children. She was desperate to know if Ralph was all right and if he was being looked after. So deep in thought was she that when a detective bent down in front of her, she jumped with fright.

'You've got to be brave now, Mrs Mosoph.' The detective's voice was gentle. 'We're taking you to the hospital to identify the body.'

'Oh, no!' Jackie cried. 'I couldn't—I just couldn't.'

'You'll have to, I'm afraid,' he insisted. 'We can't ask your husband because he's not well enough. Please be brave.'

'Will you come with me?' Jackie turned to Ada. 'I couldn't go on my own.'

'I'm sorry,' Ada looked distressed, 'I'll have to get home.' Jackie knew why Ada wouldn't come, and even in her own distress she understood. Ada had lost her husband recently and was still mourning. She just couldn't take any more.

A policewoman accompanied the detective and Jackie to the hospital. It was a nightmare drive for Jackie who dreaded what was to come. She remembered her words to Ralph this morning: 'I'm going to give our Sharon a piece of my mind for staying out all night,' and here she was, going to identify the girl's body. It couldn't be true— perhaps it wasn't Sharon's body they'd found in the canal. Even as she thought this, Jackie knew it was wishful thinking. There had never been any doubt whose body it was. When the car stopped outside the hospital, the detective took Jackie's arm and led her to the door of the morgue. 'Be brave, Mrs Mosoph,' he said quietly as he propelled her inside. As soon as they walked through the door, Jackie saw Sharon's body behind a glass window. She tried to turn away, to run, but the detective pushed her forward. 'Is that Sharon?' he asked.

Jackie looked at her stepdaughter's body and thought, she looks as though she's asleep. She felt the detective's hand on her arm and she nodded. 'Yes, that's Sharon. She didn't have those scratches

119

on her face when she left home last night, though.'

'She probably got those when she was dropped into the lock,' the detective said and tried to push Jackie nearer the window. She tried to pull away, and suddenly felt her legs going weak. Everything started to go black and her knees began to buckle under. She heard a voice in the distance say, 'That's enough now, come on,' just before she fell to the floor in a dead faint.

*   *   *

Ralph couldn't settle after Jackie had left for work. He tried doing little jobs to occupy his mind, but the feeling that something was wrong wouldn't go away. When it got to ten o'clock, he told himself that if anything were wrong, Jackie would have let him know by now. He had just convinced himself that there was no reason to worry when the phone rang and he jumped with fright. It was only Alice and he breathed a sigh of relief that it wasn't the bad news he was half expecting.

'Hello, Ralph,' she greeted him. 'How are you?'

'I'm all right,' he answered. 'I had a few words with Jackie this morning because our Sharon didn't come home all night, but I think she slept at one of her mate's houses and went straight to work. Jackie has taken her overall into her and she said she's going to give her a piece of her mind.'

'George wants to know if you'll go into Manchester with him this morning?' Alice said. 'He's got to go to John Street and he's not sure where it is.'

'Yes, I'll go with him. What time does he want to go?'

'We'll come down now, if that's all right with you? We'll be there in twenty minutes.'

It was spot on twenty minutes later when George's car pulled up outside and as he and Alice walked into the house, Ralph said, 'I'll put the kettle on for a cuppa before we go.'

'I won't have a drink,' Alice said. 'I'll just run over to the store and see Sharon, and get myself some cigarettes while I'm out.'

The two brothers watched Alice drive away and Ralph said laughingly, 'She goes everywhere in that car since she passed her test, doesn't she?'

The two brothers chatted over a cup of tea and had smoked several cigarettes, when Ralph looked at his watch. 'It's half-past eleven. Where the hell has Alice got to? She's been gone over an hour now.'

'She's probably nattering to someone, you know what women are when they start talking,' George answered, lowering his head and avoiding his brother's eyes.

Ralph stood up. 'Let's go and find her, we could be waiting all day.' He put his coat on, but George didn't make a move. 'Come on,' Ralph insisted, 'let's go.'

George seemed to hesitate, but finally he followed his brother down the path to Ralph's car. They turned off the main road, as Jackie had done a few hours earlier, and approached the canal bridge. It was when they had crossed it that they saw several policemen standing in the store's car park, and when Ralph drove inside they saw the police incident unit stationed there.

'I wonder what's going on here?' Ralph said. He didn't seem to notice that George didn't answer.

After stopping the car outside the door to the store, Ralph switched the engine off and said, 'You go and find Alice. I'll wait for you here.'

As soon as George disappeared into the store, Ralph started the engine up again. There's something happened at the canal, he thought. I've got to find out what it is. The feeling of impending tragedy, which had been with him earlier on, returned more powerfully than ever. He stopped the car near the bridge and stepped out. As he did so, a policeman walked towards him, saying politely, 'You'll have to move along, sir.'

'What's happened here?' Ralph asked.

'I'm sorry, but you'll have to move.'

Ralph was determined not to move until he knew what was going on. 'My daughter didn't come home all night.'

The policeman turned to where the incident unit was parked and shouted, 'The father's here, sir.' The officer started to walk towards the unit, but Ralph didn't move. He couldn't move; couldn't feel anything at all. It was as though his body didn't belong to him and he had no control over it. He could hear voices, but they seemed miles away— nothing to do with him. Then, like a bomb exploding in his head, came the stark, terrible truth. Sharon was dead. Never again would he see the daughter he loved so much.

Tears started to roll down his cheeks and he stepped back to lean against a wall for support. Sobbing uncontrollably, he felt himself sliding down the wall to the ground, the pain in his chest threatening to cut off his breathing. He could hear voices round him, but they meant nothing. He was alone in his grief.

'Come on, our Ralph, I'll take you home.' It was George's voice which penetrated.

'But you don't understand,' Ralph sobbed, 'our Sharon's dead.'

George took his brother's arm and pulled him up. 'Come on—the best place for you is home.'

Like a man sleepwalking, Ralph allowed himself to be led to the car. He didn't speak on the drive home but, when they were inside his house, he turned to his brother. 'Did you know about this?'

George shook his head. 'We weren't sure. Jackie rang our house this morning, but nothing definite had been said. She had to go with the police then and we've heard nothing since.'

'Why the hell wasn't I told?' Ralph demanded. 'Why did I have to find out this way?'

'Jackie was worried about you. She probably told the police not to come because of your heart condition.'

George went into the kitchen to make a pot of tea and Ralph looked round his living room. It was the same room he had left an hour earlier, but he felt like a stranger in it. It felt cold and cheerless and he shivered, thinking the house would never again be the warm, happy place it had been until this morning.

As he was drinking the tea that George insisted on making, Ralph tried to think clearly. Why would anyone want to kill Sharon? he asked himself. She had never hurt anyone in her life and hadn't any enemies. He looked over to the spot where last night she'd twirled around in front of him and Jackie, showing off her new dress and hairstyle. She had been so happy, so full of life; it didn't seem possible that a few hours later she was dead—

123

murdered! Ralph burst into tears. Putting his cup down, he covered his face with his hands. George looked on helplessly; what could he say to his brother that would relieve him of this suffering? There was a knock on the door and George motioned with his hand that Ralph should stay where he was. 'I'll answer it,' he said. A few seconds later he was followed into the room by a policeman and Ralph jumped to his feet.

'Why the hell has it taken you lot all this time to come and tell a father that his daughter has been found dead in the canal?' he screamed.

'Don't take off on me, Mr Mosoph,' the police sergeant said. 'We were told not to come and see you because of your heart condition.'

Ralph sat down heavily and, holding his head in his hands, he started to cry. He knew the sergeant was right; he was only doing his job. It was just that Ralph felt like hitting out at everyone to try and relieve his suffering. He wanted to hurt someone like he was hurting.

'What happened?' he asked quietly. 'Do you know?'

'All we know,' the sergeant told him, 'is that Sharon was murdered in the early hours of this morning. She was strangled with her own tights, then carried across a small by-wash and dropped thirty-five feet into the canal.' He looked at Ralph with compassion. 'She did put up a struggle.'

'So would I if I was fighting for my life,' Ralph said bitterly. 'Do you know who did it?'

'No, not yet,' he was told. 'But that's our job, don't you worry about it.'

The sergeant soon left after making sure that Ralph would be all right. George saw the officer out. When he came back into the room, he told Ralph, 'There's a group of reporters outside. Do you want to see them?'

'No, I don't want to see them.' Ralph was angry. 'God!' he shouted. 'How could they come here, wanting a story, when I'm nearly out of my mind with grief?'

The two brothers didn't speak much after that, both lost in their own thoughts. George was worrying about the effect this would have on his brother. Would his heart stand up to this tragedy? Ralph, sitting opposite, wasn't thinking about himself, he was worrying about how Jackie would take it, and the children. How was he going to tell them that Sharon was dead?

'Oh, my God!' He jumped up so abruptly that George gave a start. 'What about the children? Suppose someone in school gets to know and tells them?' He looked at his brother as though seeking advice. 'Do you think I should ring the school and ask them to send the two young ones home?' When George looked undecided, Ralph walked towards the phone in the hall muttering, 'I can't let them find out from strangers.'

After looking down at the phone for a few seconds, he started to rap his head with his knuckles. 'What the hell's the school number?' His brain was so confused he couldn't remember. Impatiently, he snatched up the small pad which Jackie kept by the phone and leafed through until he found the number he wanted.

The school secretary answered the call and Ralph, trying not to cry, explained what had happened. He asked that Maxine and Mark be allowed to come home early, and the secretary promised to see that this was done. Ralph replaced the receiver, then picked it up again and dialled Lester's works. He'd better get Lester home, too, because the news of the body in the canal would be all over the estate soon. Lester's boss answered the phone and Ralph could hear the surprise in his voice when he was asked if he would send Lester home.

'But Lester's not here,' he said. 'The police picked him up early this morning and we haven't seen him since.'

Ralph walked back into the living room, frowning. 'They picked Lester up early this morning and took him to the police station,' he told George. 'Why would they pick him up—he won't know anything.'

George reached for his coat. 'I'll go down and meet Mark,' he said, 'and make sure he comes straight home. Will you be all right till I come back?'

Ralph nodded and sat down heavily in a chair. He felt terrible, but what was the use of telling George that? It wouldn't solve anything, wouldn't right the terrible wrong. He was still sitting in the same position when George came back with Mark. Ralph looked at his son's happy face and thought, He doesn't know and I can't tell him. How could he tell a seven-year-old boy that his sister had been murdered and he would never see her again?

Maxine still hadn't arrived when Paul came in an hour later. The boy was so excited he didn't notice his father's tear-stained face or the tense atmosphere. 'Hey, Dad, they found a girl's naked body in the canal. They say she's been murdered. Did you know?'

'Yes, son, I knew.' Ralph looked down at his clasped hands and kept his head down as he told Paul, 'That girl was your sister, Sharon.' He didn't look up. He couldn't bear to see his son's face. Then he heard footsteps running up the stairs and raised his head.

'Paul's gone up to his bedroom,' George told him. 'I'll go up to him after, but I think I'd better go and look for Maxine first.'

Maxine had been told to go home after Ralph's phone call but, because she was in the art class and wanted to finish the lesson, she didn't do as she was told. When the lesson was over it was time to go home anyway so she waited to walk home with her friends. As they were leaving, the teacher told them they were not to go near the canal; they must go straight home.

As most children will do what they are told not to, Maxine and her friends made straight for the canal, filled with curiosity. They were prevented from getting close to it by road barriers and groups of police, and although they asked the officers what had happened, they were told very firmly to go home.

Maxine reached the end of her road and found her Uncle George waiting for her. She started to tell him about the police at the canal, but he interrupted her.

'I want you to go straight up to your bedroom, Maxine. There's something I've got to say to you. Don't go in the living room.'

They had reached the front door by this time and George pushed her towards the stairs, saying, 'I'll be up in a few minutes.'

Maxine was sitting on the bed when her uncle

127

entered the room and sat down next to her. 'Listen, Maxine,' he said gently, 'a girl has been murdered down by the canal. We are all worried because Sharon hasn't been home all night and nobody knows where she is. Now the girl who was murdered might not be Sharon—we just don't know. Your dad is very upset, so I don't want you to talk about it when you go downstairs. Will you do that for me?' When Maxine nodded, he stood up, saying, 'Auntie Alice is making some tea for you and Paul and Mark, so come on down like a good girl and have something to eat.'

The children sat eating their tea quietly. Gone were the laughter and arguments which were the usual routine at mealtimes. Ralph's mind went back twenty-four hours—to the cottage pie, the laughter and Sharon showing off her new dress. It was too much for him and the tears started to flow again. The children looked at each other. Too young to say anything to their dad that might comfort him, they sat in silence, frightened of what was to come.

A knock on the door broke the silence and George opened it to two policemen. Before they had time to say why they had come, there was another knock on the door. This time it was a relative, and from then on George was opening the door every few minutes to more relatives and friends until the house was full. The news had spread quickly and everyone had come to express their horror and offer sympathy. The room was full of cigarette smoke and conversation. Ralph sat with his head in his hands. He felt as though he was living through a nightmare—there was something unreal about it.

'Look, Ralph, is there anything I can do to help?' He looked up to see Keith, his neighbour, bending over him.

'You could take the kids for a couple of hours, if you would. This is no place for them.'

'Of course, I'll take them now.' Keith turned to the three children. 'Come on kids, you're coming home with me for a while.'

Ralph watched the children follow Keith, their eyes red-rimmed with crying and looking frightened. He wanted to go to them and put his arms around them, but he knew if he did he would break down completely. That was something he couldn't do—not yet anyway. He needed a clear mind until Jackie came home and told him what had really happened. So far he knew very little except that his daughter was dead.

*   *   *

It was 5.30 when Jackie arrived home. When she walked into the room all the talking stopped. Ralph looked at his wife's face, which was pale and drawn.

'My God, you look terrible,' he said. 'Where have you been all day?'

'I've been at the police station, then I had to go to the hospital to identify Sharon's body.' The tears were running down Jackie's face as she told him, 'She just looked as though she was asleep.'

Ralph put his arm around his wife's shoulders and could feel her trembling. 'My God,' he said, 'fancy having to go through that on your own.'

'Where's the kids?' Jackie asked. 'Do they know?'

'The two eldest ones do,' Ralph told her.

129

'They've been crying. I don't think Mark understands—he's too young. They've gone back with Keith for a few hours: I didn't think it was right to have them here. I don't know what we're going to do with them tonight, they can't be here listening to everything—it wouldn't be fair to worry and frighten them.'

'They can come home with us,' Jackie's sister, Sylvia, said. 'They'll be all right with our kids for a few days.'

'Thanks, Sylvia,' Jackie said. 'We'll come up tomorrow to see them, and we'll let the school know where they are.'

Sylvia stood up. 'We'll go now and collect our children—they'll be wanting their tea. We'll call at Keith's on the way and pick up your three.'

When Sylvia and her husband had left, Jackie turned to Ralph. 'Where's our Lester?'

'I don't know. I rang his works, but he wasn't there. They told me the police had picked him up early this morning.'

'But they wouldn't keep him there all day.' Jackie sounded worried. 'What would the police want him for anyway?'

'I'll go and ring the station to find out.' Ralph started to leave the room, and then he remembered the two policemen who'd called earlier. 'Where are those two policemen, George? I didn't see them leave.'

'They haven't left—they're sitting on the stairs.'

Ralph walked into the hall and saw the two detectives sitting on the bottom stair. 'Could you find out what's happened to Lester?' he asked. 'He's been at the police station since this morning.'

One of the detectives stood up. 'I'll try and find

something out for you. Can I use your phone?' After a short conversation the detective put the phone down and said, 'He won't be long, he's just got a few more questions to answer.'

'What!' Ralph shouted. 'After being there all day? I hope they don't think he had anything to do with it. If he's not home in an hour, I'm going to get him.'

Someone pushed a cup of tea into his hand as he walked back into the living room. 'Drink this while it's hot—it'll do you good.' The room was full of smoke and there were people everywhere. Those who couldn't find anywhere to sit were leaning against the walls. Everyone was waiting, but they didn't know what they were waiting for—what was to come?

The answer to some of their questions came with the arrival of two more police officers—both superintendents. They told Ralph and Jackie, while their friends and relations listened, that a murder hunt had been launched. Apologizing for the long delay in reporting the tragic news, they gave the reason. A man had seen the body in the canal as he walked to work and had reported it to the police. Unfortunately, after Sharon's body had been thrown into the canal, the weather had turned icy and the water in the canal had frozen over. The police had to wait until lunchtime for the ice to thaw before they were able to recover the body.

'What about my son?' Jackie asked. 'They have no right to keep him at the police station all this time. He should be home with his family at a time like this.'

One of the officers went into the hall to use the phone, but when he came back it was with the same answer as before. 'Lester will be home soon—just a few more questions to answer.'

As the officers were leaving, one said to Ralph, 'We want to ask you and your wife some questions tomorrow. We'll send a car for you and will bring you home again.' He turned as he reached the door. 'Oh, your doctor has been informed. He will be calling to see you tonight.'

A short time later the doctor came. He asked how Ralph felt—concerned about his heart condition. 'I'm all right,' Ralph told him, 'but Jackie needs something for her nerves, she's shaking like a leaf.'

The doctor gave her an injection and assured her that she would get a good night's sleep. Ralph refused any sedative, feeling he had to stay alert in case anything happened.

It was ten o'clock, friends and relations were still there, but still there was no sign of Lester.

'This is ridiculous,' Ralph said. 'I'm going down to get him.'

'I'm coming with you,' Jackie said quickly, and another voice called out, 'I'll come as well.' It was Cliff, Ralph's brother-in-law, and as the three of them drove to the police station, Jackie said. 'The poor kid will be starving with hunger. He's had nothing to eat all day.'

'I just don't understand why they've had to keep him for over twelve hours. Surely it doesn't take that long to answer questions.'

When they arrived at the police station, the desk sergeant directed them to an incident room upstairs. There they were met by a CID officer and, after telling him that they wanted to take their son home, he sent for Lester. Ralph and Jackie were deeply shocked when they saw their son. His face was ashen and he seemed drained of energy or feeling. When the officer said he could go home, they had finished questioning him, his concerned parents led him out to the car. On the way home he was very quiet and reluctant to answer any of the questions Ralph asked.

The house was still full of people when they got home and Lester seemed upset and embarrassed when Ralph demanded to know why he had been kept at the police station all day. Gradually, the reason for his reluctance and embarrassment became clear. Lester had been asked some very personal questions about his relationship with his stepsister. He was grilled about his own life: did he have a girlfriend, did he see her last night, what time did he leave her and how had he travelled home?

Ralph could feel his anger rising as he listened. 'Good God,' he muttered, 'they're treating him as though he's a suspect.' And when Lester told him that the police had taken his fingerprints and a photograph, Ralph's anger erupted. It was bad enough to have to suffer the pain of having his daughter murdered without learning that his stepson was suspected of killing her.

Jackie tried to get Lester to eat something but although he did try he just couldn't swallow the food. He was physically and mentally exhausted and more than a little afraid. The questions that had been fired at him all day, many of them very personal, had left their mark on his young mind. He couldn't believe that anyone would think he would hurt his stepsister. They were good pals, always willing to help each other and sharing all their secrets.

'You go to bed, love, you look worn out.' Jackie was concerned by her son's appearance. 'A good night's sleep will do you good.'

Lester was glad to go to bed—glad to get away from any more questions, glad to be alone to go over the events of a day which had started off like any working day but finished as a nightmare he would never forget.

* * *

It was after midnight when relatives and friends took their leave. Ralph, although tired, dreaded the time when he and Jackie would be alone. At least when the house was full of people there wasn't an opportunity to think, and Ralph didn't want to think—it was too painful. Jackie came into the room after seeing the last of the visitors out, and she and Ralph stood looking at each other for a few seconds before walking into each other's arms.

'What have we done to deserve this?' she cried.

Ralph held her close, 'I don't know, love, I just don't know.'

* * *

Helped by the injection the doctor had given her, Jackie went to sleep almost as soon as she lay down in bed. Ralph, however, tossed and turned for several hours before eventually going downstairs to make himself a cup of tea. He was glad Jackie was asleep, free for a while from the mental torment. Ralph cursed himself for not letting the doctor give him a tranquillizer, then remembered there were some sleeping tablets in the cupboard and took one. At first he thought the tablet wasn't going to work but a short time afterwards he crawled back into bed and dropped off to sleep—his head on a pillow damp with tears.

'Ralph!' Jackie was shaking his shoulder, and he sat up quickly. He couldn't make out what was happening and looked at her questioningly. 'There's someone knocking at the door,' she told him. 'Come on, we'd better get up.'

He was pulling his trousers on when Jackie shouted up the stairs, 'It's someone for you, Ralph—two men from your works.'

The men were managers from the factory and had come to offer their condolences. They told him not to worry about how long he was off work, and reassured him that his wages would be paid, no matter how long he was absent.

When Ralph was showing the two men out, after thanking them for their concern, he saw a group of reporters gathered outside the gate. He shut the door quickly before they could start asking the questions he didn't want to answer.

'Are you hungry, love?' Jackie asked.

'No, not really. I suppose I'd better eat something, though, I'll just have a piece of toast.'

Jackie heard Lester moving about upstairs and put another two slices of bread under the grill. When he came down, he ate his breakfast in silence then surprised his parents by saying he was going into work. Ralph objected at first, knowing that Lester would have to put up with everyone asking him questions. Then he realized that it had to happen sometime, and it was better to get it over with now.

135

Jackie was clearing the dishes away from the table when Ralph said, 'Don't forget, we've got to go to the police station.'

'They're sending a car for us when they're ready,' Jackie replied. 'We'd better get dressed in case they come early.'

They were ready when the detective came and he drove them to the station, a large and fairly new building. He asked Ralph and Jackie to follow him and led them between the cars parked in the reserved area to a door in the front of the building. Once inside, the detective took them in a lift up to an incident room. Jackie was told to sit down, but Ralph was asked to follow the officer to another room. Jackie felt afraid when they were separated; she needed Ralph to give her the strength to get through another distressing interview.

Although they were separated by walls, their thoughts were with each other. They answered questions quietly and automatically, and it was only when these questions became personal that their voices were raised in protest. Ralph was concerned for Jackie, and couldn't understand why they hadn't been questioned together. Surely it would have been easier for all concerned.

Jackie was relieved when the interview was over and she was taken to the room where Ralph was sitting. She was worried that his heart wouldn't stand the strain, and wanted to protect him as much as she could. The police, handling this in what to them was a routine way, were courteous and compassionate and, as soon as they had the information they needed, Jackie and Ralph were taken out to the waiting police car and driven home. It was difficult for them to talk there, with a detective present, and they sat in virtual silence until they pulled up outside their house.

'There's George's car,' Jackie said as she climbed out of the police car. 'I wonder how long he's been waiting.'

George walked towards them. 'I just called to tell you that most of the family will be down later, to see if you need anything.' He waited until Jackie had opened the front door and then followed them into the house. 'How did it go at the police station?'

'Just questions,' Ralph said. 'I wish they'd concentrate on finding out who killed Sharon instead of asking us questions. Some of them were very personal, too. It made me feel as though they suspected me.'

'That's the way I felt.' Jackie looked at him. 'They asked me if I was sure you were in bed and asleep all night.'

'They didn't ask you that, did they?' Ralph sounded horrified.

Jackie nodded. 'I told them that if you even moved in bed, I would know.' She started to cry then. 'I told them you wouldn't dream of hurting one of your children, you love them too much.'

'Don't get upset, love.' Ralph wished there was some way he could ease her pain. He knew how she felt because he was in the same hell himself. The only chance they had of surviving was to keep moving: if they cut themselves off from family and friends, kept their suffering to themselves, they would never survive. He turned to his brother. 'We're just going to have a bite to eat, George, and then we want to go and see how the kids are. We'll get back in time for the family coming.'

'My family are coming too,' Jackie said. 'They're going to sit with us tonight.'

'Thank God for family and friends,' Ralph said bitterly. 'Nobody else has been to see if we need help. Wouldn't you think the authorities would send someone to see if we are all right? Apparently they don't care what happens to people like us.'

When the car stopped in front of Sylvia's house, Jackie touched Ralph's arm. 'There's our Mark playing with the other children.'

As soon as Mark saw his mam and dad he ran towards them as fast as his legs would carry him. 'Am I coming home with you, Mam?' he asked eagerly.

Jackie started to cry and Ralph bit his lip hard to try to stem the tears that were threatening to flow. Inside the house, Maxine and Paul were playing a game at the table. As soon as they saw their parents, they jumped up. Questions poured from their mouths. Could they come home? What had happened to Sharon, and why did they have to stay away from home because of it? Ralph sat the children down and tried to answer their questions as best he could. He explained that he and Jackie were going to be very busy for a few days, and it would be better for them if they stayed with their aunt.

Sylvia interrupted then. 'I've been in touch with the headmaster of the school where our children go,' she told them, 'and he's agreed that yours can go there on a temporary basis.'

'Oh, that's great,' Jackie said. 'Thanks, Sylvia.'

When Jackie and Ralph stood up to leave, Paul asked, 'Will we be able to go to Sharon's funeral, Dad?'

138

The question hit Ralph like a blow between the eyes. He hadn't even thought about a funeral. No one had mentioned it. 'We don't know yet, son, we'll see. Me and your mam will talk about it when we get home.'

The children clung to their parents, crying. They wanted to go home and couldn't understand why they weren't being allowed to. Jackie was crying too; she couldn't bear to see them so unhappy. Ralph dug some money out of his pocket and, giving the children fifty pence each, said, 'Now be good and don't upset your mam. Go and buy yourselves some sweets.'

As soon as they arrived home, Ralph telephoned the police station and asked for Superintendent Benyon. He wanted to ask about the funeral but, when he heard the superintendent's voice on the other end of the line, couldn't find the right words. Instead, he asked if they had found the person who'd killed Sharon. There was no progress so far, the officer said, but as soon as there was any news he would notify them. Afraid that the Superintendent would ring off before he could find out what he had rung for in the first place, Ralph asked quickly, 'Can we make arrangements for the funeral?'

'No,' said the officer. 'The body is still with the police scientific department and until they have finished it cannot be released. Even when it is released, Sharon will have to be buried and not cremated. You see,' he explained, 'any defence solicitor could ask for the body to be exhumed.'

Jackie had been standing near the telephone. When Ralph replaced the receiver, she asked, 'What did he say?'

He repeated the conversation, and saw the tears in Jackie's eyes when he said the body might have to be exhumed at some later date.

'Oh, God,' she cried. 'Isn't it bad enough that she's dead, without having to go through that?'

Ralph held her close and rocked her gently, as he did with the children when they needed comforting.

*   *   *

George arrived a little later and Jackie jumped up from the settee. 'I'd better go and make the beds. I didn't have time before we went out this morning.' She ran upstairs, leaving the two brothers talking. She went into Lester's room first and, after making his bed, made her way to Sharon's. The bed was made up, as it had been when she went out two nights ago to meet her friends. How could anyone have foreseen that she was also to meet her killer?

Jackie picked up one of the pillows and held it against her face. She could smell the make-up Sharon used, and all the memories came flooding back. Sharon as a schoolgirl, the day she got her first job, the happiness on her face as she showed off her new dress and her last words when she rang to ask which bus she should get home: 'I'll tell you all the news tomorrow—'bye.'

Jackie rocked herself back and forth, crying. She wouldn't hear all the news now—she would never hear Sharon's voice again. 'Oh, dear God, what are we going to do?' she cried. 'How can we live through this?'

Suddenly she flung the pillow from her and rushed down the stairs. She made straight for the

140

medicine cabinet in the kitchen. She took out a bottle containing Mogadon tablets and walked to the sink. After filling a cup with water, Jackie emptied all the tablets out of the bottle into her hand. She had just swallowed the last of them, when Ralph came into the kitchen, alerted by the sounds of his wife crying.

'What's the matter?' He looked at her anxiously. 'Why are you crying like this?'

Jackie, hysterical by now, tried to tell him about being in Sharon's bedroom. She was sobbing about a pillow—smell—clothes—never seeing her again, and Ralph took hold of her arms to stop her outburst. It was then he noticed the empty bottle in her hand and he cried, 'What have you done? My God, what have you done?'

'It doesn't matter—nothing matters any more,' Jackie sobbed.

Ralph's head was throbbing and he tried to remember how many tablets were in the bottle last night when he took one to help him sleep. There were quite a few—almost a full bottle.

'George!' Ralph's tone was urgent, and his brother came rushing into the kitchen. 'Jackie's taken some tablets—try and make her sick, then walk her up and down. I'll open the front door to let some air in, and I'll ring the doctor.'

Ralph opened the front door just as Alice was walking up the path. 'Thank God,' he said. Alice was a nurse and would know what to do. Quickly he explained what had happened and she rushed into the kitchen. 'Make some black coffee, then ring for the doctor,' she ordered.

Within fifteen minutes he had been, telephoned for an ambulance, and Jackie was on her way to

141

hospital. Alice had gone in the ambulance with her, as the doctor had advised Ralph to stay at home. He was nearly out of his mind with worry. First Sharon and now Jackie; he felt he just couldn't take any more. Alone with George, in a house that now seemed like a stranger's, he sat with his head bowed. 'There's supposed to be a God,' he cried. 'Where is He? Sharon needed Him and I need Him now—but where is He?'

George stayed with Ralph that night. Before they went to bed, he rang the hospital. Jackie was receiving treatment, but there was no news yet. They were to ring again the next morning. 'She'll be all right,' George tried to comfort his brother. 'You get a good night's sleep, and tomorrow they'll probably tell you she can come home.'

Ralph tossed and turned for several hours before dropping off into a restless sleep. When George came into his bedroom the next morning, he was relieved the night was over. He went down to the kitchen and, after looking in the fridge, told George, 'I'm afraid there's not much in the house to eat. We haven't had any time to go to the shops.'

'What have you got?'

'Only a couple of slices of bacon.'

'That'll do fine,' George said as he put the kettle on for a pot of tea.

After breakfast, Ralph rang the hospital. His spirits lifted when he was told Jackie had responded to treatment and he could pick her up in the afternoon and bring her home. He spent an hour by the telephone, calling relatives to tell them his wife was all right, and then made the beds and tidied around. Anything to keep himself busy and his mind occupied. If he sat down for even a few minutes, Sharon's face would appear before him and the nightmare would start again.

On his way to the hospital to pick up Jackie, Ralph found himself looking at the faces of everyone he passed. One of them could be the murderer—if only he knew who'd done it and why. Surely no one would kill a girl for the few pounds she had in her bag? The police said she had been strangled with her own tights, but Ralph couldn't imagine Sharon taking her tights off and handing them over to a strange man. Perhaps it wasn't a strange man—perhaps it was someone she knew? There may have been more than one man; it could have been a gang. Ralph was torturing himself as he imagined the terrible fear Sharon must have suffered before she died. God, he wished he knew who had done it—he would like to see him suffer, as Sharon had suffered.

*　　　*　　　*

Jackie wasn't aware of anything that was happening until she came round and found herself staring at white-tiled walls. She lay for a few minutes trying to remember where she was, and then she tried to sit up. As she dug her elbows into the bed to raise herself, she realized there was a tube in her mouth. She could feel it at the back of her throat. Suddenly it all came flooding back. She could see the tablets in her hand, George walking her up and down, then Alice taking over. The floodgates opened then and she remembered why she had taken the tablets—Sharon was dead. Tears came to her eyes and she whispered, 'Why didn't they just leave me?'

Jackie looked from side to side and realized she

143

was alone in a small ward. After a while her tears stopped and she became calmer. She thought of Ralph and wondered what effect her action had had on him. God, he's got enough to put up with without me adding to his worry, she thought.

When the nurse came to remove the stomach pump, she told Jackie that she would probably be allowed to go home later in the day and promised to tell her husband when he rang. When Ralph walked into the ward it was to see his wife sitting on the bed, waiting for him. With arms outstretched, she ran towards him and he held her close.

'Are you all right, love?' he asked.

'I am now you're here,' she whispered. 'Come on, let's go home.'

*   *   *

They had only been home about an hour when Granada Television rang to ask if they would agree to be interviewed. The caller said he would like to bring a film crew to the house, and suggested that Ralph and Jackie, in their interview, could appeal to the killer, or anyone who knew him, to come forward. After first asking his wife if she felt up to the ordeal, Ralph agreed and arrangements were made for the following day.

Ralph was up early the next morning and was making breakfast for Jackie when the post came. There were quite a few letters and Ralph read through them as he drank a cup of tea. They were all letters of sympathy, and some even came from people living in different parts of the country. When Jackie came downstairs, she read the letters

144

out loud and the sympathy expressed in them caused more tears to flow.

'To think that complete strangers would write to say how sorry they are,' she sobbed. 'People are very kind.' Ralph nodded. 'One or two of them say they know how we feel. I wonder if they have gone through the same thing?'

They were both dressed and waiting when Geoff Seed from Granada TV arrived with a film crew. He asked them to sit together on the settee, and then ran through the format of the interview. He would first present the facts that were known about the murder, and then he would ask them both a few questions.

After making sure they were prepared to face the camera, Geoff Seed gave the sign and the filming began. All went well until Jackie was asked, 'What would you say to anyone watching who may know anything about the incident?'

'Please,' she pleaded, 'if anyone can help the police, get in touch with them and try to find the killer of our daughter.' She broke down then, unable to control her emotions, and the interview ended.

Geoff Seed stayed for a cup of tea while the crew dismantled their equipment. He had been affected by Jackie's distress and apologized for having to ask questions that seemed cruel and heartless. It was necessary, he said, if the public were to respond. He left soon afterwards, saying that he hoped the killer would be caught soon.

Jackie and Ralph were still unwinding after the interview when there was a knock on the door. It was a reporter from a local newspaper, who asked if Ralph would talk to him for a few minutes.

145

Apparently, the local radio had quoted Ralph as saying that if capital punishment hadn't been abolished his daughter would still be alive, and the reporter wanted to know if Ralph believed this to be true. He confirmed that, in his view, capital punishment should be applicable to those who committed murder. He had been of this opinion before Sharon was murdered; now he had more reason to believe it. Anyone who took an innocent person's life should forfeit the right to live. He told the reporter that he would start a campaign to urge the Government to hold a referendum on the issue.

The next couple of days passed quickly for Ralph and Jackie, with the help of their families. There was someone with them all the time, so they wouldn't have time to dwell on the tragedy. It was never out of their minds and they were suffering, but without the support of their families they would never have survived. There were letters every day from sympathizers and, when Ralph's interview appeared in the local paper, they were inundated with letters and phone calls offering help to raise signatures for a petition on capital punishment.

Although Ralph didn't realize it, all the activity was helping him keep his sanity. He was so busy answering phone calls and letters that the days passed quickly, and when he went to bed he was able to sleep. Jackie tried to slow him down at first, fearful of the strain on his heart. Then she decided it was the better of two evils. With nothing to do but think, and remember, he would pine away.

Then one day a phone call brought them back to reality, and the nightmare started again.

*   *   *

When the phone rang, Ralph picked it up expecting the caller to be one of the family. Instead, it was a CID officer from Oldham Police Station. He told Ralph that they were now releasing Sharon's body for burial. Ralph gripped the phone so hard that his hand started to shake. He could hear the officer talking, but wasn't listening to what he was saying. All the horror of the past few weeks flooded back in a tidal wave. He felt physically sick at the thought of having to arrange his daughter's funeral.

The voice at the other end of the phone was still talking and Ralph heard, 'You can arrange the funeral, but don't forget, you cannot have the body cremated.' He put the phone down and walked into the living room.

'What's wrong, love?' Jackie looked anxiously at her husband's deathly pale face.

'That was the police. They say we can now make the arrangements for the funeral.' They looked at each other, and each knew what the other was thinking. Where were they going to get the money from for the funeral?

'Don't worry, love,' Jackie said, 'we've got some saved for the holidays—we'll have to use that.'

'It probably won't be enough,' Ralph said. 'I don't know how much a funeral costs. We've got no insurance money to come either.'

'We'll just have to borrow if we haven't enough.' Jackie didn't like to see him so worried. 'We can still try and have a holiday because the kids will be disappointed after what we've all been through.'

As Ralph was dialling the funeral directors he thought that this was going to be the most heart-

147

breaking time of all, for everyone—when Sharon was buried. He and Jackie were going to need all their strength to see them through the next few days.

Two hours later all the arrangements had been made. The funeral directors had given a date, the rector of the local church had been contacted and the police had been informed. Ralph felt exhausted and emotionally drained. He had acted like a robot speaking to the different people on the phone: it was as though he was making arrangements to bury a stranger. It had to be that way; his mind couldn't have coped with the truth.

The days leading up to the funeral were only bearable because there was so much to do. Ralph and Jackie had very little time to themselves. Relatives on both sides had to be notified, clothes and wreaths ordered, and their three children visited every day. They were still living with their Auntie Sylvia but, as soon as the funeral was over, would be coming home.

The night before the funeral, wreaths and sheaves of flowers started to arrive at the house. They were laid on the floor of the hall and kitchen and their scent pervaded the air. Even when Jackie and Ralph went to bed the smell was there to remind them of the ordeal they faced the next day.

Neither of them could sleep, there were too many thoughts running through their heads. At six o'clock Ralph slipped out of bed to go downstairs; he needed a cup of tea and a cigarette to calm his nerves. Jackie felt him move and immediately left the bed to follow him down to the kitchen. She knew what today was going to do to him and was terrified his heart wouldn't stand up to it.

They sat in the kitchen sipping tea, surrounded by wreaths, and as they looked at each other across the table, both were thinking how different they looked. Two weeks ago they had been happy and carefree—content with their lives and family. Now they looked haggard; aged by two short weeks.

At seven o'clock the first wreath of the day was delivered and, after that, they kept arriving every five minutes. Very soon the house and garden were full of floral tributes in different colours and designs. Ralph looked at them, but blanked his mind off to the reason for them being there. Relatives and friends crowded the house and, although Ralph answered when they spoke to him, he felt as though it was all a dream. He was looking out of the window when the hearse drew up outside. As though in a trance he watched the undertakers placing wreaths on top of the coffin. He closed his eyes to try and block out the sight, but it was no use. Even with his eyes closed, he could see that wooden box and visualize the body of his beloved daughter inside. Turning from the window, he burst out crying and ran across the room to his wife. Jackie cradled him in her arms. With his head resting on her shoulder, she could feel his tears running down her neck.

Eventually the mourners left the house to go to the waiting cars and Jackie led Ralph down the path, her hand under his elbow for support. Her eyes never left his face—she didn't see their neighbours and friends lining the road to the church, didn't even see the vicar during the church service, or the reporters stationed at vantage points near the grave. Her only thoughts were for her husband and whether he was going to break down under the terrible strain.

It was at the graveside that Ralph finally did break down. He sank to his knees sobbing, 'Sharon', as though his heart would break. Jackie moved quickly. 'Come on, love,' she said gently, and pulled him to his feet. The crowd around the graveside moved to make way for them as she led him to one of the waiting cars and held him in her arms until the ceremony was over. Then, with their families, they made their way home.

*　　*　　*

With the three children back home, Ralph and Jackie worked hard at trying to live a normal life. They had talked it over and agreed it wouldn't be fair if they let their grief and bitterness spoil the lives of the children, who were too young to understand the pain they were suffering. When Ralph disappeared upstairs for hours at a time, Jackie knew he would be lying on his bed, crying out his grief alone. For weeks after the funeral she watched over him like a hawk, making sure he took his tablets and didn't get excited. The children were now back at their own school, Jackie was back at work, and one day Ralph announced that he too was going back to work. He felt it would be better if he were occupied all day, instead of sitting at home with nothing to do but think. 'Life has to go on,' he told Jackie when she suggested he wasn't fit enough yet. 'The sooner we get back to normal, the better.'

He had been back at work for three weeks and was gradually beginning to feel better. His bosses and workmates at the record company where he worked had been marvellous with him, and had really gone out of their way to help him in getting over the first few difficult days. The only part of the day he dreaded now was when he had to drive across the bridge over the canal where Sharon's body was found. He always kept his eyes straight ahead, refusing to look at the water which he knew he would never be able to pass without being reminded of his daughter.

*　　　*　　　*

Ralph walked into the office one morning and was about to greet his workmate Brian when he noticed the strange look on his face.

'What's wrong?' he asked.

Brian handed over a newspaper, saying, 'Have you seen this?'

Ralph took the paper and, looking down, saw a picture of Sharon. He felt his blood run cold as he read the headlines which said that a man was being questioned about the murders of Sharon Mosoph and Wendy Slater. Ralph remembered that Wendy was the eighteen-year-old girl who had been brutally murdered a few months before Sharon. The newspaper reported that the police were expected to charge the man with the murder of both girls.

Ralph shook the newspaper and cried out in anger, 'Why in the hell do I have to find out from this that they've caught the man who murdered my daughter?' His voice reflected the burning anger he felt. 'I'd better go home and tell Jackie, then I'm going to ring the police.'

She was just seeing the children off to school

when Ralph arrived home. Her face went pale, her first thought being that he was ill. Quickly he told her about the newspaper report, and then strode into the hall to phone the police. He didn't have to look the number up—it was etched on his mind and he would remember it until the day he died.

'Detective Superintendent Benyon, please,' Ralph asked when he was put through.

'Good morning, Mr Mosoph,' the officer said. 'I've been expecting you to ring.'

'I want to know what's going on?' Ralph demanded. 'I think it's scandalous that we have to learn from a newspaper that you've got the man who murdered our daughter. Don't you think we should have been informed before the press?'

'I agree with you,' said the officer. 'I don't know how or when the press got hold of the story, but I can tell you now, officially, that a man will be charged with Sharon's murder later.'

Ralph felt all the tension leaving his body. 'Thank God the bastard has been caught.' Jackie saw the relief on his face. When her husband put the phone down they held each other close before leaving the house together and kissing at the gate, going their separate ways to work. They couldn't not go because they needed the money.

That evening they decided to go to Ralph's mother's to tell her the news, but the children didn't want to go. They were playing in the street with their friends and pleaded with their parents to let them stay. More protective of them now than ever, Jackie and Ralph gave them strict instructions that they were to stay near the house and promised they'd only be away an hour.

It was just over an hour later when they

returned, after hearing on the radio that a man had been charged with the murder of the two girls and had been remanded in custody. Paul met them in the street and told them that a man and woman had called to the house and left a letter for them. He handed the envelope over to Jackie, who looked puzzled as she slit it open. They were inside the house by this time, and she took a card out of the envelope. After reading it, she passed it to Ralph. On the card was a passage from the Bible and, on top, a message of sympathy. It was signed by Mr and Mrs Slater who had put their address on the back of the card.

'I know that name,' Ralph said. 'They must be the parents of the other girl who was murdered. I think we should go and visit them and see what they wanted.'

'We'll have to thank them for the card,' Jackie said. 'Shall we go now?'

They walked up the path of the Slaters' house. Ralph felt very apprehensive as he knocked on the door, but this soon left him when Nora Slater opened it and invited them in. She introduced them to her husband, Joe, who immediately disappeared into the kitchen to put the kettle on.

For the first time since Sharon's murder Ralph felt that he was talking, and listening, to people who knew exactly how he felt. They felt the same pain, bitterness and heartache. The Slaters, like themselves, were nice, ordinary, working-class people who, without warning, had been robbed of a daughter they were devoted to. The two couples talked for several hours, glad to be able to unburden themselves to someone who empathized. Family and friends sympathized and shared their grief, but could not fully understand their feelings. The loss of a child through illness or accident is bad enough, but one could eventually accept it. When a child is deliberately taken from you, it is completely different and impossible to accept.

When it was time for the Mosophs to leave, both families had gained comfort from the meeting and had arranged to meet again in the near future. On the drive home, Ralph tried to explain his feelings to Jackie. 'Those people understand because they're going through the same thing themselves. But how do you explain to others how you lie in bed at night thinking never again will your eldest daughter come to you for advice? Never again will you see the face that was always smiling. Now I will never have the grandchildren that one day she would have given me. And what do you say to strangers when they ask how many children you have? How do you answer someone who, after being introduced, says, "Mosoph . . . that name rings a bell—where have I heard it before?"' He was silent for a while, and then went on. 'How do I explain to the children when I shout at them that it's because of the tension built up inside of me, and by shouting I'm trying to relieve that tension?'

It was the first time Ralph had really given voice to the torment that had been gnawing away at him since Sharon's death and, as he spoke, it seemed as though the tight band around his head eased a little. 'They've charged someone with her murder and, if he is found guilty, he will be sent to prison. He'll be relieved of all responsibility—no money or food problems, no worry about how he's going to pay the bills that keep coming in. And here's me, worrying about going to the doctor for the pills I have to have to keep me alive, in case I can't afford the prescription charge.' They were turning into their road as Ralph went on, 'Only people like the Slaters know what it is to lie awake at night with all these thoughts running through your head. Nobody else could possibly understand.'

*   *   *

On Tuesday 29 June 1976 Trevor Joseph Hardy was to appear at Oldham Magistrates' Court, to be charged with the murder of Sharon Mosoph and Wendy Slater. The night before, Ralph and Jackie couldn't sleep. It was a warm night, but it wasn't the heat that caused them to toss and turn so much as the thought of actually seeing the man who had murdered their daughter. How would they feel when they saw him—could they sit in court and watch him without wanting immediate revenge?

Nora and Joe Slater were going to the court and had offered to pick up Ralph and Jackie on the way. Jackie was tidying the kitchen after seeing the kids off to school when she saw the Slaters' car stop outside. She hurriedly slipped on her coat and, with Ralph following, walked out to meet them. As they were getting into the car, Jackie whispered to her husband, 'Have you taken your tablets?' He nodded. 'What about you—have you taken a Valium?'

'I've taken one and brought the bottle with me, in case you need one.' Jackie, as ever, was concerned about Ralph's heart condition. She was amazed he'd been able to cope so far. What would he do today, though, when he saw the man who had killed his daughter?

155

When they reached the courthouse they found many of their relatives had already arrived. They had arranged to meet early because they had been told that only so many were allowed in the courtroom. Being related to a murder victim didn't give you any special privileges. You had to take your chance along with the rest of the public.

As they were making their way down the corridors to the courtroom, Ralph could feel his heart pounding and his stomach churning. He was glad when they found the appropriate courtroom and he was able to sit down. He looked around and could see plain-clothes policemen all round the room. He recognized several who had been to his house during the enquiries.

Suddenly Ralph saw everyone standing up and realized the magistrates had entered the courtroom. Then he felt a dig in his side and Jackie whispered, 'That's him.' Three men had walked up the steps to the dock. As they passed by not five feet away from him, Ralph felt his blood turning cold. The man standing in the dock between two officers was about thirty years of age, of medium height, with a dark moustache, deep-set eyes and a balding head. Ralph didn't hear the charges read out, he was staring at the murderer's back, willing him to turn round so he could see the hatred in the eyes of his victim's father. Who the hell was he, to take away the life of a young girl?

Ralph became aware that everyone was standing up, and then he saw the man he had been watching being led past him again. Suddenly, without warning, all hell broke loose. People were screaming 'Bastard' and 'Murderer', and Ralph saw his brother George, who had been sitting behind him, jump over the seats and run towards Hardy. There were violent scuffles as everyone surged forward, trying to reach the accused man.

Ralph felt a pair of arms wrap themselves tightly around him, and as he turned his head recognized one of the detectives. 'Don't get involved,' the officer said quietly. 'It's not good for your health, and it might prejudice the trial.'

Ralph made no effort to move, knowing that the officer was right. He saw the police calming the crowd as the accused was led away, and looked round for Jackie. She wasn't in the seat next to him, and then he realized she was in the midst of the crowd who had been trying to get at Hardy.

'We nearly got him,' Jackie told him as she returned to his side. 'Your George would have landed on top of him, but someone grabbed his legs from behind.'

They made their way out of the building to see reporters and police waiting by a transit van which they knew was waiting to take Hardy back to prison. There was a group of people gathered near the van and, as the prisoner was led out of a side door with a blanket covering his head, there were shouts of 'Monster' and 'Murdering bastard'.

When the van had driven away, the crowd was advised to disperse by the police. Ralph was told by his family that Hardy was to appear in court again the following week, and they all made arrangements to meet outside on that day. As Ralph was driven home, he said quietly, 'Maybe we'll be lucky next time.'

*   *   *

157

Ralph and Jackie met their family and friends outside the courthouse on 6 July. They had arrived early, intending to find seats as near the dock as possible, but were to find their intention had been anticipated. An officer met them as they approached the courtroom and informed them that they were to sit in the balcony. Before that they were subjected to a search by the police. As they inspected Jackie's handbag and pockets, she said she felt as though she was the accused going on trial. They were leaning over the balcony when Hardy was led in by two prison warders. As Ralph looked at him, he thought he would never forget that face as long as he lived. He listened intently as the charges were read out. He then saw Hardy's solicitor rise to his feet and tell the court that his client denied the charges. The magistrate said the case would go to the Crown Court and Hardy would be remanded in custody until then.

As the prisoner was led away there were shouts of anger from the balcony, but this time they were answered by a woman sitting downstairs in the courtroom. 'My son didn't do it,' she screamed. 'He wouldn't do a thing like that.'

As a police officer led the woman out, Ralph said, 'She was allowed to sit downstairs, but we weren't. Where's the justice in that?'

*   *   *

Later that evening Ralph was reading the evening paper which carried an item on what had happened at the hearing that day. There was a photograph of Hardy being led out of the court building with a blanket covering his head. While Ralph was staring at it, his youngest son, Mark, came over and leaned on his dad's shoulder. 'What's that man got his head covered for, Dad?'

Ralph was silent for a while, and then he said, 'That's the man who killed our Sharon.' He put the paper down, thinking that Mark was too young to understand what had happened but, to his surprise, his son picked the paper up and threw it back on the floor. Then he started jumping up and down, stamping his feet all over the photograph of Hardy, as though he wanted to punish him for what he had done to 'our Sharon'.

*   *   *

Feeling that the family needed a complete break away from the house that held so many memories, Jackie had borrowed some money for a week's holiday. 'The kids need and deserve some pleasure,' she told Ralph, 'and we need a break too.' She'd booked a week at a Butlin's holiday camp and the kids were very excited as they set off in the car.

For the sake of the children, Ralph and Jackie tried to put the events of the last six months out of their minds. They joined in the fun by day. It was only at night in bed that they allowed themselves to think, and talk, about Sharon.

On Thursday 2 September Ralph was sitting in the huge dining room waiting for his breakfast, along with hundreds of other holidaymakers. He was reading the *Daily Mirror* and, as Jackie glanced at him, she saw his face drain of colour. 'What's wrong, love?'

Ralph passed the paper over. 'It's about Sharon,

159

Wendy Slater and Audrey Newton.'

Jackie looked at him. 'What? Who's Audrey Newton?'

Ralph took the paper back from her and started to read the report. The skeleton of a teenage girl had been uncovered in a shallow grave at dawn the day before, and police believed that the girl was fifteen-year-old Audrey Newton who had been missing since New Year's Eve 1974 when she had gone out to meet her boyfriend before going on to a party at a friend's house. She had never arrived. The report then went on to say that a man had been charged with the murder of Sharon Mosoph and Wendy Slater.

'It looks as though the police think Hardy killed all three girls.' Ralph saw his wife's eyes fill with tears and knew there was no way that they could stay at the holiday camp. They had tried, for the children's sake, not to mention Sharon's murder but after reading the newspaper report, he knew it wasn't possible to keep up the pretence any longer.

'We're going home today,' he said, 'I can't stay here now.' He saw the disappointment on the children's faces, but they didn't say a word. 'As soon as we've had our breakfast, we'll pack up and be ready to leave after tea tonight.' He would have preferred to go home straight away, but thought it only fair that the children should be allowed one last day's pleasure.

*   *   *

The long drive through the night was very tiring. While the children slept in the back of the car, Ralph and Jackie took turns at the wheel. He was

160

driving for the last part of the journey as they left the M6 and approached Manchester. He drove up Oldham Road towards Failsworth and passed Tenacres Lane where the skeleton of Audrey Newton had been found two days earlier. A few hundred yards further on they passed Thorp Road which joined Lightbourne Road where Wendy Slater had been murdered.

Ralph drove along, knowing there was one more grim reminder to come. He gritted his teeth as they drove along Poplar Street and passed Whelan's store, where Sharon had worked, and the car park where she had met her death. Then, eyes straight ahead, he took the bridge over the canal where her body had been found. It had been a nightmare journey, the children asleep and neither he nor Jackie in the mood for talking. He was glad when they reached home and, after taking a couple of sleeping tablets, he was able to crawl into bed, praying sleep would come quickly.

Life returned to a dull monotonous routine after their brief holiday. Ralph and Jackie went back to work and the children to school. There had been no further news after the report of the finding of Audrey Newton's body, and Ralph was beginning to despair of Hardy's ever being brought to trial. Christmas and New Year passed and still no further developments. He couldn't understand why, it was taking so long, and why they weren't kept informed of what was happening. It was almost as though they didn't exist; weren't involved. Their daughter had been murdered, but apparently they were just supposed to forget about her. Apart from the initial interviews with the police, not one person had been to see if they needed any help, if they were coping mentally and financially with the situation. Ralph had become very bitter about what he saw as the injustices suffered by victims of crime.

One evening, Jackie was alone when there was a knock on the door. She opened it to find two men standing on the step. They introduced themselves as reporters from a local radio station and explained they were gathering information on the three murders to use in a programme after the trial. They asked if Ralph would agree to being interviewed. Jackie invited them in and made them a cup of tea while they were waiting for her husband who was due home any minute.

When Ralph came in, he immediately agreed. With a tape recorder running, he answered the reporter's questions. It was when the interview was over that Ralph was asked a question which surprised him. 'Do you know where Hardy's girlfriend Shelagh Farrow lives?' the reporter asked.

Pretending he knew of the existence of this girlfriend, Ralph answered, 'No, we haven't been able to find out where she lives.'

'We wanted to interview her,' the reporter told him. 'We heard that they were living together in a flat off Smedley Road, but a neighbour told us that the police have taken her away as a witness.'

Ralph didn't pursue the matter, but as soon as the men left he rang the police station and asked an officer for some information on how Shelagh Farrow was involved with Hardy's crimes. He was told, 'Sorry, but we can make no comment.' Frustrated that he knew no more about what was happening than any other member of the public,

Ralph was forced to face each new day with the heavy burden on his mind.

*   *   *

Finally, thirteen months after Sharon's murder, it was made public that Hardy would be brought to trial on 20 April 1977 when he would be pleading 'Not Guilty' to the charges of murder. As the time drew nearer, Ralph found the tension was seriously affecting his health. He was taking more time off work because he couldn't sleep at all, even with the help of sleeping tablets, and the pains in his chest were becoming more frequent. He tried not to complain to Jackie, because he didn't want to add to her worry, but she knew him too well not to see there was something wrong and kept a close watch on him. If anything happened to him, she thought, Hardy would be responsible for another death. When she considered the trouble that monster had caused her family, she hoped he would rot in hell!

Ralph felt guilty about the time he had taken off work, and grateful to his employers who had been very understanding. The day before the trial started his boss rang to assure him that his wages were guaranteed, no matter how long he was away from work. Not everyone was so understanding, though. When he made enquiries about attending the trial, he was told that if the court were full when he and his family arrived, they wouldn't even be allowed in. Ralph was furious when he was told this and made his feelings known to the police. But it made no difference—they were to be treated the same as anybody else who wanted to attend the trial.

Ralph and Jackie had planned to go to bed early, after taking enough sleeping pills to ensure a good night's sleep, but it didn't work out that way. The phone never stopped ringing as relatives and friends called to make arrangements for meeting outside the court building the next morning. Ralph stressed that they would have to be very early, to be sure of getting in. When they finally climbed the stairs, both weary, Jackie said, 'There'll be no room for anyone else tomorrow when all our families get there.'

'That might not be a bad thing,' he answered.

*   *   *

The day of the trial dawned and Ralph and Jackie were up early. The children were given their breakfast, their clothes attended to and they were sent on their way to school. Jackie was scooping medicine bottles into her bag when Ralph walked into the kitchen.

'I've left two tablets out for you, love. One is your heart tablet and the other is the Valium.'

'Have you taken one?' he asked. 'Remember, the doctor said we should take them to calm our nerves.'

Jackie nodded. 'I've had one and I'm taking them with me in case we need them.'

After parking the car as near the court as they could, Ralph and Jackie walked towards the building. Some of their relatives were already there, even though they were very early.

'Let's go in and find out in which courtroom the trial is being held.' Ralph walked ahead of the group down the main corridor. After they'd made

164

enquiries about the Hardy trial it was Jackie who suggested going to the canteen for a cup of tea.

They were surprised to see Nora and Joe Slater already seated in the canteen, along with some of their relatives. Nora pointed out Audrey Newton's mother, Laura, to Ralph. She was seated at a table with a woman she introduced later as her mother. Looking from his own wife's face to Nora Slater's and then Laura Newton's, he said to himself, 'My God, Hardy has a lot to answer for.'

'Come on, let's get out of here,' Jackie whispered, 'I want to be sure of getting a good seat.'

Nora and Joe followed them to the courtroom door, where they were told by policemen to form a queue. When the door opened, everybody was searched before being allowed in. Ralph and Jackie were the first in and as they were climbing the stairs, he said, 'Searched like a criminal—as though we haven't been through enough.'

Followed by the Slaters, they made their way to the front row where they would be able to see and hear everything that went on. When they were seated, Jackie nudged Ralph. 'Do you want a Valium before it starts?'

Ralph, whose heart was pounding so hard he thought it was going to burst, nodded his head and held out his hand. Joe Slater, sitting next to him, saw Jackie open the bottle and pass the tablet to her husband. 'What are you taking?' he asked. Ralph explained that the doctor had prescribed the Valium to keep them calm during the trial and Joe asked if he could have one. 'I need something,' he added.

The courtroom had filled by this time. Suddenly,

Ralph was aware of a lot of activity below in the front of the court. Then he froze as he saw Hardy being brought into the courtroom from the stairs directly below them. Two warders were with the prisoner, but it was Hardy who claimed Ralph's full attention. He stared hard at the back of Hardy's head, willing him to turn around so that by some gesture he could relay his hatred to this man—this savage—who had killed three young girls. Ralph was denied this, though, as Hardy never turned his head.

Jackie touched his arm. 'There's some of our crowd down there.' She was pointing to the left of the courtroom below, and Ralph recognized their relatives. He noticed that the benches reserved for the press were all full and that the reporters had their notebooks and pens at the ready.

'Everybody be upstanding.' The clerk's voice rang out and Ralph rose to his feet as the Judge, Mr Justice Caulfield, entered the courtroom.

Everyone was quiet as the jury of six men and six women were sworn in, and Hardy indicated that he had no objection to any of the jurors. Then Mr Patrick Russell, QC, stood up to open the case for the prosecution. He addressed the jury in a clear voice, warning them that they were to hear details of the murders of three teenage girls which would make their blood run cold. 'You may experience a feeling of revulsion,' he told them, 'but I would ask you to do your best just to consider the evidence which is put before you.'

Ralph sat rigid in his seat. Although he felt cold there was sweat on his forehead and the palms of his hands. If the jury were to hear details which would make their blood run cold, what effect would those details have on the parents of the victims? Mr Russell told the jury how Hardy's story began in 1972, when he was sent to prison for five years for wounding a man called Stephen Burns with a pickaxe. He was released after serving just over two years of his sentence, and his one thought was to kill Burns whom he believed had perjured himself to convict him. Mr Russell glanced at the jury, and then continued reading from the forty-page dossier of death that Hardy had handed to the police in Strangeways Prison after he had confessed to the killing of Audrey Newton.

On New Year's Eve 1974, Audrey Newton had arranged to meet her boyfriend outside the Phoenix Hotel. From there, they were going on to a party at a friend's house. On the same day Hardy had gone to report to his parole officer, but found the office closed and returned home to arm himself with a knife. He had been told that Stephen Burns had died just before he himself was released from prison, and this news had angered him. He was living for just two reasons—one was to see Burns dead, and the other was Elizabeth Davies, the fifteen-year-old girl with whom Hardy had formed an association. While he was serving his sentence, Elizabeth had written to Hardy, telling him she no longer wanted anything to do with him and was seeing someone else. Hardy had vowed he would hunt her and Burns down, and had thought of little else in prison.

Still reading from the statement, Mr Russell went on, 'Hardy made his way towards Tenacre Lane to try and see Elizabeth. He saw a car pull up and a girl with long black hair get out and shout goodbye as the car drove off.

'Audrey Newton made her way towards the short cut across the playing fields. Hardy, who was half drunk, approached from behind and said, "Do you remember me, Beth?" Audrey turned around and said, "What do you want?"' Mr Russell stopped for a few seconds, and then continued. 'Hardy then hit her in the face and, as she fell, kicked her and drove the knife into the side of her neck.'

'"Blood just poured out of her and she started choking," Hardy said. "I just stood there and watched. I didn't care a damn after what I'd been through." He added that he'd dragged the body into a hollow and covered her with grass, then washed his plastic mac in the nearby canal, brushed his trousers and returned home. He sat watching a Hogmanay programme on TV then had a hot drink before going to bed. Later, when he knew his parents would be asleep, Hardy crept out of the house and returned to dig up the body in order to rebury it in a lonelier place.'

Ralph and Jackie were feeling sick as they listened to Mr Russell reading out the gruesome details. They were hearing for the first time the manner in which Audrey Newton had been murdered. Hardy was visible below, his expression impassive.

'The man's an inhuman savage,' Ralph said softly. 'How could anyone do such a thing?'

Mr Russell was still reading from the statement. 'The body of Audrey Newton did not remain undisturbed for long. For weeks and months after, Hardy returned to his victim and dismembered the body with an axe and his bare hands. He alleges that he threw the head into a nearby lake, later filled in by the Council. It will probably never be recovered.' Mr Russell looked up then and said, 'The Crown does not accept that this killing was a case of mistaken identity.' He went back to the papers in his hand.

'Shortly afterwards, Shelagh Ann Farrow came on the scene. She was ten years older than Hardy and, after forming a relationship with him, went to live with Hardy at his parents' house. Later they lived together in a flat in Smedley Road.' Pausing just long enough to take a breath, Mr Russell went on.

'In July 1975, Wendy Slater, eighteen years of age, became Hardy's second victim. She was attacked by him as she left for home, only a short distance away from her part-time job at the Lightbourne Hotel in Moston. She left the hotel about 2.15 a.m. on the twenty-ninth, but didn't get very far. The following morning her body was discovered on a building site near her home. She had terrible head injuries and had been strangled with her own sock. Her right nipple had been bitten off and she had been kicked in the lower parts of her body.' Another pause before Mr Russell continued, 'According to Hardy's statement, on the night Wendy Slater was killed he and Farrow had been out drinking but, because they had run short of money, he decided he would steal. He claimed that he left Farrow and followed a girl he had seen walking alone. He waylaid her and robbed her of her handbag. Hardy told the police that Farrow was anxious the girl might recognize her, and it was at her instigation, invitation and persuasion that he returned and killed Wendy Slater to stop her identifying Farrow.' Mr Russell looked up at the jury and said, 'Farrow denies this. In Hardy's

169

statement he says, "I picked up a brick and hit the girl four times in the face with it. I took it out on that girl with all the hatred and frustration I felt for that slut across the road. The thing that horrified me was that it gave me pleasure to do what I did to her."'

Ralph looked at Nora and Joe Slater and could see their pain. Further along, Laura Newton and her mother sat with tense, white faces. God, he thought, I've got to listen to what happened to Sharon. He turned to Jackie and whispered, 'Am I due for a tablet?'

She knew that, like herself, Ralph was dreading what was to come. 'Do you want to take it outside? I'll come with you.'

'No, I'll take it here. I want to know what he said about Sharon.' Ralph turned his attention back to Mr Russell, who was still reading from the papers in his hand.

'Three days after the killing, police went to Hardy's flat but were unable to find him because he was hiding in a secret cubbyhole, watching them. When he was eventually seen by the police he denied all knowledge of the murder, and his mistress, Farrow, provided him with a false alibi.

'There was another attack on a girl on the fifth of March 1976. Hardy was alleged to have indecently assaulted a young woman named Carole Connelly in the ladies' toilet of a public house. He was alleged to have gripped her throat, squeezing it so tightly that she bit off part of her own tongue. Hardy was seen by police and asked if he normally grabbed girls by the throat. He replied, "Yes, throat them. I grab them round the throat and it usually works."'

170

Mr Russell looked at the jury. 'The significance of that remark became apparent a few days later when Sharon Mosoph was killed. Hardy was on the run from the police and was trying to break into a store when he was disturbed by Sharon, who was returning home from a party held by the store Hardy was trying to break into. He told the police that Sharon said she would remember his face.

' "I hit her with the handle of a screwdriver on the forehead, just above her eye. I don't know why, but I had been in a bad mood over Shelagh Farrow and that girl in the pub. She started screaming and shouting, so I grabbed hold of her with one hand over her mouth and shoved her into the doorway. I got one hand over her throat and braced myself by putting one foot on the alcove wall behind me. I started to choke her. A couple of minutes later she went limp." '

Jackie could hear Ralph sobbing and squeezed his hand. 'Do you want to go out, love?'

'No,' he sobbed, 'it can't get any worse.'

Ralph was to be proved wrong as Mr Russell carried on. 'Hardy went on to describe how he stripped the girl, bit her left nipple then threw her naked body into the icy waters of the canal. He returned home and was smuggled in by Farrow after, he claims, he had told her what he had done. She then dried and pressed his wet trousers.

'Hardy later told the police, "I knew I would have to go back and try to hide the body because of the teeth marks." He said he returned about five-thirty a.m. and walked down the dark street where he had earlier been lurking. Sharon's naked body was still lying in the canal. He stated, "I stripped down to my underpants and swam out to

171

the body and turned it over. I managed to scrape out most of the teeth marks with a rivet."'

Mr Russell told the hushed courtroom, 'When the body of Sharon Mosoph was recovered, there were sixty-four scratch marks on it where Hardy had tried to obliterate the tell-tale signs which would connect him with the death of Wendy Slater.

'Eventually he was arrested and charged with the murders of Sharon Mosoph and Wendy Slater. In August 1976, while awaiting trial, he asked to see senior detectives at Strangeways and admitted killing fifteen-year-old Audrey Newton. Hardy, accompanied by police, took them to waste ground and showed the officers where the body was buried. Police found parts of the skeleton, but some of the bones were missing and the head has never been recovered.

'We propose,' Mr Russell announced, 'to show that in three different places, at three different times, and for perhaps three different reasons, three young, harmless and defenceless teenage girls lost their lives in circumstances of the utmost callousness and savagery.'

So ended the first day of the trial. The details which had emerged had horrified every person in the courtroom and, as Mr Russell had forecast, made their blood run cold. For the parents of the murdered girls it was as painful as any physical torture. Their hatred of Hardy was so intense that, if he weren't so well protected by warders and police, they would surely have killed him as violently as he had killed their daughters. The difference between them and Hardy was that while he had killed for no reason, they most certainly had one.

On the second day of the trial, the prosecution set about proving their case by calling different witnesses. One witness, sixty-eight-year-old Martha Lynch, was asked by Mr Russell to give an account of what she had heard in the early hours of 9 March 1975. She told the court she had gone to bed about 1 a.m. and, a little while later, heard loud, piercing screaming.

'They were terrified screams at first. I went to have a look through my bedroom window but could see nothing. The streetlights were out and it was like a dungeon out there. Then I heard a second outbreak, as though someone was really terrified. It was a young woman's voice, but still I could see no one. The first screams had come from the front of the mill opposite, the second from the rear car park. Shortly afterwards, I heard a man's and a woman's footsteps pass nearby, then after about an hour I dropped off to sleep.'

'The bastard,' Ralph whispered. He was thinking of the fear and pain his daughter must have gone through at the hands of Hardy, now sitting in the dock without a flicker of emotion on his face. There was no sign of shame or remorse from him, and Ralph had come to hate him with such intensity it frightened him.

Another witness was Hardy's brother Colin, aged twenty-three, who had been brought from prison to testify against the defendant. He told the court about a night he had gone out with his brother and Farrow to have a few drinks in the Dusty Miller public house. This was in October

1975 and Colin told the court that they had talked about the death of Wendy Slater and how he and Trevor had both been questioned by the police about their movements.

'I was asking Trevor what had been said to him, and he told me certain tests had been taken, including a saliva test. I told him if they had let him go there was nothing to worry about. He just turned round and said to me, "I done the murder." At first I thought he was bragging and trying to be clever, then he said it was an accident, that he hadn't meant to kill her, he just wanted money from her. He told me that he had used a brick on her, but she must have had a weak skull or something. He told me there was forty-eight pounds in her handbag, but I didn't believe him. I told him barmaids don't earn that much money.'

Mr Russell then asked the witness, 'Did he say anything about sex?'

Colin Hardy replied, 'Yes, he wanted to stress that he had not committed a sexual assault and had not interfered with her in any way. I asked him why he was telling me this and one of them, I don't know if it was Trevor or Shelagh, said, "It makes no difference, you can't tell anyone." Then Shelagh said, "I will swear my life away that he was with me all night."'

Colin went on to say that in October 1976, after his brother had been committed to Strangeways prison accused of the murders, he and his mother had visited Trevor in prison. 'I asked him if it was as he had told me in the pub, but his attitude was one of complete indifference. He was calm and did not deny or admit it. He was more interested in why Shelagh Farrow had not been arrested.'

Colin then told the court of an alleged statement written by his brother and smuggled out of prison by his mother, who passed it on to him. The alleged statement was produced and shown to the jury.

*   *   *

It was Monday, 25 April 1977 and Hardy's mistress, Shelagh Ann Farrow, was due to give evidence. The trial then took a dramatic turn as Mr Justice Caulfield told the jury that Hardy no longer wished to continue with the services of his counsel and wanted to defend himself. After further legal submissions, during which the jury was absent from the court, the judge agreed to an adjournment, so that Hardy could study some important evidence concerning his former lover.

When the court convened again, Justice Caulfield directed the usher to provide a table and a chair for Hardy, also a glass of water. Ralph couldn't believe that a man charged with the murder of three girls, whose imprisonment and trial was costing the taxpayers thousands of pounds, was being given what appeared to be VIP treatment.

A dark-haired woman then stood in the witness box and Mr Russell started to question her. 'Is your name Shelagh Ann Farrow?'

'Yes'

'How old are you?'

'Forty-two.'

'I believe you are married and have been separated from your husband for the last five years.'

'Yes.'

'In what way did you learn about the death, or disappearance, of Audrey Newton?'

'I went to a public house called the Grosvenor. Inside I went to the toilet and, when I came back, I noticed a photograph on the right of the bar. I asked Trevor who it was, because I thought it was some relation of the landlord's, and he told me it was Audrey Newton. We left the pub at closing time and walked down past Totals and up towards the canal.'

Mr Russell turned to the judge. 'My Lord, this might be an appropriate moment to warn the witness.'

The judge looked towards Shelagh Farrow. 'Yes. Madam, you may be asked some questions to which the answers may be incriminating for you. In other words, may put you in danger of being prosecuted yourself. Do you understand?'

'Yes, My Lord.'

'In those circumstances,' the judge told her, 'you may refuse to answer and, if you find yourself in that difficulty, you will mention the matter to me, then I will make a ruling. But I am cautioning you now that you have the right not to answer any incriminating questions—do you fully understand?'

'Yes, sir.'

Mr Russell then addressed Shelagh Farrow. 'Tell My Lord and the jury what happened next.'

'We were walking by the canal, and as we approached some hoardings near a small wall, I mentioned that I hoped they would find the girl who was missing. As we got near the wall, Trevor said, "I killed her. She's buried up there." He told me the body was buried near some white markings and only he knew exactly where. A few days later we were walking past the same spot, but in the opposite direction, and I saw a dog on the grass verge scratching on the ground. Trevor was walking a few feet in front of me and he stopped the dog which moved away, leaving no apparent marks on the ground. I asked Trevor if he was frightened that the dog may have gone near to where the girl was buried, and he answered yes.

'He didn't tell me where the girl was buried, but a few days later we were out walking again and Trevor wanted to pass urine. We were near a grass verge and there were trees along one side, which he went behind. I went up with him in case anyone came by and, when he had finished, I was stood in front of the trees. He said to me, "That's where she's buried," and I saw white markings on some boards, which had a door in the middle of them. It was near to where we had been walking when the dog had been scratching, but I couldn't see any sign of a grave or the ground having been disturbed. He didn't tell me how he had killed her, but he told me he had dismembered the body and distributed it over the nearby brick croft. I asked him why and he said, "It was so she wouldn't be identified." He told me he had used an axe, which he had borrowed from his mother, and some time later, when he went to visit his mother, she asked him where the axe was and he told her he had mislaid it.'

Mr Russell then addressed Farrow. 'We shall hear that Hardy told the police he had given you a watch taken from the body of Audrey Newton. Is there any truth in that?'

'No, sir.'

'Will you look at exhibit number sixty-two?' Mr Russell waited until the witness had examined the

177

exhibit then asked, 'Do you recognize it?'

'Yes, sir. It is similar to a watch Trevor gave me after he had done a robbery on Church Lane.'

Mr Russell then said, 'We shall hear that, in addition to that wristlet watch, Hardy alleges he gave you an engagement ring which he took from the body of the girl Audrey Newton. Would you look at exhibit number seventy-two?' The exhibit was handed to the witness. 'Have you seen that ring before?'

'Yes, sir.'

'How did you come by that ring?'

'Trevor did a robbery near the Cresta Bingo Hall.'

Mr Russell then questioned Farrow about the death of Wendy Slater and she told him that on 18 July 1975 she and Trevor were in the house at Smedley Road where they were living together. 'Trevor told me to get ready, we were going for a drink. We went to the Park Hotel and had a few drinks and left before closing time because he had spent the money I had given him, but I still had a little left in my purse. We walked down towards the bus stop and he told me I had to go home on my own. He went behind the pub and picked some roses, which he gave to me, and as we approached the bus stop, said that he was going to do a job. I told him not to be silly and come home with me, that we would manage with what money I had left, but he went into a mood and told me I was going home, and he made sure I got on the bus.'

Shelagh Farrow paused, and then went on. 'The next time I saw Trevor was between about two and three o'clock in the morning, and he was in quite a state. His trousers were wet and there was what looked like bloodstains on the sleeve of his denim jacket. He blurted out to me, "I've done a girl. I hit her with a brick." He looked tired and I asked him how he had got into such a mess. He told me that he had come through some water at the rear of a pub nearby. When we got into bed, he said, "Will you wash my clothes?" And I said I would. The following day we went to Queens Park near to where we lived, and as we walked he went into his pocket and gave me five or six pounds, saying, "I wasn't going to give you this, but it will help you out." I thought he had got this from the job he had done the previous night.'

'Did you know a girl called Wendy Slater had been killed that morning?' asked Mr Russell.

'No, sir,' replied Farrow. 'I found out later from the evening paper. When I said to Trevor that there had been a murder, he said, "I told you about it, didn't I?" I didn't want to believe him. I took his clothes to the launderette on either the Sunday or Monday and washed them.'

Farrow paused for a while, ran her tongue over her lips, and then continued. 'On Tuesday the twenty-second of July the police came to our house—a sergeant and a constable. They asked about Trevor, but he had seen them arriving through the window and was hiding behind a hole in the wall which he had made and was hidden by a chair pushed in front of it. The police asked where Trevor and I had been the night before the murder, but I said I would prefer them to ask him themselves and they left. Trevor came out when they had gone and he told me that if they returned, I was to say that he had been with me all night on the Friday and Saturday morning—the eighteenth

179

and nineteenth of July. The police returned again on the Thursday, and when they asked Trevor where he was on the night Wendy Slater was murdered, he told them he was with me and had never left my company all night. I told them that was true and Trevor asked them, did they want to see his clothes? One of the officers said yes, and when Trevor showed them, he asked, "Do you want to take them away with you?" But he was told that wouldn't be necessary. He had got rid of the boots he had been wearing that night, by putting them in a plastic bag and hiding them where they couldn't be found, behind some brambles near a wall. We were at his mother's one evening and, when we were on our way home on the bus, he pointed out to me the spot where he had killed Wendy Slater.'

Mr Russell then asked, 'Do you remember at about this time, Mrs Farrow, Trevor being asked to give an impression of his teeth?'

'That was while he was at Plant Hill, sir, at Middleton. They took him from the prison, sir, to a dental hospital.'

'When he told you this,' questioned Mr Russell, 'did you see any significance?'

'Well, he undid the top of his trousers, sir, and pulled them back and I could see a file—a nail file.'

'Did you learn from Hardy whether he had used the nail file or not?'

'I went to see him on one particular instance at Middleton, when he was being held over to appear in court that morning. His mother was with me at the time and he had shown me the nail file and made a motion with his hand towards his teeth, telling me that he was going to file his teeth.'

'Did you know at this time that Wendy Slater's

body had been mutilated by the nipple being bitten from the breast?'

Farrow shook her head. 'No, sir.'

Mr Russell went on to question Farrow at some length regarding dates and times concerning the incident with Carole Connelly, the girl Hardy had tried to throttle in the pub toilet. Then he went on to the murder of Sharon Mosoph, once more asking for details of Hardy's movements on the date in question and how she had visited him several times in Broadhurst Park when he had been on the run from the police. He was living rough and she had taken him food and clothing. After a week of living in the park, and then a derelict house, Farrow found a flat for them to share. They were living there in the April when police came to arrest Hardy.

Mr Russell addressed the judge. 'I should have shown one exhibit to this witness much earlier. It is a yellow scarf. This is going back to the Wendy Slater murder.'

He then turned to Farrow. 'Will you look at that scarf, exhibit number seventy-one. Do you recognize it?'

'It is a yellow scarf, sir.'

'When did you acquire it?'

'I got it from his mother, sir.'

'Mr Hardy, in a statement he has made, suggests that you gave him that scarf to wipe the blood from his face.'

Farrow replied, 'No, sir, never.'

Mr Russell requested of a court official, 'May she see exhibit number fifty, a pair of blue socks?' After Farrow had examined the exhibit, Mr Russell asked, 'Can you help us about those socks?'

'Yes, his mother bought Trevor those socks from a lady where she worked. He wore those while he was in the derelict building off Oldham Road.'

Mr Russell faced the judge. 'Your Lordship will recall the evidence in relation to those socks?'

Mr Justice Caulfield answered, 'Bits of material?'

'Fibres from the socks were on the body of Sharon Mosoph,' Mr Russell told him.

*   *   *

Mr Russell had questioned all the witnesses for the prosecution—Farrow being the last—and Mr Justice Caulfield told Hardy, 'You may now cross-examine the witness.'

The accused moved from his chair to face his ex-mistress and his first question was, 'You said I met you in February 1975?'

'Yes.'

'I met you on the twenty-fifth of January,' he challenged.

'You are a liar,' Farrow told him.

'I was in court on the second of January.'

'You were in court on the seventeenth of March, Trevor, and I went along.'

'I was charged on the second of February.'

Farrow didn't waver. 'I did not meet you until the twenty-sixth of February.'

It was almost as though the two former lovers were having a private argument. Question after question poured from Hardy as he faced Farrow. He seemed to relish his position as inquisitor, as though it gave him power over her. None of the questions he asked had any relevance to the case and, in the public gallery, the families of the three murdered girls were becoming frustrated and angry as Hardy continued to waste time.

He had asked sixty-three questions, none of which had any real bearing on the case, when Ralph suddenly snapped.

'What has all this got to do with it?' he shouted. Mr Justice Caulfield looked annoyed.

'Bring that gentleman down into the court.'

A police officer led Ralph down into the well of the court, to where the judge sat in his wig and red robes.

'Just keep your head,' he was warned. 'If you want to stay in court, you must be quiet. Have you not noticed how quiet the court is when evidence is being taken?'

'This is not evidence,' retorted Ralph.

'Never mind. Do not argue with me. Have you not noticed how quiet the court is? That is how it is going to stay, and if there is any interruption from you, I have powers to put you down below. Do you understand?' the judge asked.

Ralph nodded. 'Yes.'

'That may not worry you, but it is the power I have. You, like everybody else, must keep absolutely quiet. Do you want to stay in court or not?'

'I should be entitled to stay in court. It was my daughter . . .' Ralph couldn't hide his anger.

'You are only entitled to stay in court if I say so,' the judge informed him.

'It was my daughter who was murdered!'

'I understand your concern,' Mr Justice Caulfield sounded less angry now, 'but you must be quiet.'

As the police officer was leading Ralph back through the courtroom, Ralph's eyes met Hardy's and he raised his clenched fist, indicating to Hardy what his feelings were.

After another hour of Hardy questioning his ex-mistress, the judge adjourned for a break.

Over a cup of tea in the canteen, the families of the three victims discussed the evidence they had heard that morning, and expressed their own feelings on what should be the punishment of Hardy and Farrow. Although Hardy was the killer of all three girls, emotions were running high about the part Farrow had played. If she had gone to the police after Hardy had confessed to killing Audrey Newton then the other two victims would still be alive. Ralph felt as much hatred for her as he did for Hardy.

*   *   *

The court had reconvened and Farrow had resumed her place in the witness box when Hardy handed the judge a three-page letter. The judge asked Farrow to step down and ordered the usher to show the jury out of court. He then had discussions with various barristers who were called to the court. Later, he ordered the jury to be brought back, took a roll call, then sent them to a private room where two ushers were to stand guard outside to keep them incommunicado.

Two hours later, when the jury was asked to return to the courtroom, the judge told them, 'I apologize for keeping you in that room for so long, but there was a very good reason.' He then adjourned for lunch.

In the afternoon, when the trial resumed, the charges against Hardy were read out again. After each charge, he replied, 'Not guilty to murder, but guilty to manslaughter on the grounds of diminished responsibility.'

Mr Russell, for the prosecution, said the Crown did not accept that plea. The judge then said that the Crown was seeking murder convictions and the trial would continue.

Ralph felt a sense of relief when this was announced. The last thing he wanted was a charge of manslaughter for the monster who had cruelly and sadistically murdered three young girls.

*   *   *

Hardy was now to be represented by Mr B. A. Hytner, who cross-examined Shelagh Farrow. He didn't go over any of the previous ground, merely confirming by his questions that Hardy was a man of many moods, sometimes calm and easygoing but capable of flying into a rage for no apparent reason.

Then there were arguments from all kinds of professional people as to whether Hardy was fully responsible for his actions at the time of the murders, or whether he was just a cold-blooded killer who would kill again if let out of prison.

Finally, the tenth day of the trial came and it was time for the judge's summing-up. When he had finished, he told the jury that it was not for doctors to decide if Hardy was guilty of murder or not. 'You will pay great attention to all the experts, of course, but you alone will decide on the evidence you have heard whether Trevor Hardy did suffer from an abnormality of the mind.' The judge also said that the evidence of Shelagh Farrow was, at the very least, suspect, and that she may have been shielding herself. At the end of his summing-up, the judge sent the jury out to reach their verdict.

*   *   *

Ralph and Jackie, with relatives and friends, were sitting in the canteen drinking tea, as they waited for word that the jury was back. Ralph, though, was waiting for something else as well. Lester had dashed home to change from his shoes to a pair of plimsolls. This had been arranged between them the night before. It was Lester's suggestion, and Ralph had agreed. Lester and his stepsister had been best mates, and the boy missed her so much he hurt inside. So it was planned that Lester should jump from the gallery and try to get to Hardy.

Lester returned in his plimsolls and sat with his family in the canteen until there was a buzz that the jury was returning. Members of it were making their way back to their seats when Ralph stopped in his tracks. It was almost as though the police knew what they had planned because officers had been placed all along the front row of the spectators' gallery. Ralph knew then that there was no chance of Lester carrying out their plan.

The jury had been out for seventy minutes when Ralph saw the red light flashing, to indicate that they had reached their verdict. His stomach was turning over as the six men and six women filed on to the benches. He looked for signs on their faces which might tell him of the decision they had reached, but their expressions gave nothing away.

The judge made a sign to the usher, who faced the jury and asked, 'Have you elected a foreman?'

A man stood up. 'Yes.'

'Have you reached a verdict?'

'Yes.'

Ralph clenched his fists so tightly he could feel his nails digging into his palm. Please God, he prayed, let it be Guilty.

'Do you find the defendant Guilty or Not Guilty of murder?'

The voice rang out loud and clear. 'Guilty on three counts.'

The words were like music to everyone's ears and they listened intently as the judge told Hardy he sentenced him to life on each of the three charges, to run concurrently. 'This area,' the judge said, 'is a happy place, but now it will be a lot happier without you.'

Uproar broke out in the gallery as Hardy was led away. There were cries of, 'Bastard! Send him up here and we'll kill him,' from emotional families and friends. Ralph stood there watching as Hardy was led away to serve his life sentence. There had been no recommendation on tariff from the judge, and Ralph hoped that the guilty man would rot in jail for the rest of his life.

His attention turned then to Shelagh Farrow. Surely to God she was to be punished too. It was her fault that Sharon was dead and she deserved to be imprisoned. However, he learned that for helping the police, and acting as a witness for them, she had been promised immunity and was not to be charged, even though the judge had said she must be treated as an accomplice. He learned later that the police had put her on a train straight after the trial to take her away from the district to a safe address they had found for her.

Filled with rage at this injustice, he vowed that someday he would find Shelagh Farrow and make her pay. She had kept quiet about the first murder and surely must take some blame for the deaths of Wendy Slater and his beloved Sharon. To him she was as guilty, and deserved the same punishment, as the 'Beast of the Night'.

*   *   *

Ralph and Jackie tried everything they could to bring Shelagh Farrow back to court, to be tried for the part she'd played in Trevor Hardy's murder of their daughter. But Farrow had been promised immunity from prosecution for giving evidence against her former lover and, although Ralph worked ceaselessly for two years, he came up against a brick wall at every turn. He wrote to everyone he thought could or should help, including the then Home Secretary, the police, MPs and solicitors.

He was told eventually that the only way Farrow could be brought to justice was if he took out a private prosecution against her. He was warned that this would cost in the region of £15,000, and where would an ordinary working man find that sort of money? He tried asking businessmen and local clubs and pubs to help and did manage to raise some money, but only a drop in the ocean compared to the amount he needed. He tried to get legal aid but his request was turned down. Ironic, really, because if he had raised enough money to bring about a private prosecution, Farrow would have received legal aid to defend herself.

Angry and bitter, Ralph gave up the fight to bring Hardy's ex-mistress to court to receive the punishment she rightly deserved. But he has never given up the thought that one day he will meet her and, with the face of his beloved Sharon always in his mind, who knows what would happen then? As long as Shelagh Farrow walks free, Ralph will always feel that justice has not been seen to be done.

CHAPTER SEVEN

1977

Stasia Delahunty was causing concern again. She had seemed to be improving after her visit to Stephen Sherlock but, apparently, the man who had attacked her had decided to play tricks on her. One morning, about two months after the incident, her son tripped over an object that had been left outside the front door. It was still dark and Tony, who worked in the fruit market and had to start work early, fell over it before he could stop himself. It turned out to be the bag that had been stolen from Stasia, and the shock threw her back into a depression.

'Why would he do that?' she asked.

'I don't know,' I told her. 'He must be a nutcase.'

'So now he knows where I live, what's he going to do?'

'He probably won't do anything—what could he do?' I tried to reassure her, but I was puzzled myself.

It was a few days later, on the Sunday, that I received a phone call from Stasia's daughter Carol. She was distressed and worried because her mother had gone out on the Saturday afternoon to do some shopping for the weekend, and hadn't come back.

'Has she ever done anything like this before?' I asked.

'No, she's always back from the shops by teatime,' Carol insisted. 'But she was so upset yesterday that I'm worried.'

'Why was she upset?' I asked.

'Her name was in the death notices in the *Echo*. It said she had passed away peacefully in hospital.' Carol was almost in tears. 'We didn't know until my auntie rang to sympathize with me. Then we had lots of calls from relatives who had seen the notice and had to explain that it must have been a joke. My mum was very upset.'

'I'm not surprised. I think you should ring the police, Carol, just to be on the safe side.'

I didn't want to worry the girl more than she was already, but I was very concerned over Stasia. The state she was in, she was likely to do anything. She was eventually found in hospital; she had been wandering the streets, not knowing who or where she was, and the police had taken her there on the Saturday night. When Carol rang me to tell me the news, I told her I'd get to the hospital the following day.

Stasia was in the psychiatric ward, and this made me feel so angry towards the thug who was the cause of her being there. I was determined he wasn't going to ruin her life. The day after she came out of hospital I called to take her with me on my rounds.

Seeing Stephen had helped her last time, and I was glad that the new victims I took her to see had the same effect. She listened to what had happened to them, and then she would tell them her own story. Who better to help and sympathize than someone who had also suffered?

*   *   *

Soon after this I received an invitation from Radio City to take part in a phone-in on the punishment of offenders. Roger Blythe would be the presenter, and opposing my views would be a David Mathieson of the Probation Service. It was explained to me that the two panellists would be asked to state their views, and then the telephone lines would be open to the public. I accepted the invitation and agreed to be at the studio by 2.30 the following afternoon.

Next morning I heard on the radio that there was a bus strike, and thinking that all those who worked in the city would be taking their cars in, decided it would be advisable to go by train in case all the parking spaces were full. I arrived at the radio station early and, after taking my name, the receptionist asked me to sit down. I hadn't been seated long when I noticed a man walk to the desk, and watched as he was directed to take a seat next to mine. The receptionist called over to ask if I would like a cup of coffee, and the man seated next to me closed his newspaper and turned to me.

'Hello, Mrs Jonker,' he said. 'I'm David Mathieson.'

After shaking hands, for want of something to

say I remarked, 'I didn't think it advisable to bring the car in today so I came by train and it got me here early.'

He must have misunderstood my reason for not bringing the car because he said, 'I don't blame you, I had a brick put through the window of my car last week.'

I opened my mouth to sympathize but, before I could utter a word, he went on, 'But it was my own fault.'

I gazed at him in amazement and said, 'How do you mean, it was your own fault?'

'Well,' he told me, 'I had left a cassette recorder on the back seat.'

This statement left me even more amazed.

'But wasn't it your own property, inside your own property?' I asked.

'Yes,' he said, 'but it was a temptation.'

The logic of this left me almost speechless. 'So it was your own fault that someone stole from you,' I squeaked.

'Well, it was a temptation,' he repeated.

Good grief, I thought, I've known him for two minutes and already I'm in disagreement.

'If you are telling the young people who come through your hands that it isn't their fault if they steal from someone, then it's no wonder we're in the state we are in.'

At that moment someone came to take us through to the studio. I was now in exactly the right frame of mind for a discussion on crime and punishment.

I was simmering gently through the introduction and my own explanation of why I considered that offenders should be punished. Then David

Mathieson gave his reasons for thinking rehabilitation was the answer, and not the sort of punishment I was talking about. I endured his waffle until we were able to challenge each other on why we thought our opponent was wrong. Unfortunately for David, who is a quiet person, I didn't pull any punches and told him exactly what I thought of him and his crazy ideas, and also that I believed it was people like him who were ruining our society and its youth.

The phone calls were predictable; there were a couple in favour of David's views, but the majority were on my side. I then asked Roger Blythe to find out what David would do if he went out of the studio today and saw an elderly lady being attacked by a young man.

'You heard what Joan said, David,' Roger put it to him. 'What would you do if you walked out of the studio today and saw an elderly lady being mugged?'

There was deathly silence in the studio as we all waited for his answer. It was several seconds before Roger, realizing he wasn't going to get a reply, said, 'Come on, David, we're waiting.'

'It's too late now, Roger,' I said, 'the old lady has been mugged and is lying on the ground.'

'David,' Roger insisted.

'Well, I would have to consider . . .' was as far as David got before I burst out, 'Consider what, for heaven's sake?'

Roger Blythe relieved the tension with a chuckle. 'I'll play a record before Joan hits David on the head with her umbrella.'

After the programme I spoke with David for some time and found him quite charming and friendly. Unfortunately, we were a million miles apart in our views and I could not pretend otherwise. During our conversation I mentioned punishment and he seemed to find the very idea distasteful.

'We don't use the word "punishment" any more,' he told me. 'In Probation Service literature the word has been changed to "rehabilitation".'

'I have no objection to rehabilitation,' I told him, 'as long as it comes after they have been punished.'

'But punishment doesn't do any good,' he argued.

'It didn't do me any harm, nor all the people of my generation. If I was naughty, I didn't just get punished, I expected it.'

We parted without convincing each other.

*   *   *

The lobby of Parliament on law and order planned for November was taking shape now; I had been in touch with Graham Page who confirmed the hall had been booked, MPs had agreed to speak and the police had been notified. Most of the MPs who had agreed to speak were like-minded as regards corporal and capital punishment, and this I found rather a dull prospect. It was like preaching to the converted and I didn't see any point in five hundred people going to London to hear someone tell them what they already knew. So we notified all Members with constituents taking part in the lobby to make themselves available to meet their constituents. That done, I contacted British Rail and booked several coaches on the London train.

There were still a few weeks to go so I was now

able to concentrate on arranging the coach trip for elderly victims, which would include lunch in Kendal and tea in Morecambe. It turned out to be a most successful day, enjoyed by everyone. It may have been quiet on the coach for the first half-hour, but when I had been down the aisle introducing people to each other that soon changed, and the rest of the journey was accompanied by chatter and laughter. Stasia had come along, although she didn't really want to, and I was glad of her help with those who had difficulty in walking.

Actually, I didn't give Stasia much choice: she was the youngest on the coach, able-bodied and able to help, so I took advantage. It paid dividends, too, because on the way home, when everyone was singing the songs that were popular many years ago, I could hear Stasia's voice as loud and clear as could be.

The day after the coach trip I was determined to get home early from my visits and have an exotic meal ready for Tony and Philip. I was feeling very guilty about being away from home so much; I kept saying I would cut down on my activities, but never did. The meal was a huge success and I was just carrying the coffee cups through to the lounge, determined that we should sit and enjoy the television as a whole family for one night, when the phone rang.

The caller apologized for ringing in the evening but had, unfortunately, not been able to contact me during the day. She went on to explain that she worked for *Woman* magazine; they had heard of my work with victims and thought it would make a nice human-interest story. After many questions about the type of people I visited and in what way I could help them, she said she was very interested and would get a feature writer to contact me in the next few days. Knowing the mass circulation of *Woman* I was very excited. The researcher seemed very caring and concerned when I explained that all the people I visited were ordinary working-class and often left penniless after a robbery. If the writer could get the concern I felt into a story then perhaps, at last, someone would not only sit up and take notice but would do something. I was so excited at the prospect that I almost stayed at home the next day in case the *Woman* writer phoned, but common sense prevailed when I realized it could be weeks, if ever, before I heard. So it was business as usual.

When the journalist from *Woman* did ring a few days later, she told me her name was Penny Baker and asked me to tell her something about the work I did. As it happened, the evening she rang I was feeling angry and distressed because of the new cases I had seen that day. Although I tried not to let it get to me, I would have had to be made of stone not to be affected by the sight of elderly people crying, and all the emotion I felt was conveyed to Penny.

'I'm really looking forward to coming to Liverpool,' she told me, 'this should make a marvellous story.'

It was arranged that she should come the following week and stay for three days. *Woman* booked her into the Adelphi Hotel, and Penny asked whether, if she arrived in the city early enough, I would go down on the first evening to have a meal with her and then we could talk.

Penny was roughly about the same age as myself, in her early-fifties, small and petite and very gentle. Over dinner we chatted generally about weather, food, changes in society, rising prices. Everything, in fact, that two females would talk about. It was later in her room, with her tape recorder switched on, that she started to ask me questions. 'Forget about the tape,' she told me. 'Pretend it isn't there.'

We talked of my childhood, where I was educated, my parents, marriage, and views on what was happening in our society, and lastly how I came to be involved with helping victims. It was decided that Penny would write a better story if she could see for herself the conditions in which the victims lived and if she could hear their stories first-hand. So starting off at ten o'clock the next morning we were able to visit six victims during the day. Penny then wanted to visit the casualty ward of a local hospital to ask the staff what their reaction was to wounded victims being brought in. After that she had an interview with someone in the Chief Constable's office to try and broaden the story.

To say that Penny was moved by what she saw and heard would be completely inadequate—she was so affected that she said she would like nothing better than to stay in Liverpool and get involved. She was full of admiration for the courage and spirit of the victims. 'This story needs to be told,' she said. 'I hope I tell it well.'

It was only about a week after she came to Liverpool that I received a letter from her and a draft of the story she had written for me to check. She begged that I send it back immediately as she'd been told to do it fast. It was very moving and well written, and I sent it back unchanged the same day.

197

The only thing I argued with was that she made me out to be some sort of Joan of Arc, and even my best friends wouldn't call me that!

The following week I received a phone call from a photographer who had been commissioned to take photographs of the victims and myself for inclusion in the article. When he arrived, complete with lots of camera equipment, he had a copy of the story Penny had written.

Underneath each of the victim's names were suggestions on how the photographs should be taken. For instance, they wanted Stephen posed looking at his television set—the best friend he has. Ethel Attwood was to be shown looking through her lace curtains into the street which she could no longer walk down alone.

At first it was just a routine job for John; he sat the victim in the desired position and took shots from all angles, but I noticed after a while that his attitude seemed to change. He no longer just took photographs, he listened to the victims' stories and, as he listened, I could sense him taking note of their lack of material possessions.

It was when work was over and we sat having coffee before he caught the train back to London that I realized how deeply he had been affected. He told me he had travelled the earth on different assignments, covered some of the atrocities committed during the wars that were raging in different parts of the world. He had worked for some of the best-known magazines, including *Time*, but told me quite sincerely he'd never been as deeply affected as he had been this afternoon, seeing the elderly victims of crime.

'You expect to see pain and suffering when

there's a war on, but you don't expect to see pain and suffering in your own country when the sole cause is greed.'

Penny had told me it would be at least three or four months before the article appeared in *Woman* because they work so far in advance, so all I could do was sit back and be patient.

I was visiting Ethel one day and, as we sat drinking tea, she was reminiscing about the old days. She used to love going to afternoon tea dances in Reece's, and her eyes would brighten up as she told me about the friends she would go with. Old photographs showed me that she had been a very attractive, clothes-conscious woman. I felt so sorry for her now—since the attack she wasn't able to go out on her own, needing an arm to lean on. Her hearing and eyesight had deteriorated, and she wasn't able to do even little jobs around the house.

We started talking about Christmas, which was rapidly approaching, and suddenly I had a brainwave. 'How would you like it if we had a Christmas party?' I asked.

Her eyes lit up. 'Oh, that would be lovely,' she said. 'Could Vicky come?'

Vicky was the little lady next door who had been with Ethel when she was attacked.

'Of course. We'll have as big a party as we can.'

The only person I knew who could help with expenses was Charles Oxley, so that night I put my idea to him and asked for his help. As always he didn't hesitate, and the plans for a Christmas party got under way. It was a mad scramble to get round all the victims to tell them there was to be one and to ask if they would like to come. I hadn't made any enquiries as to where we could hold the party

199

because I had no idea of the numbers involved. However, it was soon obvious that we would need quite a large room because everybody accepted our invitation. I rang a friend who was chairman of a pensioners' club and she agreed to ask the committee if we could hire the hall she used for her bingo sessions. When she rang me back it was to say that the committee had not only agreed but had offered the hall free. On top of that they had offered to supply some ladies to help with the food and the washing-up afterwards.

I enjoyed all the hustle and bustle, and it was doing Stasia a power of good because I had her buying Christmas presents and wrapping them in colourful paper. She seemed to have taken on a new lease of life and was cheerful and happy.

When I added up the number of victims who were coming to the party I was surprised to find it was a hundred and twenty. Many of them couldn't get to the hall under their own steam, so I had promised that they would be picked up. I thought this would cause a problem but, after a few phone calls, I had six people with cars who agreed to help out. A local baker supplied the pies, sausage rolls and bread rolls, all at a very reduced price.

The day before the party I rang the *Echo* news desk and they promised to send a reporter along; then on impulse I rang the BBC studios in Manchester. I was promised that they would send a crew if possible, but they couldn't say for sure in case something more newsworthy turned up.

The party had been in full swing for about an hour when I saw a man with a camera walk in, followed by Alistair McDonald. I remembered Alistair from the time he worked at Radio

200

Merseyside. He seemed amazed when he saw how many people there were.

'Are these all victims?' he asked.

'Yes, a hundred and twenty of them,' I told him.

'Where did you find them all?' he wanted to know.

'I went out and looked for them. This is only the tip of the iceberg,' I said. 'There must be many thousands more like them up and down the country.'

As Alistair, microphone in hand, talked to some of the victims I could see the disbelief on his face. Some of the old people still bore the evidence of an attack—arm in plaster, bandages on wounds or bruises. I think what shocked him more than anything was their age, anything from seventy to ninety years. However they soon proved to him that, while they might be frail in body, they were certainly not frail in spirit, and when Alistair told everyone that they would be on television that night at about six they started watching the clock so that they could get home in time to see themselves.

I, too, made sure I was home in time to watch the programme, and sitting on the couch next to Tony, pointed out the victims I had told him about. It was lovely to see their happy, smiling faces, and I thought how little it needed to make them happy. This thought moved me to tears, and Tony's arm came around my shoulder.

'Come on, love, look how much they're enjoying themselves,' he said. 'Don't cry.'

Little did he know that never a day passed when I didn't cry. I couldn't sit and watch an elderly victim cry with pain, fear or hopelessness without shedding tears with them.

I was glad there were only a few days left till Christmas because I was very tired. It wasn't purely physical tiredness, more a mental weariness. Although in public I was laughing and full of high spirits, it didn't present a true picture of the way I felt. I tried not to be affected by the misery and heartache I saw each day, but I wouldn't be human if I wasn't moved by it. Two years ago I would never have believed that there was so much sadness and loneliness in the world. Nor would I have believed that much of that sadness was deliberately caused by greed and heartlessness. I could see no light at the end of the tunnel either because it seemed to me that the situation could only get worse, with higher crime figures and more heartache and misery for innocent people. Why was it that they were made to suffer? There are always those who will fight for the offender, but there was no one to fight for the victim.

Christmas had always been my favourite time of the year; I loved the excitement of dressing the tree, wrapping the presents to arrange beneath it and watching the faces of my family as they opened them. Since my younger son had been married, he and his wife Pauline always came for Christmas Eve and stayed the night, so we could all be together when the presents were given out. They were expecting their first child in about six weeks' time, and I was already looking forward to the Christmas after this when I would have my first grandchild to buy for. It would take on a new meaning then.

This year, however, although I joined in the festivities with gusto, I kept thinking of some of the old people who would be alone. Particularly those new victims I had met who had been robbed of all their money the week before the holiday started. There would be no Christmas fare for them. In fact, those without family members to help them would have little in the way of food. Stasia and I had made up some hampers with food given to us by friends and well-wishers, but it amounted to very little really. We had tried to make the hampers festive, with Christmas crackers and a little gift put in with the food, and the victims were more than grateful, but I felt sad because it was so inadequate compared with their real needs.

CHAPTER EIGHT

1978

On the day Tony and Philip returned to work, I started back in my routine. I made my first call of the day to Stasia to see how she fared over the holiday, and was relieved to find her in good spirits and eager to show me the presents the children had given her. The scar on her cheek was fading, as was the memory of the incident which had caused so much heartache.

My next call was to an elderly lady I had first met the week before Christmas when her handbag was stolen. She told me there had been a spate of bag snatching in the area, saying that the thieves kept watch outside the post office as pensioners drew their pension, then jumped them on the way home. Unfortunately, there were two weeks' pension to be drawn that week because of the Christmas closure, so people who were robbed would have no money for a fortnight. It was a bleak Christmas for the poor lady, she told me, but a rich one for the thugs. Although it was no laughing matter, I couldn't prevent a smile when she said, 'I hope he choked on the wishbone.' Before I left, she gave me the address of a neighbour who had been injured during a robbery.

I called to see that lady, whose name was Elsie, and found that although her wrist had been broken and she was covered in bruises, she wasn't as unfortunate as most of the victims I met because she had a husband. Not that it made her pain or fear any less, but at least she had someone to comfort her. I had a supply of application forms for criminal injuries compensation in the car, so I filled one in for her and told her I would send it off.

It was on that visit I realized there needn't be just one victim when a crime of violence is committed. Though untouched himself, Elsie's husband was really upset. He was suffering as any loving and protective man would. 'She'll not go out on her own again,' he said, 'I'll be going with her.'

'Don't be silly,' his wife said. 'You can't come everywhere with me.'

Both Elsie and her husband were in their late-seventies, and even together they couldn't fight off a thug who was determined to get money for drink or drugs. But to tell them that would dent the old man's pride. In his day, men protected their wives. 'Let him walk to the shops with you, Elsie, you'll both feel better.'

The husband came to the door with me. 'What's happening in society when an old woman isn't safe on the streets? They should bring back the birch, that would stop them.'

*   *   *

I was living in anticipation these days: for the article to appear in *Woman*, and to hear that our application for charitable status had been successful. Sir William Butlin still kept in touch with me and couldn't understand the delay. It was nine months since Charles Oxley had applied, and still our licence wasn't through.

A phone call one morning explained the reason for the delay. We were using our Campaign for Law and Order letterheads in our correspondence with the Charity Commission, which had caused problems. The commission objected to our registration on the grounds that they could not give charitable status to an organization dedicated to changing the law of the land. We would have to prove that our work with victims was completely separate from the CLO work.

A meeting was arranged between Charles Oxley, Olive Fairman and myself, and at that time we arranged to separate the organizations. We agreed the new charity would be called Victims of Violence, and within days had a new letterhead, and a written constitution which was sent off to the Charity Commission with the promise that in future the organizations would be kept strictly apart. Very soon after this we received notification that our application had been accepted and were given our registration number.

Sir William was delighted, and he and Lady Butlin became our first Patrons.

There was more good news and happiness for Tony and me when our first grandchild was born.

205

Pauline gave birth to a son, and we were over the moon. The proud parents chose the name Mark, and as Paul also wanted to include one of Tony's names there were weeks of discussion on the subject. Mark Anthony didn't sound right, so after much debate everyone settled for Mark Anton. It was a happy time for me because, to some degree, the birth compensated for all the sadness I came across in my work.

The more victims I saw, the more vocal I became. I grabbed every opportunity to get publicity for what I saw as the authorities' complete lack of understanding of the problems of victims. It seemed as though a plot had been hatched by all those in local and national government to ignore them. Did they think that by turning their back on the problem it would go away? Anyone with half an ounce of intelligence could see that, far from doing so, the problem was escalating and this would continue until the powers that be had the guts to say 'Enough is enough'.

My visits were not confined to elderly victims now, and my workload was growing rapidly. A five-year-old girl was sexually assaulted in a park and the trauma left her too afraid to go out; she was having nightmares and had started wetting the bed, which was adding to her distress. Her parents were devastated.

A bus driver had been beaten up several times by gangs of youths travelling on his bus. He was only one of many drivers being attacked by youths, just for the hell of it. And because they were beginning to realize that no matter what they did, they wouldn't be punished for it.

A woman of eighty I called on told me she'd

been a victim seven times. She never went to bed now, she was too frightened. She slept in a chair all night and every night. What a way to have to live at her age. And how many other elderly people were forced to do as she did?

It was at that time I had the idea of possibly liaising with the police to obtain the names of victims who needed help. Charles Oxley and Olive Fairman were enthusiastic when I suggested it so the next day I sent a letter off to the Chief Constable, Kenneth Oxford, asking if he would agree to an interview to discuss the subject.

Little did I know I was soon to find out from personal experience what it felt like to become a victim of crime.

*   *   *

I had been visiting a friend one lunchtime, and we chatted at the front door for a few minutes before I said my farewells and turned away. I heard Norma's door close, then suddenly felt someone tugging at my handbag. Thinking it was one of Norma's children fooling around, I turned with a smile. It wasn't a child, though, it was a youth of about eighteen, and the vicious look on his face made me freeze in alarm. Automatically I held on tighter to the handles of my bag, and each time the youth tugged, I pulled it back. I had my car keys in my hand and they were cutting into my skin, but I was too frightened to feel the pain. I was determined he wasn't going to get the bag, though, and the pulling backwards and forwards seemed to go on for ever, with me staring into his snarling face. Suddenly the struggle ended and, as I gave a

207

last wrench, I fell backwards on to the ground, the youth bending over me and still holding on to the bag. I could feel the pain in the back of my hand where I had grazed it on the wall when I fell, but still I clung on to those handles. Then, to my horror, I saw him raise his leg and his foot swung towards me. Desperately I rolled to one side to try and avoid the boot, but one sharp tug twisted the bag from my grip and he was away.

As I struggled to my feet, two women came around the corner, one pushing a pram. They watched as I stood up. Quickly I pointed to my attacker, who was still in sight, explained that he had stolen my bag, and asked if they would watch while I fetched my friend.

Norma's face showed surprise when she saw my appearance, but she quickly followed me as I told her what had happened. We caught up with one of the women outside a block of flats, which she said the youth had run into. Her friend, she said, had gone to ring for the police. Within minutes a panda car arrived and two police officers got out. I was shaking with shock, but very angry, and told the officers that the youth had gone into those flats and I was going after him. Though appreciating how I felt, one of the policemen said it would do me no good. The thief would be well away by now, probably having gone in the front door of the flats and out the back. Apart from which, the officer said he would have dropped my bag once he had taken what he wanted from it. He and his colleague helped Norma and me search the nearby gardens and bushes, but there was no sign of my bag.

I was trembling visibly by now and my arms and legs were stiff and sore. Fortunately I was wearing trousers, or the cuts and scratches on my legs would have been worse, but my hands were bleeding. Probably because I had used muscles I hadn't used in years, my shoulders felt as though I had been carrying ton weights.

Norma came with me in the car—thank goodness I had kept my car keys in my hand and not in my bag—and we followed the patrol car to the police station. I was given a cup of tea which revived me a little and then gave the officers details of what had happened.

After giving a description of my assailant, who I thought would be etched on my mind forever, I was given a book of 'mug shots' to look through.

After the first book came a second and a third, until all the faces started to look the same. My reading glasses had been in my bag and now my eyes were tired by the strain of looking at so many photographs. I felt miserable and forlorn sitting in that police room, and all I wanted was to get home to Tony. So I asked the police officer if I could ring my husband because he'd worry when he got home from work and I wasn't there. I made the phone call brief, just saying I'd had my bag snatched and would be home soon. Then Norma and I left, with the police saying they would contact me if my bag was found, but not to expect any valuables or money to be returned.

Walking to my car, Norma said, 'Why didn't you scream or shout? I'd have heard you and been out like a shot.'

I sighed. 'I didn't even think of it. I was too intent on hanging on to my bag.'

'What'll you tell Tony?' she asked.

'No more than I told him on the phone, that my

209

bag was stolen. I won't tell him the lot because he would only worry.'

'You won't have to tell him, Joan, he'll only have to look at you to know it was more than just a bag snatch. Your trousers are torn and dirty, your hands are bleeding and you're as white as a sheet.'

'Norma, I couldn't look any worse than I feel. Thank you for coming with me, you're a pal.'

I was shaking as I drove home, and when I finally got out of the car outside the house I felt like bursting into tears. Thank God my house keys were on the same ring as my car keys, and I didn't have to knock. But Tony had been watching for me, worry written on his face, and the door was open before I could put the key in the lock. I tried to make light of it because Philip was listening, but I knew from the way Tony was looking at me that while Philip believed what I said, he didn't. I did get him to promise not to tell any of my family, though, because I didn't want my mum and dad worried.

In bed I tossed and turned, the whole nightmare vivid in my mind. I could still see the snarling face bending over me. Sensing my distress, Tony put his arm around me, and I immediately felt secure and safe. 'Now I know what it's like to be a victim,' I sighed.

'God forbid,' he whispered in my ear, 'but if it ever happens again, just let them have the bag.'

I shook my head on the pillow. 'No, love, I will never willingly give my bag to a thug. They may take it from me forcibly, but I'll never hand it over. What's mine is mine, and no one has the right to take it from me.'

It was days later that Tony, without thinking, let

slip to one of my sisters that I had been mugged, and it spread like wildfire through the family. They were convinced I had been attacked because of my outspoken views, but I didn't agree. Bag snatchers are spur-of-the-moment criminals, acting when an opportunity presents itself. Poor Tony was sorry he'd let the cat out of the bag because all the family had a go at him. He was told he should insist on my not speaking my mind in public, but argued that no one could, or should, try and stop me from doing something I thought was right.

One Saturday afternoon, after I'd been out to visit a new victim the police were concerned about, I returned home to find there had been a phone call for me. Tony said the woman had sounded drunk and he couldn't understand what she was saying, so he had suggested she should ring back.

It was seven o'clock when the phone rang, and as soon as I answered I knew at once it was the same woman because her voice was low and her speech slurred, but somehow I didn't think she was drunk. She spoke in such a posh voice I thought one of my friends was playing a joke on me for a moment, but she told me her name was Prudence Webster and that she had been mugged six times. In four of the incidents she had been injured, but when I asked about criminal injuries compensation, she had never heard of it. I offered to call and see her, and when I called her 'Mrs Webster' she answered in a low drawl, 'Call me Prue, darling.'

I asked for her address and as I was writing it down, she said, 'Just push the front door open, darling, and come straight upstairs because I'll probably still be in bed.'

I was so amazed and intrigued by our

211

conversation, I arrived at her house on the Monday morning eager to meet the person behind the voice.

The street of tall Victorian houses had once been elegant, but now many had been pulled down and those that were left were boarded up or derelict shells. I pushed open the front door and stared in dismay at the cheerless, neglected state of the hall. Wallpaper hanging in shreds showed the stains where damp had come through from leaks, and the remnants of a once handsome chandelier hung forlornly from the ceiling, devoid of bulbs or shades

My call from the bottom of the stairs was answered by, 'Come up, darling!' I grinned as I went up, thinking anyone who lived alone in this house deserved a medal. I followed the direction of her voice and it led me to a door on the landing. Pushing it open, what I saw stopped me in my tracks. On the wall to my right was a sideboard piled high with bundled-up clothes, two tins of cat food and a tin opener. Along the bottom wall was the oldest gas fire I have ever seen in my life, set into an even older fireplace. In front of this, on a box, was a two-ring gas cooker with spent matches all around.

All this flashed before my eyes before I fully entered the room, and when I poked my head around the door I didn't know whether to laugh or cry. Propped up in the bed with two cats at her side was Prue Webster. Around her shoulders was draped a fur coat which, even to my inexperienced eyes, looked like the real thing. She wore it as though there was nothing unusual in wearing a fur coat in bed. A small hospital table stood at the side

212

of the bed and carried a bottle of whisky, a glass, cigarettes and an ashtray. Her dark auburn hair looked as though it had just been set, but I was to realize quite soon that she was wearing a wig.

Sweeping the cats to the floor with a wave of her hand, she invited me to, 'Sit on the bed, darling.' Looking around the room, I saw I didn't have much choice since there were no chairs.

'Have a whisky, Mrs Jonker.' Her hand reached out for the bottle.

'Good Lord, no,' I laughed.' I couldn't drink at eleven o'clock in the morning.'

'Only thing that keeps me going,' Prue stated, pulling her fur coat tighter round her shoulders.

I was having difficulty believing my eyes and ears. I felt as though I was on stage taking part in a comedy but didn't know what my next lines were. Most of the houses I had visited were in working-class areas, some of them poorly furnished. But I had never seen anything like this, I just couldn't take it in.

Between sips of whisky, Prue Webster's story began to unfold, and I found that although she seemed eccentric, she was also intelligent, proud and courageous. Her husband had been a well-known doctor and they'd come to live in this house forty two years ago, when the area was very fashionable and housed many well-to-do medical men and shipping merchants. It was the 'in' place to live for wealthy local people, who had maids and entertained a lot. Life had been good to Prue and her husband, and she told me of the lavish parties they had had in the large house.

When her husband had died many years ago, Prue had tried to continue with the same lifestyle and had, over a period of years, sold all her possessions one by one. Even now, when she was living on a pension, she refused to see that anything had changed. She didn't see the houses all around that were empty and falling down, she still saw things as they were years ago because that was the only way she could survive.

She told me she had been attacked six times, each time near her home. She was an easy target, would stick out like a sore thumb in that area with her posh voice and the fur coat. Each time she had been robbed her bag had contained her pension money which she could ill afford to lose. Several times she had ended up in hospital, but when I asked her for dates, thinking it might still be possible to claim compensation, I couldn't get any definite information from her. She couldn't remember dates as it had happened so often and she had been in four of the hospitals in the city. She promised to try and remember, and said she would write any information down. I arranged to call the following week and was told once again, 'Just walk in, darling, because I will probably be in bed.' She said she had tummy trouble and it was the whisky that kept her going. I gathered she went out each evening to the local pub and it didn't take much intelligence to figure out that her movements were watched by the local thieves.

During that day when I thought of Prue, which was quite often, it was with admiration and compassion. She had a tremendous spirit and was far braver than I, staying in that big house with no neighbours either side. I had thought of asking her why she didn't move out, but where would she move to—she would be completely out of place and unhappy in a flat in one of the concrete jungles. Crazy as it may seem, Prue was happier where she was, with her dreams of the past.

*   *   *

I received a very pleasant surprise one day in the form of an invitation to lunch at the Adelphi Hotel. I had been nominated, along with five other people, for the Merseyside Gold Medal Award for Achievement. I felt very honoured that so many people had seen fit to nominate me, and it was with pleasure that I went along to the lunch. When I arrived I was introduced to the other nominees, and as soon as I saw John Moores, founder of Littlewoods Pools, I knew he was the obvious winner. I was delighted when I was proved right because his firm had, over the years, given employment to thousands of people on Merseyside. I congratulated him warmly, and the smile on his face showed genuine pleasure.

A few days later I received an answer to the letter I had written to Chief Constable Ken Oxford, and was so pleased that he had agreed to a meeting to discuss the possibility of police liaison with our organization. Charles Oxley had a prior engagement, so it was myself, Olive Fairman and the Rev. Martin Garner who turned up at Police Headquarters.

The Chief Constable was very friendly and helpful, showing great interest in the scheme we had in mind which would mean that victims referred to us by the police would receive a visit within twenty-four hours. As it would be the first scheme of its kind on Merseyside, it would take a while to select the trial area and set the wheels in motion. Superintendent Laurie Blackburn was to monitor the scheme and report back to Ken Oxford. Until we were given a date when the liaison would start I would have to find the victims in the usual way via radio, newspaper reports and the grapevine.

*   *   *

There were many times I would say that a particular crime was the worst I had seen, and within days encounter something even worse. I was beginning to think there was nothing the thugs would stop at to get what they wanted.

In one particularly vicious crime which I heard reported on a radio news bulletin, an elderly man had answered a knock on his door one night and been stabbed with a pitchfork. It seemed the old man was a bit of a recluse and kept the pitchfork in his hallway as a protection against burglars. Unfortunately it was used against him, and he was stabbed several times with it. I had the name of the road where the victim lived from the radio, but no name or house number. By now I was quite used to knocking on doors to trace the whereabouts of victims and was no longer nervous about it, so on this occasion I just knocked on the door of the first house in the road. Before I had time to ask the lady who opened the door any questions, she said, 'Aren't you Joan Jonker?'

I nodded, surprised that she should recognize my face and more surprised that she pronounced my difficult name correctly.

'My husband and I often talk about you,' she

216

said. 'We agree with everything you say.'

'Thank you! It's nice to know someone feels the same as me,' I told her, then went on, 'I'm looking for the man who was attacked yesterday and wondered if you knew him.'

'He lives next door,' she said, 'but he's in hospital. Come in anyway and meet my husband.'

I sat talking to the couple for a while, and heard that robberies in the area were now commonplace. They themselves had been robbed several times. On one terrifying occasion they had been confronted in their kitchen by two men who had manhandled the woman and slashed her husband across the face with a razor when he tried to protect her. When I was leaving, the couple promised to ring me when their neighbour came out of hospital. However, I was never to meet Mr Glossop because he died two days later in hospital from the puncture wounds he had suffered all over his body. Just another crime statistic no one seemed to care about. It never made the headlines.

*   *   *

Although my family had expressed their concern about my airing my views in public, I had never feared possible retaliation. So when I answered the phone one Thursday afternoon about a quarter to five, I was unprepared for what was to come.

'Is that Joan Jonker?' a voice asked.

When I said it was, there came such a torrent of abuse that my stomach churned with fear. 'You f— b—' The voice was harsh with threat. 'You want the f— birch, do you? Well, we'll get you and your f— family.' There was more venom to come. 'There won't be a brick left standing in your house, just you wait, you f— b—'

The phone went dead and I stayed still for a while, the receiver to my ear. God knows how long I stood there before replacing it and going back to the kitchen to pick up the potato knife I had put down when the phone rang. My mind was in a whirl, uppermost being fear for the safety of Tony and Philip. I wanted to sit down and cry, but if Tony saw how worried I was, that would definitely be the end of my work with victims.

I have never been the kind who is easily frightened or intimidated, sometimes being far too quick to defend what I think is right, but that abusive phone call could very easily have scared me off. Gradually, however, as I prepared the dinner that night, my fear turned to anger. I could hazard a guess that the owner of that voice was in his mid-teens, and if I was going to let a youngster like that dictate to me then I might as well crawl into a corner and give up now.

I had half decided not to tell Tony about the phone call, but then I realized he had every right to know. I waited until we'd had our meal, and, trying to sound casual, repeated the conversation. When I had finished, he asked, 'Has he frightened you?'

'I was shaken at first, because of the bad language, but I'm most afraid for you and Philip. You shouldn't have to suffer because of my views.'

'I share your views, love, as I believe ninety per cent of the population do, so don't worry about me. Anyway, I don't think the caller has any real intention of carrying out his threats, I believe he was just trying to frighten you off. But if you're worried, then I think you should call the police in the morning and see what they think.'

So I rang the local police station the next morning, and the sergeant on the desk promised to send an officer round to listen to my story. Within the hour, I was sitting facing a policeman and going over the conversation word for word. I told him how horrified I'd been by the venom in the lad's voice.

'Mrs Jonker, it's very unusual for prior warning to be given before an attack. I don't think you have anything to worry about, and doubt you'll hear from the bloke again. If you do, though, contact me immediately.'

The officer's words certainly had a calming effect on me, and I had almost forgotten the incident when, exactly a week later, at the same time, the second call came. As soon as I heard the voice I recognized it, and this time I wasn't caught off balance. I interrupted his torrent of abuse by shouting down the phone that if he didn't shut up I was going to put the phone down. There was complete silence for a few seconds, and when he spoke it was in a much softer, calmer voice.

'You want to birch boys who steal because they have no money,' he said. 'They can't buy anything because they've got nothing to pay for it with.'

'So they go out and mug an old lady who has even less than they have?' I asked angrily. 'Listen, love, only cowards mug old people, and they deserve to be birched.'

'But the pigs pick on young people, especially blacks.'

'That's no excuse for stealing, no matter what you say.'

Then came a question which astonished me.

219

'Why don't you join our party? Everyone knows you and if you joined us, people would listen.' He then mentioned a party with very extreme views.

'I'm not interested in politics,' I told him firmly. 'I'm only interested in stopping thugs robbing elderly people.' With that I put the phone down, wondering why I bothered to talk to him at all.

I expected the phone to ring again, but thanked my lucky stars when it didn't. Not until the following week, same day same time, and right away I knew who to expect. As soon as I heard his voice I knew that, unless I put a stop to it now, these calls would continue, and the only way to stop it was to tell the caller something he would understand. 'Sod off, love,' I said, banging the phone down. I never heard from him again.

*   *   *

It was over seven months since Penny Baker had come to Liverpool to interview me for *Woman* magazine and I resigned myself to the fact that they were not going to publish the story, for some unknown reason. So I was surprised and pleased when I received a phone call from Mary Hampson. She said she worked for the magazine and they were now getting ready to publish Penny's article. Because of the delay, they were afraid there might have been changes in the circumstances of some of the people interviewed and this was the reason for Mary Hampson's call. In my mind I quickly went over all the victims who had been interviewed and told Mary that there were no changes. Then I remembered the change in my own life, the birth of Mark, and passed on the information that I was

220

now a very proud grandmother. We chatted for about fifteen minutes and before we said our farewells I asked if I could be notified of the date of publication and Mary promised to let me know.

Because I believe that most people are fair and honest, and any promise they make will be kept, I was surprised when Charles Oxley rang one morning to ask if I'd bought that week's edition of *Woman*. I said I hadn't because I didn't take the magazine regularly, and anyway I'd been promised they would notify me in advance.

'My wife's copy arrived this morning,' he told me, 'and I'm very angry at what they've done to you.'

I felt a shiver of apprehension. 'Why, what have they done?'

'I suggest you buy the magazine as soon as you can,' he said, 'and ring me and let me know what you intend doing.'

It all sounded very mysterious and ominous, and within five minutes I was driving down to the newsagent's to buy a copy of the magazine. I couldn't wait to get home to read it, so I sat in the car and leafed through looking for the obvious signs of a story on victims. I reached the end without seeing anything that looked like Penny Baker's article and then checked the date on the front cover. Once again I started to turn the pages over, but more slowly this time. It was when I reached the centre spread that the word 'violence' caught my eye, and underneath, in heavy black print, 'The Facts and the Frenzy'. I didn't connect it with the article I was looking for, but started to read the first paragraph, headed 'Bring Back the Cat'. My heart froze. All the words I had ever used on punishment and some I hadn't were in that first paragraph. There was no mention of my work with victims; in fact the word 'victim' didn't appear in the whole paragraph, which was devoted to my views on the punishment of offenders. It didn't say why I held these views, and so made me appear hard and without compassion. What enraged me initially was the heading 'Bring Back the Cat' because I had never in my life used those words.

It was a three-page article, and two and a half of those pages were given over to people who disagreed with my views and were involved in the rehabilitation of offenders—the so-called do-gooders who, in my opinion, were the very ones ruining our society. What a pity they didn't live in the real world. The last paragraph in the article was the worst, and it was this that upset me most. It said: 'But there are people who care about victims of crime. People like Mrs Catherine Hawkins from Bristol who rings the police each day and is given the names of victims. Their names are passed to a band of helpers who visit the victims.'

To my dismay, two of the victims I had helped on Merseyside, and who had been interviewed for the original story by Penny Baker, were then listed as having been helped by Catherine Hawkins from Bristol.

I couldn't believe that a magazine like *Woman* would resort to such deception, nor did I think they should be allowed to use people as they had used me. There was no mention of Penny Baker's name on the article, and I wondered if she knew what had happened. Surely, after seeing the victims and their suffering, and writing such a moving story, she wouldn't have had any part in betraying them.

I threw the magazine on to the passenger seat and headed for home. Once there I picked up the phone and dialled Penny's number. When she answered, she said she'd been waiting for my call. She shared my feelings about the article and said that, although she knew something had gone wrong because she'd expected her article to be published months before, she had been unable to find out why this had happened.

Apparently, since Penny had written the article, there had been a change of editor, and Penny could only conclude that her sympathies lay in the opposite direction to mine. She was, in fact, in favour of being lenient with offenders. It was quite easy, Penny said, completely to change the slant of an article by clever editing. She was angry and upset at what had been done, and swore she would never work for that magazine again. She also urged me to do something about the article, which, she said, had twisted the words of her original story.

'But what can I do?' I asked, almost in tears.

'Complain to the Press Council,' she advised. 'What *Woman* has done to you is wrong and you should take the matter as high as you can.'

I sat for a long time after putting down the phone, thinking about what I should do. I was convinced I had been used, that the powers that be at *Woman* were morally wrong, but what could I, an ordinary housewife, do against the power of a mass-circulation magazine? Then, gradually, my fighting spirit came to the fore. How dare they treat me, or anyone else, in this way? Powerful magazine or no powerful magazine, they shouldn't be allowed to ride roughshod over the feelings of someone they thought wouldn't have the guts or the know-how to fight back. Well, this was one time they'd have a fight on their hands.

In the right frame of mind now, I decided not to delay and rang Directory Enquiries for the phone number of the Press Council. Before my resolve could weaken, I rang the office. The man I spoke to listened to my story in full, from the first phone call from *Woman* saying they had heard of my work with victims and asked if I would cooperate in the 'heart warming' story they had in mind, right through to 'The Facts and the Frenzy' article in that week's edition. When I had finished, the gentleman advised me to put the whole story, just as I had told him, in writing, and send it to the Press Council. They would consider it carefully and advise me if I had cause for complaint.

It took me over an hour to type the letter to the Press Council—tearing up several attempts when they didn't satisfy. Ten minutes later I watched the letter disappear into the dark interior of the letterbox, and crossed my fingers for luck, just as I had when a child.

CHAPTER NINE

I was still smarting over my experience at the hands of *Woman* when, a week after the article appeared, I received a phone call from the BBC. As the girl explained they were interested in interviewing some victims of crime, my heart sank. Her words had an unpleasantly familiar ring. The conversation was one-sided until I heard the name of Roger Cook and pricked up my ears. He would, it seemed, be presenting a series of Checkpoint programmes, which would be going out nationwide, and one of these programmes would be on victims. Now I was interested, because I knew of the good work Roger Cook did in tackling injustice, and I also knew that he would approach the subject with honesty and compassion. I realized that if victims were shown on television the public would see the real story behind the crime statistics, so when the researcher said they were keen to start work the following week, I readily agreed to arrange interviews with six elderly victims.

Many of them I knew well, so was aware who would be willing to tell their story on television. Ethel was a natural choice as she was friendly, articulate and able to express her feelings. Stephen, although less articulate, had to be my second choice for his story alone which, because he was a legless cripple, would make a big impact. Both Ethel and Stephen agreed at once, as did the other four people I approached. I promised each one that if he or she should find the prospect too daunting they could opt out at the last minute, they were under no pressure.

I needn't have worried, though, because when Roger arrived I found he was warm and friendly, and I knew he would put the victims at their ease. He was absolutely marvellous with them, and not only did none of the elderly people dry up in front of the cameras, they thoroughly enjoyed themselves. I could see that Roger was deeply affected by what he saw and heard and hoped that, when the film was shown on television, the whole nation would share his feelings.

While the equipment was being dismantled, I

told Roger about Prue ('darling') Webster. I hadn't put her on the list to be interviewed because I did not think she would come across well, but to point out how many people were ignorant of the existence of the Criminal Injuries Board, Roger thought it would be a good idea to try her.

I rang her and, as expected, she was delighted and told me to tell Roger to 'come straight upstairs'. I could not go with him on that occasion because of a prior commitment and it was the next day before I found out how he had fared. He was full of enthusiasm about his meeting with Prue and agreed that I was right when I said she didn't see the squalor in which she lived.

'What a marvellous character she is,' he said. 'She was sitting up in bed, drinking whisky, and there were police cars, with sirens going, flying up and down the road outside. I looked out of the window and it was like a scene from a cops and robbers film, with youths climbing over walls and the police chasing them.'

I found it a pleasure to be working with Roger; he was open, honest, forthright, and with a good sense of humour. I felt the programme he was making could only be good for victims up and down the country.

A week later, when it was transmitted, Prue came across well on the small screen, as did the other elderly victims. I was so proud of them that I cried as I watched the programme. Although I knew all their stories so well, they could still reduce me to tears.

The programme had barely finished when the phone calls started, and they kept coming until eleven o'clock. Both Ethel and Stephen phoned, so excited at having seen themselves on telly. Other calls were from well-wishers, some from friends, others from people I had never met. These reactions told me of the programme's success in showing the plight of victims and the sufferings they endured. Two days later the letters started to flood in. They came from all over the country, offering sympathy and financial help to those who had appeared on the programme.

Keeping pace with all the mail was quite a task as I answered each letter myself. This meant writing all evening and into the early hours, stopping only when Tony insisted I go to bed.

One letter which pleased me particularly was from the Criminal Injuries Compensation Board. The programme had brought to their attention the case of Prue Webster and they promised to deal with any claim from her, provided the injuries had been sustained during the last two years. They asked for details of hospital treatment, police reports and relevant dates.

The day the letter arrived, I went to give Prue the good news but found her ill and in a distressed state. I offered to make her a cup of tea but she refused, preferring her glass of whisky. To see her alone in this cold, cheerless room made me very sad and I tried to cheer her up by telling her the news about the CICB, but she was vague and didn't understand the need for all the details.

Suddenly she called out, 'Sinbad!' I thought she was delirious, because I didn't think there was anyone else in the house. When the door opened and a man's head appeared, I nearly died of fright. He had a shock of white hair and a huge white beard, but the brilliant blue eyes that smiled at me were not those of an old man.

After Prue introduced us, I was told he lived in one of the downstairs rooms and helped her with the shopping and cooking. He had been a sailor, but had given up the sea because he was an alcoholic and often missed his ship when he was drunk. This fascinating and attractive man was articulate and clearly well educated, and his clothes, although way out for a man of his age, were clean. He told me he had no home but slept anywhere he was allowed.

Thinking she was not receiving her fair share of attention, Prue interrupted the story of his travels and sent him down to the shops for a bottle of her favourite medicine—whisky. While he was away I asked if it was wise of her to have a strange man living in the house, but she told me she could not do without him. He did her shopping, washed her clothes and helped her to the bathroom.

When I left, I made sure Sinbad came to the front door with me. The only way of expressing my concern for Prue's safety was to be honest so I told him of my fears. He listened until I'd finished then assured me that I had no cause to worry, he would look after Prue and make sure she came to no harm. As he grasped my hand in a bearlike grip, I knew I could trust him.

When I got home later in the afternoon, I decided to try and trace Prue's hospital records myself. If she was entitled to compensation, she should have it—heaven knows, she deserved it. Two of the hospitals at which she had been treated had since closed down and their records had been transferred to the new Royal Liverpool Teaching Hospital. After being passed from one official to another, I was put through to the Administrator. When I explained what I wanted, the poor man nearly had a heart attack. He asked if I realized just what I was requesting? Many older hospitals had closed down and all the records had been sent to the Royal, which meant they now had thousands of files going back decades. It would take years to complete the mammoth task of collating the information. I refused to be put off and, when I explained the urgency of the situation due to Prue's ill health, the official asked for a week's grace to see what he could do.

*   *   *

A few weeks after I had sent my letter to the Press Council I received one from Dee Remington, assistant editor of *Woman*, explaining why they had changed the format of the original article. As her letter failed even to mention any of the points to which I had objected, namely that I had been misquoted and misrepresented, and that the victims of Merseyside I had been involved with had been placed in a paragraph describing the work done in Bristol by Catherine Hawkins, I did not accept this reply.

The Press Council asked both the editor of Woman, Jo Sandilands, and myself to go to arbitration, with the Council as mediators, and to this we agreed. I found the Press Council understanding and helpful, which is more than I could say about Jo Sandilands, who refused to admit to any fault on the part of the magazine. The Council sent me a copy of her letter, asking if I was satisfied with the explanation, but I was angered by the way Jo Sandilands seemed to shrug off the whole matter as being unimportant.

(1) They had changed the format of the article, but this was their decision and they had not thought I would mind.
(2) They had used the words, 'Bring Back the Cat' because the word 'Cat' is emotive and that was the effect they wanted. (They did not mention that the word had wrongly been credited to me.)
(3) They had used my victims in a paragraph about Catherine Hawkins because they wanted to involve different parts of the country in the article and they could not understand my objection.

The letter contained not one word of regret for their distortion of the facts or the distress I had been caused. Having gone this far, I was not going to give in, so I refused to accept Jo Sandilands' vague explanation. Mediation having failed, my formal complaint went before the Press Council.

I had to wait many months for the outcome but, when it came, I was quite satisfied. The Press Council upheld my complaint against *Woman*, and the editor, having been informed of its decision, was asked to print the Council's findings as soon as possible, which they duly did.

*   *   *

Christmas 1978 was approaching and, now that we had received money from Sir William Butlin, I was able to plan a party for the victims without worrying unduly about the cost. I blessed the Butlins for their generosity because I could not have coped with the expense without them. The previous year's party had been held in a Conservative club, so this year I asked permission to hold the party in a Labour club, so that I couldn't be accused of being political. One hundred and fifty victims were coming and, again, I coaxed friends into transporting those who had difficulty in walking. Charles Oxley collected Stephen in a mini-bus, as we couldn't manage his wheelchair in a car, and promised to take him home again.

It was lovely to see all the old people dancing and singing—many of them over the microphone. Even Stephen insisted on my wheeling his chair into the middle of the floor so he could sing over the mike. When it was over, everyone clapped and cheered and he was delighted. I was worried that he was drinking too much for everyone was buying him drinks, but he promised me he would be all right. It was only when the hall was emptying and I went over to him that I realized he was not asleep, as I thought, but drunk. I couldn't rouse him and was terrified of what Charles Oxley would say because he had strong religious objections to alcohol. He was very understanding, though, and I breathed a sigh of relief as I watched him lift Stephen into the mini-bus. I offered to go with them, but Mr Oxley said he could manage and would put Stephen to bed. I went home happy that everyone had enjoyed themselves because, for some of them, it would be the only celebration they enjoyed that Christmas.

My own enjoyment of the festivities with family and friends was soon forgotten when I started visiting again. There had been so many attacks and robberies over the Christmas period that I was kept fully occupied visiting new victims. Most of them were elderly and lived alone, and although the method of robbery was different in each case, the result was always the same. I saw so much misery and distress that it began to affect me and I was getting very short-tempered, though never with the victims.

At home I would flare up for no apparent reason and, although I knew it wasn't being fair to Tony, I was finding it impossible to switch off at five o'clock at night. Unfortunately my work was not like an office job where it was possible to put a cover on your typewriter and forget about it until the next morning. Even if I had been able to clear my mind of the victims' plight, I had only to pick up the evening newspaper and it was all brought back again.

One night I was talking to Sir William Butlin on the phone and mentioned an idea I'd had in mind for a while. If MPs would not come to the victims, then surely it would be a good idea to take the victims to the House of Commons. Five minutes later I came off the phone bewildered by the speed with which everything had been agreed. Sir William was so keen on the idea he had offered to arrange everything. All I had to do was to find out how many people wished to attend and make sure they were representative of all Merseyside areas. Sir William would arrange for coaches to meet us at

Euston and take us across London.

I made an appointment to see my MP Graham Page to ask his help and advice. He offered to notify the police so that the victims, all pensioners, could be guided straight into the House of Commons and would not be tangled up in the milling crowds outside.

Within a week I had a hundred victims who wanted to make the trip and had reserved seats on the London train. Sir William had arranged for two coaches to meet us at the station. When we arrived at Euston, I found not only the coaches but also a taxi for me so that I could go ahead and be there waiting to help people off the coaches. There was much laughing and joking when the ladies had to have their handbags searched at the House of Commons, something that had never happened to them before but which they took in their stride.

I took one lady from each group across to fill in the green card which would be taken through to the relevant MP. All those we wanted to see had been notified in advance and only a couple had pleaded prior engagements, so there should be a good response. As the MPs appeared in the main hall, they were shown to their own group and introduced. I wandered from group to group listening to snippets of conversation, much of which was about rising crime figures and the leniency shown to offenders. Because, to them, an MP was an important person, all the ladies treated them with respect, but looking at the smiling faces of most of the MPs it seemed to me that they were being condescending, acting as if they were bestowing favours on children. I watched the old ladies' faces as their elected representatives told them that they were wrong in their belief that stiffer penalties would reduce the crime figures. They were too polite and too overawed to argue, but their bewilderment and disappointment were evident.

I saw Robert Kilroy-Silk in a side corridor with his constituents and hovered on the edge of the group, interested in what he had to say.

Several of the ladies told him they had been mugged or burgled and were frightened to go out because of the thugs roaming the streets. His reply was incredible: 'Not my lovely boys, they don't do things like that.' It was as if he was telling these ladies that they had not been mugged or robbed at all. There was no anger in the voices of the victims; they simply told him that the thugs should be birched. Although they were his constituents, he was not going to listen to that, and turning away abruptly he bumped into me. He glared at me before making his escape. 'You talk about law and order, but just listen to them,' he cried.

As he moved across the main hall, one of the women shouted after him, 'I hope *you* get mugged sometime, then you'll know what it's like!' There was a certain humour in his hasty retreat from a group of women whose average age was seventy-five.

Eric Heffer was sitting on a bench with his constituents when I walked over and introduced myself. 'I imagine we come from the same sort of background, Mr Heffer, a two-up, two-down, lavatory down the bottom of the yard,' I said.

'Not exactly, we had a toilet in the house,' he answered primly.

'Then you were lucky, but I imagine there wasn't

too much money about when you were young.' When there was no reply, I went on, 'If anyone had tried to steal what little I had, I would have fought like mad to keep it. These people are too old to fight back, though, so society should do it for them.'

One of the old ladies said, 'They should bring back the birch.'

Mr Heffer shook his head. 'I don't agree with you. You can't fight violence with violence.'

'There is a difference, Mr Heffer,' I pointed out. 'The criminal uses violence for gain. Society punishes.'

The group from Huyton was still waiting for Harold Wilson, who hadn't yet put in an appearance. Enquiries had twice been made at the desk and we had been told he was still in the House, so would probably be down soon. There was only half an hour left before the coaches were due to pick us up, so I went over to the desk to enquire again. I was told that the green card had gone from the rack, which meant that it must be in his possession, so at least he knew we were there.

Graham Page came down and we stood together watching the various groups. I was convinced most of the MPs were not taking the victims seriously. They had only put in an appearance because these people were their constituents and they needed their vote.

'Just look at the supercilious expressions on some of the MPs' faces,' I said to Graham Page. 'These old people have more sense in their little finger than the politicians have in their whole body. They have brought up families, known hardship and they deserve more sympathy and understanding than they're getting here this afternoon.'

'Don't upset yourself, Joan,' he advised, 'you're doing all you can.'

'To be quite honest, I don't know why I bother,' I replied. 'Sometimes I feel like throwing the towel in, and this is one of those times.'

'Don't think of it like that,' urged Graham. 'It's like water dripping on a stone. It takes a long time, but eventually the water wears away the stone. Someone has to speak for the victims, and one day your voice will be heard.'

The coaches arrived, but Harold Wilson did not. Just as we were leaving, a note came down to the effect that he had had to leave the House. His constituents were angry and disappointed for he had known about the visit for over three weeks and had not seen fit to let anyone know he would not be attending. On the journey home I found that, without exception, every victim had lost respect for his or her MP. I got the impression that most of them wouldn't even bother to vote in future.

*   *   *

For a few weeks after the London trip I was so despondent that I asked myself if there was any point in carrying on. If our elected representatives were not concerned, how were we ever going to change anything? It was only the thought of the victims that made me carry on.

Another reason that kept me going was the knowledge that some people would be only too delighted if I gave up, and I was not about to afford them that pleasure. I was a thorn in the flesh of the penal reformers, who wanted the subject of victims brushed under the carpet. Being stubborn over anything about which I felt strongly, especially injustice, I was not going to give in.

* * *

Leaving hospital one afternoon with Stasia, after visiting a woman who had been injured in a bag snatch, I met the Reverend Martin Garner who was on his way to visit one of his parishioners. He seemed over-pleased to see me, and I was amazed when I learned the reason. There was a by-election coming up, and Martin staggered me by suggesting that I should stand as a candidate. I really thought he was joking until he explained that, as a Law and Order candidate, it would bring the whole subject out into the open and force the other candidates to express their views. I told him that I couldn't do it, even if I wanted to, because my husband would go mad at the idea. He was so persistent that in the end I promised to think it over. I could see his point, but I really thought the idea was too far-fetched.

I didn't give the matter much thought until a meeting of the CLO later that week when Martin brought the subject up. The members present had mixed feelings at first, but his reasoning for my doing it caught on and they warmed to the idea. Charles Oxley, however, remained strongly opposed. He objected on the grounds that it was too late to get properly organized as the by-election was only four weeks off, but his main objection was that, although we knew we would only be doing it for publicity, it would give our opponents ammunition to fire at us.

'You can't fight an election without a party machine behind you,' Charles warned. 'You need an office and you need public meetings.'

'But we only want the publicity,' Martin argued. 'We just want to bring Law and Order out into the open.' Still Charles Oxley was adamant.

'They'll use it against you,' he warned again. 'Why not wait for the General Election and then we'd have more time to organize things?'

'Only a fool would think we expected to win,' I told him, 'and I don't mind standing up for what I believe in.'

Charles's objections had only served to make me favour Martin's suggestion. If it meant publicity for our views then I would have a go. Martin was delighted, but I warned that I still hadn't mentioned the matter to Tony and if he objected then we could forget the whole thing.

Bringing myself to tell my husband wasn't easy; I wasn't sure whether he would be angry or think I was crazy. But he heard me out before agreeing to the suggestion, if that was what I wanted. The next morning I rang a friend, Frank Moody, in Yorkshire and asked his advice. Not only did he think it a great idea, he also offered to pay all my expenses. When I pointed out that he would lose the money, he said he would regard it as his contribution.

Being prepared to do it and knowing what to do was another matter, so I rang Mr Williams, the Election Officer, and explained the situation. He was kind and patient, explaining that I needed the signatures of six people resident in the area to support my application. I must then take my application form to his office, together with the

£150 deposit, and I would be formally accepted as a candidate in the by-election.

As I didn't know the exact boundaries of the Edge Hill constituency, he promised to send me a map and offered any further help I might need. I went to six victims I knew in the area and, as they were all keen to help, I was given the six signatures I needed. The next thing was to have leaflets printed for distribution to every house in the constituency, so I called at a local printer's and got advice as to how a leaflet should be set out.

On the morning of my official acceptance as a candidate, I met my Labour and Conservative rivals. After being introduced, we drank a glass of sherry with the Election Officer and wished each other well—all very civilized! I went on to the printer's to talk about the leaflet, which we decided should be four pages, printed in brown on white as a contrast to what the other candidates would choose.

By the next day I had to provide the text for the leaflet and let the printer know how many to print. I began to realize how much easier it was for the other candidates with the weight of a big party machine to back them, but they had to worry about winning while I did not.

I sketched out my ideas for the leaflet. On the first page was my photograph and the slogan 'Law and Order Candidate'. The other pages contained my views on crime and punishment, with the return of corporal punishment as my main theme. I also strongly criticized successive governments for their failure to deal with the rising crime figures.

I had no problem enlisting the help of friends in delivering the leaflets and, with photocopies of the

239

area map, I drove them round the constituency, which we decided to split into four sections.

My first leaflet brought some interesting reactions from the press, two of which in particular spring to mind. The first in the *Daily Express* was headlined 'Joan's Brave Stand Against Violence', and the reporter said that, although I wouldn't win, he was sure many people would be grateful to me for raising an issue that had had less attention than it deserved. The second was by Anne Robinson, who, before her television fame, worked on the *Liverpool Echo*. She gave her opinion of all five candidates; of me she wrote that, although I had joined the race very late, I had produced a very professional leaflet and, for someone whose views on punishment were only slightly less severe than the Ayatollah Khomeini, I was a remarkably nice woman. I thought the comparison absolutely hilarious.

There were many incidents during the campaign. One friend, Rose, toiled up hundreds of steps to deliver to the top floor of a block of flats. She had just reached the ground floor again, when a man from one of the top flats called to her. As she looked up, he tore the leaflet into shreds and threw them down to her. She was so angry that she started to argue with the man, who said some very unpleasant things about me. Loyal Rose wasn't going to have that, and a heated argument followed. I made her promise that she wouldn't get involved in any more arguments that might threaten her personal safety; I didn't want her to finish up a victim.

Long before Election Day arrived it was obvious who was going to win. Posters bearing photographs of the Liberal Candidate, David Alton, were displayed in three out of every six houses in the constituency. I had not then met him, but knew of his popularity and his reputation as a hard worker.

On the day itself I looked forward to a rest after the rushing round of the last three weeks, but when I rang Mr Williams, the Election Officer, to thank him for his help, he said he would see me, no doubt, at the count. I told him I wasn't intending to come but he said I should, I would find the experience interesting. Afraid of being thought churlish, I arranged with Tony, Rose, an ex-victim called Mrs Hodson and my sister Elsie that we would go. We went out for a meal first, then on to St George's Hall for the count.

In the entrance hall I was met by Gordon Burns from Granada Television who asked if he could interview me with Bob Wareing, the Labour Candidate. After this we were directed to the room where the count was in progress and were told that we couldn't leave the room until it had finished. There was a small canteen next door, so we wouldn't be short of refreshments.

Rose was busy running up and down looking at the piles of votes already counted and was disturbed that she could not see any with my name on, but I told her that, as I only knew twenty-three people in the area, I couldn't honestly expect any more votes than that.

David Alton hadn't yet arrived, but it was clear that he was going to win handsomely. Clement Freud came over, shook hands with me and told me that although he didn't agree with my views, he admired me for fighting for them. My sister remarked in disgust that she couldn't understand what I was doing with this lot, but everyone was kind and friendly. David Alton's agent suggested that if I became a councillor first, I would stand more chance of getting into Parliament. I told him I had no wish to be involved with politics and had only put my name forward to gain publicity for the plight of victims and the injustices suffered by them.

David Alton arrived looking happy and relaxed only minutes before the result was announced. He had every reason to look that way for it promised to be a landslide victory for him. We were called on to the platform for the official announcement, which did indeed bear this out. My own 337 votes were 314 more than I expected and I felt quite happy. I went over to congratulate David Alton, and then I was free to go home and enjoy a good night's sleep. Before I drifted off I wondered why anyone wanted to be a politician—was it a genuine desire to serve the people, or was it to satisfy their own ego? Unfortunately, the voters had no way of knowing.

CHAPTER TEN

I was fast becoming as hard as nails, for, although I had been brought up to respect people and not to be rude to them, I was learning that being nice was going to get me nowhere. I had to be hard and loudmouthed if I was going to make people listen. Because I was outspoken and pulled no punches, I was labelled an activist by those who disagreed with my views, but my support from the general public was growing. There was evidence of this every day when I visited victims who said they had heard me on the radio or read about me in the papers and agreed with my views. I couldn't understand why MPs seemed so out of touch with the views of their constituents. By what right were they to be seen as correct and everyone else wrong? Did they think people were too stupid to know what was right for them?

My collection of horror stories was growing all the time, four of the most recent additions being particularly brutal. Stasia rang one night to say that a young man who lived near her had been attacked with a knife and was in hospital with facial injuries. Coming home on sick leave from the army, he had arrived in Liverpool late at night and as he waited for a taxi someone slashed his face with a knife. I asked Stasia if we could visit the victim, and she said it would be all right as she had already asked the boy's mother.

Although Stasia had told me Paul's face had been badly slashed, I wasn't prepared for the horrific scar which stretched from his left eye down to his chin. It stood out against a pale face still very badly swollen. He told us that as he waited for a taxi a man had come up behind him and had put his hand out as though to stroke his face. As he turned, Paul said, the man took to his heels and hurried away. It was only when he had touched what seemed like rain on his chin that he had realized it was blood. There seemed to be no motive for the attack; he had not been robbed. The police had told him the wound was inflicted with a Stanley knife and forty-six painful stitches had been inserted. Seventeen-year-old Paul would be scarred for life. What a prospect.

Our next visit was to Elaine, who was eighteen and eight months pregnant. She had been dragged down an entry and, on pleading for mercy, kneed in the stomach and almost strangled. Her young attacker had snatched a gold chain off her neck before leaving her on the ground, frightened for the life of her unborn baby.

Then I visited Tom, a twenty-eight-year-old father of two young children. He had been walking home from his afternoon shift and, as he passed a fish-and-chip shop, a youth had dashed out of the shop, colliding with Tom and almost knocking him over.

'Watch it, mate,' Tom said, and carried on walking. He had only walked a few yards further on when he was pushed from behind and fell to the ground. Bending over him, with two other youths, was the one who had collided with him, a knife in his hand. Before Tom knew what was happening, the youth had slashed his throat. The doctor who stitched up Tom's wound told him he had been a quarter of an inch from death.

It was the next day that I knocked on the door of Mrs Winstanley, an eighty-three-year-old who kept herself and her flat spotlessly clean. This woman anyone would be proud to call 'Mother' or 'Grandma' had opened her flat door to find two young teenagers standing there, and before she could speak they had bundled her back into her living room where one of the youths kept beating her about the head while his accomplice ransacked each of her rooms.

The boy kept on brutally punching her until his mate told him to stop. They took all her money and jewellery, even pulling her wedding ring from her finger. Then they fled, leaving her bruised, bleeding, distressed and terrified. I felt very sad when she told me the wedding ring had been on her finger for over sixty years. For her, that was the most distressing thing. And in a tearful voice she said, 'They didn't have to hit me like that, I couldn't have done anything to stop them taking what they wanted.'

Driving home I could still see her battered face in my mind, and couldn't keep my tears back. What cowards these thugs were.

*   *   *

Once again I found myself on the shortlist for the Merseyside Gold Medal Award for Achievement, this time with Ken Dodd, Bob Paisley and Kay Kelly. The winner, announced at a dinner at the Adelphi Hotel, was Kay Kelly, a housewife who, though suffering from cancer herself, had raised a quarter of a million pounds for a hospital cancer unit. She really was a worthy winner.

A few days after the dinner, I received a phone call from Yorkshire Television inviting me to take part in one of David Frost's Global Village programmes. I was asked if I could take ten victims with me and told we would be put up in a Leeds hotel overnight as the live programme was screened during the evening.

The subject was the punishment of offenders, and victims would be asked for their views. I accepted the invitation and thought about who to invite. I decided to take Ethel and Sally but, because of the long journey, thought it would be better if the other victims were younger and could look after themselves. Mr and Mrs Aldis agreed to come together with four others who were in their sixties, and Stasia was to come as a helper as well as a victim.

The day after the call from Yorkshire TV I had another one, this time from BBC Radio One, asking if I would take part in a Talk About discussion on capital punishment. As it was the day after the David Frost programme I said I wouldn't be able to manage it, but the girl was very persuasive, saying that my pro-capital punishment views would greatly contribute to the balance. Canon Paul Oerstreicher was to oppose my views but, as I had never heard of him, this didn't help to persuade me. In the end I agreed to reconsider and, making sure I could get a train from Leeds that would get me to London on time, I agreed to do the programme.

When we arrived in Leeds we took taxis to the Dragonara Hotel and were very impressed when it turned out to be five-star. As we were registering Sally was gazing round, and her eyes popped out of her head when I took her to the room she was sharing with her daughter, Helen. I told them I was next door if they should need me.

Stasia went off with Ethel, with whom she had agreed to share a room in case she needed help, and the rest of the group retired to their respective rooms. I had asked them all to be down in the dining room at six o'clock when the girl from the studio was coming to have a meal with us. I had just plonked myself on the bed in my room when, suddenly, Sally's head appeared round the door, her eyes dancing with excitement.

246

'I've got me own bathroom,' she announced grandly.

'Don't brag, Sally, so have I.'

She came into the room and shut the door behind her.

'I've never been inside a place like this before. There's mirrors everywhere. Every time I look round I get a fright, but it's only me.'

'Do you know you can make tea and coffee in your room?' I asked.

'Yes, but I'm not messing about with those machines,' she replied flatly.

'Shall I make you one here?' I asked, but she shook her head.

'No, I'm going back to me own room. I'm going to make the most of it while I'm here 'cos I'll never have the chance again. Fancy me having me own bathroom.'

'You never know, Sally,' I laughed again, 'you might meet a rich man while you're here.'

She turned towards me, one hand on her hip, the other behind her head, and wiggled her way to the door with an exaggerated walk. I was shaking with giggles.

'Sally, you're priceless,' I gasped. Seconds after the door had closed it opened again and her head popped round.

'I've got shampoo in me bathroom, but I'm not goin' to wash me hair. I'm goin' to take the shampoo home with me!' With that parting shot, she finally disappeared.

Later, down in the dining room, Sally's humour came to the fore again when she was handed a menu almost as big as herself. Gazing at it for quite a few seconds, she said, 'It's all in foreign, I can't understand a word. I'll have a plate of scouse. At least I'll know what I'm eating.'

We all ordered soup to be followed by steak and, for the next half-hour, roared with laughter at Sally's antics. When a waiter appeared at her side carrying a huge silver tray she gaped as he put the whole helping on her plate. Her eyes were like saucers as she looked at the size of the steak.

'Is this all for me? I thought it was for all of us.' As we laughed she added, 'I don't have this much meat in a month at home.'

Ethel was having problems with the size of her steak, too, asking someone to take some from her because it was a sin to waste it. Sally and Ethel were the only two who were concerned about the food left on our plates and I could understand why. Like many old-age pensioners who had known poverty, and now only had their state pension, they didn't like to see good food go to waste.

While we were having coffee, the researcher made a note of all the names before going off to make arrangements for taxis to take us to the studios. The room where the programme was to be staged was massive, with tier after tier of wooden benches arranged across one half of it and a stairway up the centre. We were directed to the sixth row and had great difficulty getting Sally and Ethel up the steps. We were just settled when I was asked to change places with Ethel. I protested that it was dangerous to move her as there was no room for her feet and a steep drop in front, but it was explained that David Frost had to know where everyone was sitting. The seats had nearly all filled up and it seemed as if there was an audience of between one hundred and fifty and two hundred.

When it had been checked that we were all in the right places, a man I assumed was the producer explained the format of the programme which was to be in three parts. David Frost would explain more fully and we should clap every time he came in. We dutifully did so as David Frost came out from behind the camera equipment. He explained that in the first part of the programme a film from America would be shown. It had been shown before and I had seen it. Called 'Scared Straight', it showed an experiment there where young first offenders were put in prison alongside hardened criminals, in an effort literally to scare them into going straight.

The second part of the programme would concentrate on the front three rows, occupied by people who had been criminals. They would be asked for their views on the American experiment. The third part of the programme, in which we would be included, would deal with the views and comments of the rest of the studio audience.

I had objected to the film the first time I had seen it because of the obscene language and constant references to homosexuality. Now I was glad that both Sally and Ethel were shortsighted and hard of hearing.

After the first commercial break David Frost introduced some of the people in the front rows; there were some well-known names among them, including John McVicar and Wally Probyn. To our left, David explained, were young offenders, some of whom were accompanied by prison officers.

Within seconds of David's asking for the criminals' views on the film that had been shown, it seemed as if all hell had been let loose. In language

249

bad enough to make your hair curl they called the police and prison officers every dirty name in the book, accusing them of using violence against prisoners. John McVicar took reams of paper out of his briefcase and, waving them over his head, claimed they contained details of acts of violence against prisoners. Another man was on his feet shouting about the violence of the 'screws' when David Frost interrupted him to ask, 'But you're a violent man yourself, aren't you? Didn't you bite off a man's ear in a fight?'

I was eager for our chance to speak so I was stunned when, as music started to play in the background, David Frost walked towards the audience, saying, 'That's all from this week's Global Village. Please join us next week . . .'

Almost before I realized it I was on my feet, shouting, 'Mr Frost, you have to be joking! The only people to speak have been those criminals.'

I could see him looking at me in amazement as he muttered something about a party political broadcast. I was more incensed still when Wally Probyn shouted to me, 'You've got a mouth on you, haven't you, missus?'

'Not as big or as foul as yours!' I shouted.

When I turned back to speak to David Frost I saw only his back as he left the studio. Wally Probyn and a couple of other men were still shouting up to me and I called back, 'I didn't come here just to listen to the likes of you!'

'You want to open your mouth then, missus!' shouted another voice.

'I will. Just you stay there!' I shouted. I turned to Stasia and asked her to bring Ethel down the steps while I kept the men there, then I had to struggle down through the departing crowds to reach Probyn, McVicar and another man called Tony who had been introduced as having been in prison for his involvement in armed robberies.

'Why should you be the only ones to speak?' I demanded as I reached them. 'What about the parents of a murdered child or an old lady who's been mugged?'

'You should have spoken up,' said Tony.

'You didn't give anyone a chance,' I retorted, fishing in my bag for the photograph of Ethel's injuries and, thrusting it under their noses, demanded, 'What excuse have you got for the thug who did that?'

Their expressions were serious as they studied the picture, and I went on, 'It was people like that I wanted to talk about and I'm furious victims weren't mentioned.' I indicated Ethel who was approaching. 'Here's the lady herself—isn't the man who could attack her a coward?' Ethel was smiling, unaware of the contents of the programme and the identities of these men.

'Whoever touched her wants a bloody good hiding,' Tony said. Wally Probyn took Ethel's hand and said to her, 'Anyone mugging you again, darlin', I'll put out a contract on him.' Ethel was enjoying all the attention and I didn't want to spoil it for her by telling her the truth. She was smiling sweetly as Wally Probyn bent over to tell her how nice she was. And I suddenly realized that we were all alone in the studio—John McVicar had disappeared when Ethel came on the scene.

'For all anyone knows we could be killing each other,' I remarked. 'They don't seem to care if we get out of here or not.'

251

Wally Probyn put Ethel's arm through his own, saying, 'Come on, darlin', I'll look after you.' He helped her step over all the cables that were lying around, leaving Stasia and me to follow with Tony. We never found out his surname. He was quite a handsome man, probably in his thirties, and full of humour. Our conversation as we went down the corridor was unbelievable.

'Were you really a bank robber?' I asked.

'Yes.' He grinned, swinging his briefcase.

'Then you deserved to go to prison.'

'I only robbed banks, not people,' he said calmly.

'The money must have belonged to someone,' snapped Stasia.

'Was it worth it?' I asked.

'Of course.' He smiled. 'My children go to private schools.'

'How did you manage to keep the money you stole?' I asked.

'That would be telling,' he chuckled.

'When your children come out of their posh school with their posh accents, aren't you afraid they'll be ashamed of their bank-robber father?'

'Won't happen,' he said calmly.

'I wouldn't be too sure of that,' I warned him as we reached the foyer, which was crowded. People were waiting for taxis or queuing to collect travel expenses. Tony pointed to a door nearby. 'Coming in for a drink, Joan? There's plenty of free booze in there.'

I shook my head and, gathering my group together, asked them to wait there while I joined the queue to collect expenses for train fares and taxis. While I was standing there, Tony came over again, glass of whisky in his hand, and tried once more to persuade me to take my group into the hospitality room where the drink was flowing freely. But I shook my head. I just wanted to get everyone back safely to the hotel.

After being paid our expenses, we were waiting for our taxis when we saw Tony in the expenses queue.

'He's already been paid,' Stasia said. 'What's he doing in the queue again?'

We watched as a flustered clerk searched through the receipts in her book. Then she told him, 'You've been paid out already.'

Not in the least embarrassed, Tony lifted his glass to her.

'Just testing your efficiency.'

As he turned back, I called, 'I see you haven't changed.'

'No harm in trying,' he laughed, making his way back to the free booze.

*　　　*　　　*

Back at the hotel Stasia and I saw the old people to bed then sat mulling over the evening's events. I was angry that, after coming all this way, it had been a waste of time. Why was it that only the wrongdoers were ever allowed to air their views? We ended the night laughing, though, because it really had been funny the way we had been left with Wally Probyn and Tony. We both liked them, too!

Next morning we were down to breakfast early because I wanted to see my charges on to the train home before I crossed the platform to catch the London train. At the table I found that Sally was missing and her daughter told me she was running round the hotel trying to buy a postcard of it.

I found her at the reception desk, disappointed that there were no postcards with pictures of the hotel on.

'No one will believe me when I tell them how posh it was,' she said. And back in the dining room she looked round at the luxurious décor. 'I've had to live to ninety before I see how the other half lives.'

At the station I found I didn't have time to see them on to the train, but had to dash across to catch my own. It was a long journey, and when I arrived at Euston I felt tired and lonely. I took a taxi to Broadcasting House where I gave my name to the receptionist and was asked to wait for someone to come down to see me. Twenty minutes later a girl came down and apologized for keeping me waiting, saying she had had trouble booking me into a hotel. Having finally done so, she had organized a taxi to take me there and gave me the address, asking me to be back at the studio by seven o'clock. The hotel turned out to be a tall Victorian terraced building, and when the door was opened by a young woman, I explained that the BBC had sent me.

Going over to a small table in the hall she wrote something on a piece of paper and said over her shoulder, 'That will be fifteen pounds and thirty pence.'

'You mean, you want me to pay now?' I asked. 'I'm not even in the hotel yet.'

'Those are the rules.'

'I thought the BBC would be paying you.'

'I'm sorry, but you'll have to pay me now,' she

insisted.

I sighed as I took out my purse to pay her. I was tired and hungry and not in the mood to argue. As I followed the woman up the stairs I noticed the drab decorations and threadbare carpets, but the surroundings seemed to match my mood.

Worse was to come; she threw open a door and ushered me into a room with an old-fashioned bed with a badly stained cover draped over it, a chair standing by the wash basin and a battered wardrobe. I dropped my case on the bed, my thoughts unprintable.

Feeling hungry, I asked what time dinner was served, only to be told that they didn't serve meals. My expression must have been comical as I asked if I could have a sandwich if I went to the dining room.

'We don't have a dining room,' she told me. 'We only cater for bed and breakfast.'

'And where do we eat breakfast?' I asked, dreading the answer.

'On the chair or the bed.'

Well, that explained the stains on the bed cover, I thought. When she told me there were no restaurants nearby, I wished there was someone there from the BBC to vent my anger on.

I had to throw myself on the woman's mercy and asked if, perhaps, she could make me a sandwich. I pointed out that I was starving and would be in no fit state to take part in a broadcast if I did not eat. She said she would go down to the kitchen and see what there was and ring me back. Five minutes later the phone at the head of the bed rang and I was told there was only bacon and yogurt in the fridge.

'Oh, could I have a bacon butty?' I pleaded.

A peal of laughter came down the phone as the woman repeated, 'A bacon butty?'

Never before have bacon butties tasted so good, and now completely thawed out the woman told me the reason for the payment in advance rule. Catering for tourists, they used to find that some stayed the night before slipping away in the morning without paying the bill. Before she left me, I asked if she would order me a taxi for 6.30.

I found the loo the final straw and felt laughter bubbling up as I surveyed it. Facing me on a high pedestal was the most ancient loo I have ever seen and one needed the skill of an athlete just to sit on it. Fortunately, the bacon butties had restored my sense of humour and I was now able to see the funny side of things.

*   *   *

When I arrived at Broadcasting House at seven o'clock, I was met by the girl who had booked me into the hotel and lost no time in telling her what I thought of the place. I was still telling her when we reached the hospitality room and I was introduced to the producer, David Winter. He too was told about the hotel and asked the girl to make sure that next time guests were put up in a decent one. While he was talking my eyes widened in sheer disbelief as I saw a man lying full-length on the huge table in the centre of the room. David Winter was trying to tell me the format of the programme but my attention kept straying to the man on the table, a sight which, oddly enough, no one else seemed to consider strange. David was still talking, telling me that I was to have two panellists and Canon Paul Oerstreicher was to have the same. While both of Paul's panellists had arrived, only one of mine had so far turned up; this caused me some concern until I was introduced to him.

I was delighted to see that it was William Hague who, two years ago, when just sixteen, had received a standing ovation for a brilliant speech at the Conservative Conference. I had shared a platform with him on several occasions and we made a good team. Out of the corner of my eye, I saw the man on the table slide his legs over the edge and slowly sit up. Still mesmerized by the sight, I said to David Winter that I hoped his programme wasn't going to be one-sided, especially after Global Village the night before. David promised it would not be. The man who had been lying on the table was walking towards us and, if I thought his actions had been odd, his appearance was even more so. He was wearing an off-white sweater, which almost reached his knees, a pale pink fluorescent tie and boots in baby pink and blue stripes. David introduced him as Den Heggarty, the presenter of the programme.

When Paul Oerstreicher arrived we went through into the studio. I wasn't worried that my other panellist hadn't turned up; William and I could manage very well provided we were given a fair chance. There was a pretty young woman in the studio whose job was to keep the show ticking over and time the questions, so that the intervals for pop music would come at the right moment. We were told not to worry about hesitations as the programme was being recorded and could be edited before transmission in two days' time.

At a sign from David Winter in his glass-fronted box, Den Heggarty opened the show. He told how one night he had gone to a pub with a friend for a glass of beer. They had been sitting there, minding their own business, when two huge policemen had come over and taken them outside for questioning. They were told they fitted the description of two men who had committed an offence. He claimed they had been really frightened but, fortunately, the policemen had recognized him and let them go. What, he asked, would have happened if he had not been famous? How could an ordinary man in the street prove that he was not the man they were looking for? By the time he had finished I was ready for him.

'What was the point of your story?' I asked. 'Do you think the police shouldn't question you if you fit the description of someone they're looking for? If my house is burgled it's the job of the police to find the guilty person, and if you fit the description they should question you. If you're innocent why should you object?' Paul Oerstreicher, who spoke next, was not the person to defuse my anger. He spoke in a pious, holier-than-thou manner about the sanctity of life, even that of the most vicious murderer, but made no mention of the sanctity of life in the case of innocent victims.

The panellists were allowed to state their views and, as usual, William was brilliant. After an interval it was my turn again. I told of the victims I had seen and their suffering. I reminded everyone that the offender had a choice, while the victim had none.

Paul Oerstreicher, in a sickly-sweet voice, said he did admire the work I was doing with victims, for whom he felt so much sympathy, but we must love and forgive our fellow men, even those who commit the most atrocious crimes. He would never agree with the taking of a life, even that of a murderer to whom he would show forgiveness and compassion.

I'd heard it all before so many times and, though it wasn't my turn to speak, I had to interrupt.

'People like you make me sick! Every day I see victims of crime—old people with broken limbs and broken hearts. Parents of murdered children sentenced to a life of pain and misery. But people like you want to protect the thugs who do this. You are encouraging crime and ruining our society.'

I could see David Winter smiling broadly in the control room. Controversy brings a programme to life and this was what they wanted. I have noticed that pacifists never show any emotion, they seem devoid of feeling, and Paul Oerstreicher was no exception. During the next interval we were told that we would have one more chance to state our views, then Den Heggarty would close the programme with his summing-up. He did so with a vengeance.

'Before this programme started I had no definite views on capital punishment but, after hearing Joan's venomous remarks . . .'

'Don't you dare say that!' I interrupted angrily. The girl was waving anxiously, telling me that I mustn't say any more, but I went on, 'If you think I'm going to sit here and let him call me venomous, you can think again.'

David Winter was waving his arms at me to keep me quiet, but I shook my head furiously. A moment later he burst into the studio. He

259

remonstrated with me about going on talking, but I repeated that I was not going to sit there silently and let Den Heggarty call me venomous.

'If his words are left in this programme when it's transmitted, I'll make sure you have a whole lot of bad publicity. I'm not moving from here without a promise of fair play.' I did not feel as hard and self-assured as I must have sounded. I honestly felt like running away and crying. David hesitated, but he turned to Den Heggarty and told him to start his summing-up again, leaving out the remarks about me. He then held out his hand to me and invited me to go for a drink. I refused, saying I wanted to hear what Den was going to say, but David sounded so sincere and friendly that I allowed myself to be led to the hospitality room. We were followed by Paul Oerstreicher and the other panellists who had remained silent during the argument but were now all talking at once. When Paul offered to drive me back to the hotel, I accepted and found him a charming companion though definitely not my cup of tea. He was no friend to victims.

*   *   *

Back home again I took two days off to recover from my three days away. I was very tired and had to catch up on my housework. When the Talk About programme was transmitted, Tony and I listened and he thought William and I came out of it very well. Den Heggarty's summing-up contained none of the words I had objected to.

I was busy cleaning the kitchen the next morning when the doorbell rang and I found a man standing

260

on the doorstep smiling at me. In his hand was a cellophane box containing a single, long-stemmed red rose. He handed me the box.

'Congratulations, Mrs Jonker. You have been nominated our Rose of the Week.'

'It's beautiful,' I said. 'Thank you very much.'

'You were nominated by the readers of our paper,' he told me, 'and we are delighted to present it to you.'

Looking down at my scruffy appearance, I laughed 'I look more like a wilted petunia than a red rose.'

CHAPTER ELEVEN

I had applied to the Youth Opportunities Programme for a young girl to help with visits, because Stasia and I were finding it increasingly difficult to keep up with new victims while trying to follow up old ones too. I didn't intend to let a young girl visit new victims, but she could help by doing some back-up calls.

When Tina came to work with me, I suggested she come out each day for the first few weeks, so that I could tell whether she had the right attitude and approach. One morning, before I picked her up, I rang the Royal to see if they had managed to trace Prue Webster's files. The last time I had seen her, I had been shocked by the change in her. Her health had deteriorated so much that she no longer cared about her appearance and, for the first time, I had seen her without her wig, which made her look twenty years older. The hospital authorities told me they were making progress and asked me to give them another week. I stressed the urgency and was promised they were doing their best.

After Tina and I had been on a few calls, I suggested we should go to visit Prue, to see how she was. I was surprised to find her front door locked. It never had been before. I knocked several times but there was no sign of life so Tina and I walked back to the car. Then I saw Sinbad talking to another man on the corner of the street and called to him. I think Tina thought I had gone mad because I heard her saying 'Sinbad?' to herself.

'What's happened?' I asked as he joined us. 'Has Prue gone out?'

He looked surprised. 'Haven't you heard? She died at the weekend. It was her funeral yesterday.'

'Oh, no, poor Prue,' I said. I felt shocked and sad. She had been such a colourful character and I had grown very fond of her. I felt as though I had lost a dear friend. Sinbad invited us in and we joined him for a few minutes so that I could hear what had happened to Prue. I could see Tina was fascinated by him as he went over the events of the previous few weeks. Apparently Prue had been very ill and he had done everything for her because there was no one else. He had fed, washed her, and sat up with her at night when she was in too much pain to sleep.

'Prue told me how grateful she was to you,' I told him. 'I think you've been smashing.'

'She was fond of you too,' Sinbad told me, 'and she asked me to see you got this.'

He handed me a flat box. Inside was a very old lace and linen tablecloth. Although some of the lace was torn, I vowed to have it repaired and to use the cloth on special occasions. I could clearly imagine it covering a huge dining table as Prue entertained her friends in those halcyon days of long ago.

Sinbad had been given a week to get out of the house because Prue no longer owned it. She had been forced to sell it years before, to raise cash, and allowed to pay rent on it afterwards.

'Where will you go?' I asked.

'Wander round as I always have. I'll probably go to another town.'

'Surely you could get a job and settle down. You're intelligent and of good appearance.' I was angry at such a waste of a life. Sinbad was emphatic, though.

'Wouldn't stick it. I'm an alcoholic and I can't change.'

'Where do you get the money from and what do you drink?' I asked. He pointed to a row of empty bottles under the table.

'As I've no money, I'm on cider and meths.'

'Good God! You'll kill yourself,' I protested.

He shrugged his shoulders, then asked, 'Would you buy this? I only want three quid for it.' He pointed to a hostess tray with three compartments.

'You'll only blow it on drink,' I told him. He didn't argue, but I gave him the three pounds anyway. I felt sad saying goodbye—Prue had gone and now Sinbad was leaving. I felt that my life would be the poorer for the loss of two very colourful characters.

As I was putting the hostess tray in the boot of the car, Tina said, 'You've made a bargain there.'

'It's useless, Tina,' I laughed. 'The elements and sockets are missing. It's just an empty shell.'

'Why did you buy it, then?' she asked in surprise.

'It was little enough to pay for all his kindness to Prue. I know he'll spend it on drink, but who am I to judge?'

When I got home I rang the hospital to tell them there was no need to search further for Prue's files, as they wouldn't be needed now. As I put the phone down, I remembered the first time I had spoken to her and she had said, 'Call me Prue, darling.' I would never forget her.

*   *   *

Tony and I had been invited on holiday in Jersey again and were looking forward to it immensely. I felt I needed a complete break from my work for a couple of weeks, and it would be bliss not to hear a constantly ringing telephone. Ten or twelve calls a night was not unusual and I never saw a television programme in its entirety. I was tempted to take the phone off the hook sometimes, but there would have been little point. People would only keep ringing until they reached me.

A week before we were due to leave for Jersey, I saw several victims who were so badly injured both mentally and physically that it had a really adverse effect on my own mental state. An old lady of eighty-seven, who had been robbed many times in the past, was held with a knife at her throat until she told the thugs where her measly few pounds were hidden. The next victim was a barber aged seventy-eight who had worked in his shop for forty-eight years. He was quite content to earn fifty pence for each short-back-and-sides and only opened the shop for a few hours each morning.

One day three youths pretending to be customers beat him up and robbed him. He was badly injured, but it was his mental anguish which most saddened and angered me. Those thugs had broken his pride, his spirit and feeling of independence, for after the attack he was too frightened to open up his shop again.

How could anyone see people like this day after day and not be affected? If I had learned nothing else in the last two years, I had learned to recognize when things were getting on top of me and to know when a diversion was called for. One thing certain to cheer me up was shopping, so I decided to take a day off and buy some presents for Ray and Ruth, our hosts in Jersey. When I had bought those, I thought it would be nice to buy something for Sir William and Lady Butlin. I couldn't afford anything expensive, but I knew it was the thought that counted. Marks and Spencer was my favourite shop for quality goods that were not too expensive, but what did you buy for someone who had everything? I finally decided on a waist slip for Lady Butlin, a tie and initialled handkerchiefs for Sir William, and talc and aftershave for their children Jacqui and Bill Junior.

We had decided to fly to Jersey this time and I was a nervous wreck by the time we landed owing to my fear of flying. Ray met us at the airport and when we reached our destination I had a stiff drink to calm me down. After some hours chatting with our friends I was back in the land of the living, my fear forgotten for the time being. Then, with my gifts under my arm, I made my way to the big house to pay my respects to the Butlins. Lady Butlin was glad to see me and gave me a warm welcome. I had just given her my gifts when Sir William came into the kitchen and, after exchanging kisses of greeting, his first question was how my work with victims was progressing. Lady Butlin handed him his present, saying 'Look, Bill, Joan has bought presents for us all.' Pleasure was written all over his face as he turned over the small parcel and sniffed it, trying to guess what was inside.

'We've had a lot of alterations done since you were last here,' said Lady Butlin. 'Come and look at Bill's apartment.' I followed her upstairs and into a truly magnificent apartment. Wide windows overlooked the gardens Sir William loved so much, and beautiful furniture stood on deep-pile carpets. The bathroom was an absolute dream, with gold fittings on the bath and washbasin. I was gazing round in admiration when Sir William came in with a boyish grin, wearing the tie I had bought him. Twirling round in front of us he asked, 'Don't I look handsome?' My respect and affection for him grew in leaps and bounds at that moment. The tie he had been wearing when I arrived had probably cost many times my small gift, but his pleasure was genuine. 'I've got hankies, too,' he told Lady Butlin. She smiled.

'Have you, love? Joan's bought presents for the children as well, wasn't that kind of her?' I had been right in my belief that it was the thought that counted with these people.

I was to see the Butlins almost every day during our stay. Sometimes when I was having a cup of tea with Lady Butlin, Sir William would join us and we would discuss the frightening increase in crimes of violence. At other times he would be watering his garden in his shirt sleeves and would tell us proudly of the new plants and trees he had put in. On the day we were to leave Jersey, the Butlins were to open a garden fête and, as our plane was not leaving until six, we were able to attend. A horse-drawn carriage picked them up and Lady Butlin waved gaily as they passed us by. After an hour spent going round the various stalls with Jacqui and Bill Junior, it was time to say our goodbyes ready for the dreaded flight home. It had been a lovely restful holiday and Tony and I felt refreshed and on top of the world.

*   *   *

Two days after our return I had a phone call from Superintendent Laurie Blackburn to say that the police were ready to start the liaison scheme in Toxteth. I knew the area well as I had visited over a hundred victims there and made many friends. The officer with whom I was to liaise every morning was Pip Mosely so on the Monday morning I made my first call to him. There were no referrals but I wasn't disappointed because it would obviously be some time before the scheme would take off. The policemen on the beat would have to get used to the idea of having a Victim Support Scheme in the area. I had made it clear that, although I would help anyone who was in need, my main concern was for the elderly victims, particularly those who lived alone.

Although there were no referrals that first week, it didn't mean I was inactive because I was still hearing of victims on the grapevine. It was on the Monday of the second week that I got my first police referral, an elderly man whose home had

267

been burgled. It was the same story I had heard hundreds of times: an old person who had so little in the way of material possessions that it angered me deeply to think heartless thugs could steal the last few pounds he had in the world.

Two days later came my second referral: a Somali whose arm had been broken trying to protect himself from muggers who had stolen his watch and wallet. His name was Ali and he had a café which, I found, was a meeting place for many of the Somalis living in the area. Over a cup of tea he told me what had happened and, as I listened, I could sense the interest my presence was creating. It was unusual for a strange white woman to be sitting in the café and, although I could not understand the language they were speaking, it was clear they were worried about the reasons for my presence. Ali, whose arm was in plaster, told me he had been in touch with a solicitor about claiming damages for his injuries and, although his English was not fluent, we chatted for about half an hour. When I left I promised to call again in about a week and, addressing all the men who were regarding me with such obvious curiosity, I said, 'Goodbye gentlemen.' Immediately, their faces lit up with smiles and there was a chorus of goodbyes.

When I saw Ali the following week, I was surprised that he asked me to help him fill in a criminal injuries claim-form, as I'd thought that was his reason for consulting a solicitor. Unfortunately, I had no forms with me, though I promised to call back the next day with the required form.

The next day, however, there was a strange man behind the counter who told me that Ali had 'gone away'. When I asked if he was coming back, the man shrugged as if he neither knew nor cared. The café was full of Somalis who were all smiling at me in a friendly manner, so I went over to a table to enquire about Ali's whereabouts. Immediately a chair was pulled out for me and I was brought a cup of tea. Everyone started talking at once and I was bombarded with information. It seemed Ali had got himself into some sort of trouble and had just taken off: where to, no one seemed to know. Suddenly a man who had been sitting nearby came across waving a piece of paper at me saying, 'You help me?' It was a letter from a firm of solicitors saying that his appeal hearing before the Criminal Injuries Compensation Board was on a certain date, but the solicitor needed £30 from him before they were prepared to represent him at the hearing.

'You'll have to pay them,' I told him.

'But I have no money,' he replied.

I hesitated for a moment. 'Can I take this letter? I'll ring the solicitor and find out what is going on.' I had to explain again to make him understand but, eventually, he agreed and I told him to be in the café at one o'clock the next day—meanwhile I would see what I could find out. When I rang the solicitor, he told me that he had spent quite a lot of time applying for compensation on Mohammed's behalf, and he was not prepared to proceed further without some payment. Apparently the Criminal Injuries Compensation Board had turned down the first application and when I asked the solicitor if he thought the appeal would be successful, he said his firm didn't and that was why they did not want to represent the client. If he had no money to pay

269

them now, he would not be able to afford a higher bill later. The solicitor had no objection to my helping Mohammed and was even prepared to send me all the relevant correspondence so I would know why the Board had turned down his original application for compensation.

I met Mohammed at the Municipal Annexe where the appeal hearings were conducted and went over all the details with him. It was difficult because of the language problem, but I managed at length to get a clear picture of the incident in which he had been injured. Walking home about eleven o'clock after having a drink, he had been attacked by a group of youths. He was badly beaten, robbed and left lying dazed on the ground, where two friends found him. Thinking he was drunk, they took him home and left him to sleep off his drunkenness. For three days he lay there, too ill to get up. On the fourth day he managed to get to the hospital and have his wounds attended to, then he went to the police station to report the attack. His application for compensation had been turned down because of the four days' delay between the attack and the report to the police.

I approached a man whom I had seen taking names of other people in the hall, gave him Mohammed's name and one of my visiting cards.

'Are you representing him?' he asked and, when I nodded, he added, 'What are your qualifications for doing so?'

He caught me by surprise. I hesitated for a few seconds. 'Common sense,' I told him. 'Do I need anything else?'

He smiled. 'No, I don't suppose you do.'

After an hour's wait, which made me

increasingly nervous, Mohammed's name was finally called and we were led through to the courtroom. The board members were sitting on the judges' bench and the atmosphere, just like that in a court of law, was enough to ensure that both Mohammed and I were nervous. One of the board repeated their reasons for turning down the application, then started to question Mohammed, which proved almost impossible because of his limited knowledge of English. All that came out was his insistence that he was telling the truth. I could see that they were not satisfied and one of the board said to him, 'You say on your application form that you were unconscious for three days. We find that impossible to believe.'

So far I had contributed nothing because, at first, it is up to the victim to present his own case, but now I was asked if I had anything to say before the members of the board retired to consider their verdict. Swallowing hard from sheer fright, I began to speak far too quickly.

'I think the board should ask Mohammed the meaning of the word "unconscious". They'll find he doesn't know it. The solicitor who filled the form in for him used the word. Mohammed was not unconscious for three days, he was just too ill to get out of bed to visit the hospital. He lives alone and there was no one to help because his friends didn't know what had happened to him. That was the reason for the delay. Mohammed was just too ill as a result of the attack.'

After conferring together, the members of the board decided that he was telling the truth and awarded him £300. He was delighted, and I was pleased that I hadn't made a complete fool of myself. Everyone had been so kind and I knew that, should there be a next time, I wouldn't be so nervous.

*　　*　　*

During the run-up to the 1979 General Election the Conservatives pledged that, if they came to power, they would have a free vote on the reintroduction of capital punishment. On the day the vote was being held several countrywide organizations campaigning for the return of capital punishment sent representatives down to London to demonstrate outside the House of Commons. It was only to be a small demonstration because of the cost of involving large numbers of people—about one hundred and fifty attended, including twelve families of murder victims.

The Merseyside contingent travelled down by coach but, because the driver was unfamiliar with the London streets, we were the last to arrive. There were many placards calling for the return of capital punishment and some bearing the words 'My Child Was Murdered'. It took a while to greet all the different groups and, on my way round, I was surprised to see Ann West with the Manchester group. I knew that Ann's health had not been good for a while, and it had been thought that she would not be able to make the trip. Her depth of conviction had clearly given her the strength to come after all.

Eldon Griffiths came out to talk to us, as promised, but it was clear that he did not expect the pro-capital punishment lobby to win. While I was listening to him, Martin Garner drew me aside.

'I think you should go after Mrs West. She doesn't look very well,' he said.

I looked helplessly round the crowd. 'Where is she?'

'Lord Longford walked past and she ran after him.'

I pushed my way through the crowd and eventually spotted Ann West about thirty yards away, talking to Lord Longford. As Martin and I approached, a group ran past us and joined them. They were families from Manchester whose children had been murdered. Their voices were raised as they fired questions at Lord Longford.

'Why are you only interested in helping murderers?'

'Why don't you help the victims' families?'

They were all shouting at once and Martin and I stayed a few yards away, not wanting to be involved.

'I am not going to speak to you in the street,' said Lord Longford. 'If you want to talk to me you must make an appointment.'

This did not prevent the families from going on in loud, emotional voices. I was about to suggest to Martin that we intervene when Ann West moved them all away. After they had passed us Martin and I went up to Lord Longford, who was watching the retreating backs of the bereaved parents.

'Do you know they want to hang people?' he asked.

'Lord Longford, I disassociate myself from their language but not from their views.'

He turned and looked at me then. 'We have met,' I told him, 'on Brass Tacks.'

To my amazement he took hold of my hand and

273

said, 'I bet you're a Roman Catholic.'

'I don't see what my religion has to do with it,' I said.

'But you are a Roman Catholic, aren't you?' he insisted.

This is crazy, I thought, as I looked at Martin Garner and shrugged my shoulders. He too seemed surprised. 'I don't see what religion has to do with visiting victims. Those people you've just been talking to are the parents of murdered children and, like them, I'd like to know why you have so much sympathy for the murderers and not for the victims.'

'That is untrue,' Lord Longford insisted. 'I do quite a lot to help victims. I'm the chairman of a committee set up to help them.'

'How many victims have you met?' I challenged. 'And if you haven't met any, how do you know what help they need?'

'I realize you have more experience of visiting than I have,' he admitted. 'Perhaps you could join our committee?'

'I don't have time to sit on committees unless something constructive comes out of it. I'm too busy visiting victims,' I told him. Lord Longford took out a card and handed it to me.

'Ring me tomorrow and we'll discuss it. Of course I'll have to put it to the committee.'

After I had promised to ring him the next day, Martin and I rejoined the demonstrators.

I rang Lord Longford as promised. Although I arranged to meet him in London in ten days' time, I was only half-hearted about the meeting, for two reasons. One was that Tony would be on holiday at that time, and would be none too happy about me spending a day in London, and the other was that I really did not believe that Lord Longford was sincere about helping victims. On the other hand he was a well-known figure and, if he were sincere about helping, he was in a far better position to do so than I was.

Three days before I was supposed to meet him there was a CLO meeting and there I met with strong opposition when I told them of my intentions. The strongest protests came from Charles Oxley. The strength of his views increased my own doubts, so I decided to give myself more time for consideration and the following day rang Lord Longford's office to cancel the appointment. I promised to ring again in a few days to arrange another date.

*   *   *

The Police Liaison Scheme was beginning to show results now, and each morning when I rang Pip Mosely he would pass on the names of new victims; sometimes only one, sometimes three or four. Stasia in particular was a great help because, having been a victim herself, she knew just how to sympathize. I was confident that if I had to take part in a radio or television programme or speak at a meeting, people would be left in good hands. Her work was a great help to Stasia too. Her daughter told me that she had been much happier since she had been visiting victims. Each night we would ring each other and discuss the day's visits, and pass on the details to Olive who would fill in cards for filing.

Increasingly often I was coming across people

275

who had been victims more than once, and their reactions both surprised and saddened me. After the first time they seemed resigned to being targets and I considered it a terrible indictment of our society that anyone should consider themselves a natural victim.

Mrs Mac, for example, had been a victim no less than five times by the time she was referred to me. She lived in a small council flat and when I visited her the place was freezing because there was no heating on. She could no longer afford to pay for it. Originally she had had an electricity meter, but that had been robbed and she was still trying to pay off the money that was stolen. After two more robberies from it, she had reached the stage where she would never be able to catch up. Now she was terrified of turning on the electricity and increasing the debt. I was able to give her twenty pounds towards her outstanding bill, and I wished I could have done the same for all the elderly people in the same predicament. It was heartbreaking to know that there were many of them sitting in the cold and, I suspected, not eating properly either. It was now early-December and the worst of the weather was yet to come.

Worrying about this problem brought me back to the subject of Lord Longford. I had to get through to the Government and perhaps I could do so through him. Deciding there was nothing to lose, I rang Lord Longford and arranged another appointment. He was very pleasant and suggested that if I came to London, he would take me to lunch and we could talk over a meal.

It was a lovely mild, sunny day when I arrived at his office and he suggested we should walk to the restaurant, which was only about five minutes away. He was clearly well known there and, when we had been shown to our table and our order had been taken, I settled down to business. I told him about some of my victims and produced photographs to drive home my point about their injuries. He only glanced at them before passing them back quickly. Without making any reference to what I had just said, or to the photographs, he surprised me by saying, 'Look, if you come on our committee [the National Committee for Victims] you won't keep jumping up shouting "Hang 'em," will you?'

I tried to keep calm and answered, 'My feelings on crime and punishment are not allowed to interfere with my work with victims. For over two years I have been visiting them and have been horrified that they receive no help whatsoever from any official sources. Unless they are physically injured, there's no compensation for them at all.'

'Well, I'll put it to the committee at our next meeting,' he said, and proceeded to tell me about some of the committee members and their occupations and how they had been given a cash grant. During the excellent meal, I tried to bring up the subject of victims many times, but each time the issue was sidetracked. Realizing that time was running out, I decided on bluntness.

'Lord Longford, how can you help victims if you don't know any? When you and your committee have some knowledge, first-hand knowledge, of the victims' suffering, then you might know what help is needed.' When this brought no reaction I went on, 'Why don't you come to Liverpool and see for yourself? I could take you to see six or seven

277

victims in one day and give you a real insight into the injustice in our society.'

I could not persuade him, though, and left with a feeling of complete frustration. Nothing constructive had come out of the meeting, and I felt it had been a waste of time.

*   *   *

Christmas 1979 was only two weeks off and Stasia and I were busy making preparations for the party which this year was to be held at Scarisbrick Hall School. Charles Oxley and his wife were supplying the food and the entertainment, so all there was left for Stasia and me to do was the wrapping of presents and the writing of cards to those who were attending. We also had to make up hampers for those not well enough to come to the party, which we would deliver a few days before Christmas.

I was given a new name and address by the police, Christine Turner, aged sixty-seven, and told she was the victim of a bag snatch. I knocked at her door several times and, when there was no answer, was about to leave when I heard a shuffling noise inside and the door opened slowly to show a tall, thin woman wearing a nightdress and dressing gown. After explaining who I was, I was invited inside and followed Christine down the hall, a slow process because she had to support herself on the wall. Although she had difficulty walking, I noticed how straight she held herself.

When we were seated I asked if she had been injured in the robbery, but she told me that, although badly shaken, she had not been manhandled. The illness from which she was suffering, and she did look ghastly, was a result of being mugged twelve months previously, when she had been attacked by a group of men who had kicked and punched her after throwing her to the ground. Her bag and jewellery had been stolen and she had been left helpless in the gutter. Severe damage had been done to her stomach and she had been in and out of hospital ever since.

Clearly she had once been a great beauty because, even now, with her face showing the ravages of pain, she was still attractive. She had fine cheekbones and lovely white hair combed up into a coil on the top of her head. Only a week ago she had received an interim payment from the Criminal Injuries Board of £300, but £200 of that had been stolen in the latest attack.

'I'd only drawn the money out of the bank the day before,' she told me bitterly. 'I was going to have the flat redecorated and get new curtains. Now, thanks to them, I've nothing left.' Before I went, I asked Christine if she would like to come to our Christmas party and she was delighted. The only difficulty would be getting there, as she wasn't well enough to travel on public transport, but I promised to arrange to get her there and back.

I was wrapping the last of our Christmas presents for the party when the phone rang. It was Kathy Hollis, who introduced herself as a researcher with BBC's Man Alive. It seemed they were planning a programme on William Whitelaw's 'short sharp shock' treatment for offenders, and she asked if I would be prepared to take part. I was told that Leon Brittan, Robert Kilroy-Silk, Jim Jardine and a university lecturer would be on the panel, and they would like me to represent the

279

public. They would also be interviewing young offenders from the two centres where the treatment was already being tried out.

'How many victims are on the programme?' I asked.

'There won't be any,' she told me. 'It's about the short sharp shock.'

'How can you talk about punishment of offenders if you haven't seen the victim of that offender?' I asked.

Kathy sounded as if she was trying to be very patient with me.

'The programme is about the punishment of offenders, not about victims. You will be able to mention them if you wish.'

'Look, Kathy, I'm fed up with this kind of programme about how to punish offenders, particularly if there are penal reformers involved. I don't want to be rude, but I think it's arrogant of people to discuss punishment when they haven't seen the reason for it. You have to see the result of the crime.' I couldn't hold back. All the frustrations of the past few years were pouring out. I told her that when a person was found guilty of burglary it didn't seem such a serious crime to those who hadn't seen the pain and distress of the victim.

'Before any offender is punished, the court should see the victim of his crime; then, perhaps, we would see realistic sentences being given.'

Kathy was very quiet and I realized that it was unfair of me to take out my frustrations on her; she was only doing her job.

'I'm sorry, but unless you have a victim on the programme, I don't want to take part.'

After saying that she would relay my feelings to

the producer, Kathy rang off. Thinking that was the end of it, I was surprised when half an hour later she rang back with the news that she had told the producer about our conversation and he wanted to speak to me.

'Mrs Jonker, I'm Desmond Lapsley, producer of Man Alive. I'm very interested in what you said to Kathy. Tell me about your victims.'

That sympathetic request was all I needed to pour out what was in my heart. I ended by saying, 'Now you know why I don't feel I can take part in your programme. I'm sick of do-gooders telling us that we can't punish offenders realistically because it's degrading. No one is interested in victims—they don't want to know.'

'I'm interested,' Desmond told me. 'And I would very much like to meet your victims. If I come up to Liverpool and meet these people, will you agree to come on my programme?' When I hesitated, he added, 'If we let you bring a victim with you?'

'With pleasure,' I told him happily, amazed that here at last was someone who was willing to listen.

The programme was to be recorded on 8 January and transmitted on the 17th. Desmond suggested he should come up to Liverpool on the 3rd so that we could meet before the recording. I promised to arrange meetings with eight elderly victims in their homes for it was important that he should see a true picture of the injustices dealt with every day. Although the conversation with Desmond had lifted my flagging spirits, I filed it away at the back of my mind until the hustle and bustle of Christmas and the New Year were over.

*   *   *

281

The day before his visit I went to see the victims I wanted him to meet, and Christine Turner was one of them. I asked her if she would like to come on the 'short sharp shock' programme with me, although I was a little doubtful about the wisdom of her making the journey to London. However, she assured me that she would be all right if she didn't have to do too much walking. That would be no problem, as we could take taxis to and from the station and would be staying at a hotel overnight. This news made Christine determined to come, as she didn't go out much and was very excited at the prospect of 'living it up'.

I was waiting for Desmond and Kathy at the station, and, as soon as I saw him walking towards me with a big grin on his face, I knew I was going to like him. There were no awkward pauses, as there are sometimes when people meet for the first time, and once we had driven to the house of the first victim I felt as if I had known him all my life. Kathy, a quiet and gentle girl, did not say much but was taking it all in, which I imagined was part of her job as a researcher. I was so used to seeing the victims in their own surroundings that it didn't have the same impact as it did on Desmond, seeing them for the first time. For him and Kathy it was an eye-opener, and I could see it was having a profound effect. They were welcomed with warmth and friendliness in each of the houses we visited, and each victim told of her experiences without bitterness or self-pity. I watched Desmond as he was listening, and sometimes he looked round the room and shook his head as if he couldn't take in what he was hearing.

Driving from one home to another, I listened as Desmond told me of his admiration for their courage and spirit and his sadness that, poor as they were, things had been stolen from them. As we drove to our last call it was getting dark, and I was concerned that Mrs Parker wouldn't open the door to us. She had already been robbed seven times and, like most elderly people in the area, didn't open the door to anyone after four o'clock.

As I locked the car door outside the block of flats where she lived, I prayed silently that it would still be there when we came out. The streetlights were on, but the street was quite deserted as we walked up the flight of concrete steps to the first floor. The atmosphere was quite eerie. I knocked at the door five or six times and shouted through the letterbox before Mrs Parker opened the door slightly and peeped out. When she had checked it was me, she invited us inside.

The last attack had only been two days ago and signs of her injuries were still visible. A plaster hid the wound on her forehead which had required three stitches and her face was badly bruised. She had returned from shopping to find a gang of youths coming out of her flat. They had pushed her violently against the wall. Although she was eighty years of age, small and thin, she had plenty of spirit and this was evident as she told Desmond of the other attacks. It was only when she spoke of the latest robbery that her voice became tearful.

'One of the boys had a case in his hand with bedding and clothes in.' Her voice was choked. 'What worries me most is that they stole my two budgies.' We saw the two empty birdcages on the sideboard.

'They stole the birds?' said Desmond incredulously. She nodded tearfully.

'When I came in the flat the cages were empty.'

He looked at me and shook his head in disbelief.

'Will they have killed them?' pleaded Mrs Parker.

'No, they won't,' Desmond and I said together.

'They must have stuffed them in their pockets which would have killed them. They weren't holding them in their hands or I would have seen them.'

'How long have you had them?' asked Desmond.

'Three years. They were all I had and I used to talk to them. I've no family, you see,' she said sadly.

When we had said our farewells to Mrs Parker, we stood under a streetlight buttoning our coats against the cold and, as we looked up and down the deserted street, Desmond said, 'I had no idea.'

'No one has,' I agreed. 'Now you can understand why I get so angry at all the publicity given to the offenders. How can anyone properly punish someone who has committed a crime without seeing the damage he's done?'

'I've got to do a programme on victims,' said Desmond. 'As you said, Joan, you have to see the victims and hear the stories behind the crime statistics.'

Kathy Hollis had been very quiet during each of the day's visits but now, standing under a streetlight in that totally deserted street, in an area with one of the highest crime rates in the country, she voiced her sadness and distress at the things she had seen and heard.

'I couldn't do what you do,' she told me. 'It would upset me too much.'

'Well, I'm going to have a word with my boss,' announced Desmond. 'I must do a programme on victims.'

CHAPTER TWELVE

Christine and I had been booked into the Kensington Hilton, and we had time to settle in before taking a taxi to the studio. Christine looked very elegant as we left for the studio. Although in constant pain, she held her head high and her eyes sparkled with pleasure and excitement. It was her first time inside a television studio and she was like a child being given a treat. In the make-up room she giggled as the girl powdered her face, and the expression on her face as she watched Robert Kilroy-Silk sit in a chair nearby to have his face made up was comical. In case she should make some remark about a man wearing make-up, I went outside to wait for her, and when she emerged we both burst out laughing.

Until now I had not been nervous, but when we were both taken our different ways I felt the butterflies starting. I was placed in the middle chair of five with Leon Brittan and Jim Jardine on my left, and Robert Kilroy-Silk and his colleague on my right. Facing us across the studio was Jack Pizzey, who was presenting the programme.

The first part was taken up with a film showing the camps where the treatment was being tried as an experiment, and then there were interviews with prison officers and young offenders. Christine, in another studio, was interviewed next and came across well, giving no impression of being nervous. Leon Brittan and Jim Jardine spoke in favour of the experiment, and then Kilroy-Silk and his colleague spoke of their opposition. Kilroy-Silk is a skilful speaker who can out-talk anyone, but what he says is so predictable: punishment is humiliating and degrading and has no place in a civilized society.

Rehabilitation, not punishment, was the answer according to him. Jack Pizzey then asked for my views and I took a deep breath before asking, 'Why is Mr Kilroy-Silk so concerned with preventing the punishment of offenders? Are victims not degraded and humiliated? No one has mentioned the victims—' At this point I was interrupted by Kilroy-Silk, who did not like my criticism and was not about to let me get away with it. Knowing his trick of not letting anyone finish, I carried on talking but was interrupted again, this time by Jack Pizzey who said, 'Let Mr Kilroy-Silk answer the criticism, Mrs Jonker.' I was about to say that Kilroy-Silk doesn't answer questions, he makes speeches, when the man in question started to do just that. All I could do for the rest of the programme was sit there fuming, and as soon as we returned to the hospitality room, I rounded on Desmond and the editor. They both agreed that Jack Pizzey had been wrong to interrupt, because it was his job to see that all the speakers had a fair share of the time and, on this occasion, we had not. When Christine joined us, she was so furious that she wanted to give Mr Kilroy-Silk a piece of her mind. Looking round the room, I saw the man who had caused her anger sitting with two of the studio girls, laughing. How he loves an audience, I thought, and walked over to the group.

'Mr Kilroy-Silk.' He turned his head, still smiling. 'Next time I'm on a programme with you, I'm going to bring a rubber hammer with me because it's the only way to shut you up.' Giving him a sweet smile, I walked away feeling much better.

When I rejoined Christine and Desmond, the editor of the programme said, 'I don't know what you have done to Desmond in Liverpool but he's never stopped talking about it. He's persuading me to let him take a team up there to film some victims.'

'It's about time someone took an interest in them,' I replied, taking out my photographs of Ethel, Sally and Stephen and handing them to him. He studied them in silence for a few moments, then handed them back, saying, 'You've convinced me. He's very determined to do this programme so I suppose I'd better let him.' I don't know whose smile was the broader, Desmond's or mine.

It would be several months before a crew was available, but Desmond promised to keep in touch during that time. As we parted he was as happy as a sandboy and couldn't wait to get back to Liverpool.

*   *   *

Life settled into a routine after the London trip and my days were full. We had started to liaise with another police district and every morning I would ring Admiral Street and Eaton Road for referrals. I no longer read the papers or listened to the radio to hear of victims because, apart from the police referrals, I was being contacted by the victims themselves or their relatives. I was so busy that I was drifting away from the CLO and seldom attended meetings now. It just wasn't possible to be committed to both CLO and Victims of Violence and I felt that the latter was more important. I wasn't moving mountains in my efforts, but I was getting a lot of publicity and some day someone might listen.

Three weeks after the Man Alive programme, I received a phone call from Granda Television asking me to take part in a programme presented by Gordon Burns called Double Vision. The subject was capital and corporal punishment and I was keen to agree until Gordon Burns told me that Robert Kilroy-Silk was one of the opposition. I told him of my past experiences at the hands of Kilroy-Silk and Gordon promised me it would not happen on this programme. He suggested that this was my chance to get my own back. Like a fool, I fell for it and promised to be at the studios at six o'clock on the night the programme was to be recorded. I asked if I could take Stasia for company and Gordon agreed, saying she could watch the recording from the Visitors' Room.

The buffet in the hospitality room at Granada was much more lavish than that at the BBC and Stasia and I were helping ourselves when Kilroy-Silk arrived. He joined the other two people who were on his panel, and they soon had their heads together. Gordon Burns joined Stasia and me to explain the format of the programme. The studio audience would be asked, at the start of the programme, to vote on capital punishment. It was then up to the leaders of the two panels to state their case and they would be allowed to question

288

the opposition. This had to be done with the panellists sitting in what Gordon Burns called the 'witness box'. At the end of the programme the audience would be asked to vote again to see if any of them had been persuaded to change their minds. Ivor Lawrence, the MP on my panel, had not yet arrived; neither had my other panellist. Gordon was clearly worried by the late arrivals and I was beginning to worry too.

'I told you what Kilroy-Silk did to me a few weeks ago,' I reminded him. 'I hope you aren't going to let him do it again.'

'I think you're quite capable of holding your own,' he told me, 'but when you're in the witness box you're only allowed to answer questions, not ask them.'

When 7.30 came and Ivor Lawrence and our other panellist still hadn't arrived, I became concerned and angry. 'Kilroy-Silk will make mincemeat out of us. He's had an hour and a half with his team,' I told Gordon. 'He'll have it all pat and I don't even know my panellists.' Gordon agreed that it was unfair and kept going out to enquire if Ivor Lawrence had arrived.

It was 7.45 when he sailed in, unconcerned that we had been waiting since six o'clock, and brushed aside the protests of Gordon and myself. 'Kilroy-Silk will crucify us,' I told him. 'It will be like lambs to the slaughter.'

'Nonsense,' he said cheerfully. 'We have the whole country on our side. We can't lose.'

'You don't know Kilroy-Silk,' I warned him grimly. We were on our way into the studio when I met our other panellist but I didn't even hear her name. Gordon Burns' desk was in the middle of the

289

studio facing the audience at the far end and the two panels were on either side. In the centre was the dreaded witness chair, with a spotlight shining down on it. The audience was asked to vote on capital punishment and the majority was in favour. Then Kilroy-Silk began; he has such a flair for making speeches that he is undeniably impressive, if you don't listen to what he has to say. Ivor Lawrence was a good speaker too but lacked his opponent's flair. If he had met some families of murder victims he would probably have spoken with more conviction. When Gordon Burns asked me to take the witness box, I felt as if I was in a court of law. It was a terrifying experience sitting under that harsh light watching Kilroy-Silk walking towards me.

His first words belied the smile on his face. 'Mrs Jonker, did you not stand in the Edge Hill by-election as Law and Order Candidate?' So that's the way he's going to play it, I thought, as I answered in the affirmative, stressing his double-barrelled name. 'And is it true that you received 373 votes? If that is the case, your claim that most of the country agree with your views can't be true, can it, or they would have voted for you.'

'You're very generous, Mr Kilroy-Silk, I only received 337 votes,' I answered.

He smiled sweetly, but gave me no time to say any more. As he spoke he prowled around my chair like a tiger getting ready for the kill. I thought grimly, Oh, no, you don't. I then opened my mouth and started talking. To this day I have no recollection of what I said, but I carried on regardless, spurred by his supercilious grin and sarcastic voice. I kept it up until I returned to my

290

seat, furious at his rude and ungentlemanly behaviour, but I could get my own back yet. On a piece of notepaper I wrote down what I would have asked Kilroy-Silk had I been allowed, and passed it down to Ivor Lawrence. I had written, 'Ask him if it isn't true that he lost 10,000 votes at the last election. If 650 more people had changed their votes wouldn't he have lost his seat? I gained 337. He lost 10,000.'

Ivor Lawrence was surprised at the professional approach of the other panel and I think he was regretting his late arrival. When he summed up he made no mention of the facts in my note, though, probably thinking it was hitting below the belt. He didn't realize that, had the positions been reversed, Kilroy-Silk would have had no such qualms. The vote at the end was still in favour of capital punishment, but the majority was reduced, purely because of our lack of a planned campaign.

Stasia's face was flushed with anger when we met in the hospitality room. She was threatening to give Kilroy-Silk a piece of her mind when Gordon Burns came over and heard me telling her that she must not. 'It was all your fault,' I told him. 'You had no right to let him make a fool of me. You should have stopped him and given me a chance to speak.'

Gordon was quite unrepentant and delighted with the way the programme had gone. 'Wonderful television,' he said. 'The sparks were literally flashing from your eyes. You'll be pleased when you see the programme next Friday.'

'I'm dreading it, and even if you think it was good television, I still think you were wrong. You let Kilroy-Silk do it again, but I'll tell you this,

291

Gordon, never again will I let him, or anyone else, make a fool of me—even if it means walking out in the middle of a programme.'

'We'll get a tremendous response from the viewers,' he said.

'That still doesn't alter the fact that you allowed me to be treated unfairly by a man who was rude and insulting,' I snapped.

'I promise you that you will feel differently when you see the reaction to the programme,' he insisted.

I believe that he was by that time feeling guilty about what had happened but, as a professional, he first of all wanted good television and the scene between Kilroy-Silk and myself had been just that. Before leaving the hospitality room I told Stasia I must go and say goodbye to my tormentor; I thought she was going to choke.

'You're not going to speak to him after what he did to you?'

'Watch me,' I said, walking over to where the cause of my anger was, as usual, enjoying the attention of his colleagues. He was in a jolly mood, probably pleased with his performance and laughing now with his friends.

'Goodnight, Mr Kilroy-Silk,' I said politely. 'Goodnight, gentlemen.'

'There you are,' said some bright spark. 'They're really good friends.'

'Let's say friendly enemies,' I suggested as I walked away. That night I promised myself that I would never again be out-talked or ridiculed by anyone, and that is a promise I have kept.

I was dreading watching the screening of the programme on the Friday night and warned Tony what to expect. I died a thousand deaths as I saw myself walk across to that witness chair and would have fled the room if it weren't for Tony. I forced myself to watch as Kilroy-Silk prowled around me like a panther about to pounce on his kill.

Tony was blazing with anger. 'Why the hell didn't you stop him?' he demanded.

'What should I have done—run out of the place crying?'

I was always annoyed when someone offered me advice on how to behave on television, particularly when that person wouldn't have had the nerve himself to appear on the small screen.

No sooner had the programme finished than the phone started to ring, and the calls kept on coming until 11.30 when I took the phone off the hook. Each caller offered sympathy for the way I had been treated, and some were so angry that I wondered Kilroy-Silk's ears were not burning.

On the following Wednesday, I received a phone call from Gordon Burns at 10.30 at night.

'You're not still working, are you?' I asked in surprise.

'I often work until this time of night. At the moment I'm trying to sort out the mail we've had since the programme. It's the biggest response we've had—over a thousand letters—and you'll like the contents. Watch this Friday. I'll be reading some of them out.' He couldn't resist adding, 'I told you so, didn't I?'

'I know there's been a big response because my phone has never stopped ringing. Kilroy-Silk certainly did himself a lot of harm that night.'

True to his word, during the programme the following Friday night Gordon Burns told the viewers of the huge stack of mail they had received and read out some of the letters. Tony and I roared with laughter because they were bluntly critical of Kilroy-Silk. Even Gordon Burns didn't escape. He was told he should have stopped my persecutor, one woman going so far as to suggest a wedge in the gentleman's mouth. I may not have been able to stop Kilroy-Silk on the programme, but the viewers had certainly given him the two-finger sign.

CHAPTER THIRTEEN

1980

When I heard on the radio that Sir William Butlin had died I was very sad. It was like losing an old friend because he and Lady Butlin had been good to me. Genuinely concerned about the plight of elderly people, they were always around when I needed them. They had become Patrons of our charity years earlier, along with Sir Kenneth and Lady Stoddart and Ken Dodd. Our committee consisted of David Alton MP, Malcolm Thornton MP, and David Irving, who was a serving police constable at West Derby Road police station. My own title was chairman, organizer and fundraiser. They wanted to put me down on the letterheads as 'founder', but I thought that sounded like a staid Victorian lady so it never came about. Ringing Lady Butlin wasn't easy—what could you say to someone who's just lost her husband?—but I had to pay my respects. She was absolutely devastated, and my heart went out to her as she talked about her Bill. Over the years he had given so much away to charities that there must be thousands like myself who had cause to be grateful to him.

Several things happened at that time which made me both sad and angry. My home was broken into, and my wedding and engagement rings and a gold watch stolen. The police told me there had been a spate of burglaries in the area and they believed they were all committed by one man. It seemed the thief gained entry through the garden into back kitchens where, because women were in the habit of leaving their bags around, he usually managed to steal something. In some cases he only had a small haul; in my case he had a field day. I was very distressed because I had owned those rings for thirty-five years and, although Tony bought me new ones, they could never really replace the originals.

During the same week I went to visit Maggie Matthews, a police referral. When she was pulled down a flight of concrete steps in a bag snatch, Maggie had sustained a cut on her head which had needed stitching. I had been back several times to check that she was all right, but this time I found her very nervous because of a letter she had received from the police, asking her to attend a juvenile court on the Monday morning. The name of the youth whom the police believed had attacked her was on the form, and they wanted Maggie there for his court appearance. She was terrified at the prospect as she had never been in a court in her life before. I calmed her down and said I would go with her. Because Philip's bus didn't pick him up until nine o'clock, I could not pick Maggie up and be at the court in time so I suggested she take a taxi and I would meet her there. It was a mad rush for me anyway, but it was made worse by the heavy traffic at that time in the morning and I was hot and bothered by the time I reached the court. I made my way upstairs and into a room bursting at the seams with teenagers. Expecting Maggie's white hair to make her stand out, I looked again, more carefully; I saw that most of the young people had adults with them. Probably they were parents, solicitors or probation officers; still I couldn't see any sign of Maggie.

A court usher came out of a side room and as soon as she saw me came over. 'Aren't you Joan Jonker?' she asked, and when I nodded, she said, 'I'm very glad to meet you. You're doing a grand job and I agree with everything you say.' I thanked her, and then asked if she knew anything about Mrs Matthews. 'I'm sorry,' she said, 'but we only have the names of the offenders.'

'I know the name of the offender—can you tell me anything from that?' I asked hopefully. After I gave the name the usher disappeared for a few minutes and then returned with news for me. 'He was in court last Thursday,' she told me. 'He was up on four charges and asked for Mrs Matthews' case to be taken into consideration, so it was dealt with at the same time.'

'What happened to him?' I asked.

'He was fined twenty-five pounds.'

'For five offences?' I almost shouted. 'Mrs Matthews was dragged down a flight of steps and had her head split open, and he gets fined twenty-five pounds? That's five pounds per offence. Who says crime doesn't pay?'

'You want to be here every day and see what happens,' she told me. 'I've been here fourteen

296

years and I used to enjoy it, but now I'll be glad to leave. You see kids coming out of here laughing their heads off.'

I drove straight from the court to Maggie's and my anger was mixed with pity when she opened the door and I saw her frailty. She was surprised to see me as she had been informed by the police that she would not be needed in court and they had promised I would be informed. What worried her most was that I had been inconvenienced for nothing. Poor Maggie. I was only glad she didn't know that the thug who had attacked her had been fined just £25.

*   *   *

Lord Longford's committee reared up again in the shape of one of its members, Michael Whittaker, who rang me from his home in Leeds to say he was interested in starting a Victim Support Scheme in his area and would like some advice on how to go about it. After I had explained the kind of help we gave, he asked if he could come down one day and accompany me on my calls, so it was agreed he would come down the following week. Michael and his wife had first hand experience of suffering; only a few years ago their eight-year-old daughter had been raped and murdered. Who better to sympathize with people than someone who had suffered too? Even so, he was deeply affected by the sight of so many elderly victims. Time after time Michael expressed his horror at the callousness of the thugs who had attacked and robbed them. He was even more determined to start a support scheme in his own area.

Back home, while I was preparing the evening meal, he told me of his disillusionment with the committee of which Lord Longford was chairman. While he had great respect for his colleagues, he was concerned that they seemed to be getting nowhere. Knowing of my meeting with Lord Longford, he said that if I joined them on the committee he felt sure that, between the two of us, we could stir them into some sort of action.

'I really don't think I could work with Lord Longford,' I told him. 'I don't have the time to attend meetings in London if nothing constructive is going to come out of them.'

'If you join the committee, I'll stay on and we can work together. Otherwise I'm resigning,' he announced. 'I've seen a little of the work you do and that's the way I want to help victims.'

Michael did resign, and sent me a copy of the letter he had written to Lord Longford, expressing the disillusionment and disappointment he felt at the lack of achievement of the National Committee for Victims. Because distance made it impossible for Michael to be involved with our organization, he decided to start his own scheme in Leeds.

*   *   *

It was three months before I heard from the BBC that Desmond Lapsley would be coming to Liverpool for a few days with a researcher. They wanted to visit as many victims as possible in order to find in advance those who would be most suitable to appear on the proposed programme. Some of the victims, although prepared to talk to Desmond, were frightened of appearing on the

298

television because of possible reprisals, and others could not be used because their voices would not be clear enough. I tried to draw up a list of possibilities ready for when Desmond arrived with Mandy Temple, his new researcher. From the start, Mandy and I got on like a house on fire and the three of us were like the Three Musketeers, sharing the sadness, the injustices and the laughter. The Scouse humour, with which I had lived all my life, was new to Desmond and Mandy, who were amazed that people who had suffered so much could still find so much to laugh about. Desmond had the knack of putting people at ease and they made tea for him while they told their stories.

'I can't wait to start filming,' he told me. 'It's going to make a wonderful programme.'

'They've all been making fun of him in the office,' said Mandy. 'He never stops talking about Liverpool and the people there.'

'I don't mind that. I just want everyone to see these people, then perhaps something will be done.'

I told Desmond about an idea I'd been toying with for a while, that I should take a group of elderly victims away for a few days' holiday. Many of them never went out at all because they were too frightened, so a few days right away from Liverpool would do them a world of good. A friend in Yorkshire, Frank Moody, had offered to help in any way that was needed. I was thinking of asking him to help towards the cost of the holiday. Desmond was interested at once because he thought that if I could fit in the holiday with his filming dates it would make a marvellous end to the film. 'We could show how, in spite of all they

299

have gone through, they still know how to enjoy themselves.'

We agreed that I should wait for the start of filming date before booking the holiday, but first I rang Frank to ask if he would help with the finances. He agreed at once to pay the full hotel bill, and I was delighted.

This was a happy time for me because it seemed that at last some people were beginning to see things from where I stood. It was a real breakthrough, and I walked with a spring in my step and a heart that was lighter than it had been for several years.

I only had to wait a few days for Desmond to confirm the filming dates in Liverpool, and then I rang a person I knew on the Blackpool Hoteliers' Association Committee. He was able to suggest a small hotel overlooking the sea where the prices would be within our range. That same night I booked in twenty-four people at the Wembley Hotel for the Monday after Desmond reckoned the main filming would be finished.

The following week was hectic as I called on new victims referred to me by the police, and organized those who were to be interviewed for the television programme. In addition, I had to organize the twenty-two who would be going to Blackpool with Stasia and myself. It was tiring working all day and making phone calls until late in the evening, and at one point Tony remarked that if I didn't slow down I'd be heading for a nervous breakdown. I always intended to slow down the next week, but the next week never seemed to come.

At last it was time for Desmond and Mandy to arrive with the film crew and Michael Dean, who

300

was to present the programme. For the next four days I was to lead a convoy of four cars to calls spread across the city. Several times I lost sight of the last car in my rear-view mirror and had to pull in until it caught up. The first day was rather tense as Michael Dean and the camera crew were strangers to me, but, because of the warmth and friendliness of the victims, it wasn't long before the atmosphere became more relaxed and, in between the serious interviews, there was much joking and laughter. Michael was handsome, reserved, and possessed a lovely voice. He handled the interviews with an understanding and compassion to which the elderly people responded whole-heartedly. Several victims cried when they related their experiences, and I could see how it affected everyone's emotions. How I loved those old people, and how proud I was of the way they conducted themselves before the cameras.

On Desmond's previous visit, I had taken him to see an old lady called Cathy who had been robbed eight times, but I hadn't included her in the list of people to be interviewed because her strong Scouse accent made her difficult to understand, except by another Scouser. Desmond wanted to try, though, as he thought her story worth telling, so, reluctantly, I led the convoy to Cathy's flat. The hour that followed was one of the most hilarious of my life. Desmond wanted to film the interview in Cathy's kitchen, where the window was boarded up after the last break-in. Cathy, a large lady with short white hair, stood by the sink, her arms folded, and Michael stood in front of her. The clapperboard was held in front of the camera and someone called 'Take one'. Michael, in his

301

beautifully modulated voice, said, 'Tell me what happened to you, Cathy.' Her reply was understood by no one except me, and I started to giggle at the sight of the puzzled looks exchanged by the others, who hadn't understood a word.

'Cut!' called Desmond. There followed a whispered discussion on how best to tackle this interview then came the clapperboard and 'Take two'.

'Cathy, can you tell me what happened to you?' invited Michael.

'Ah bin to me dorter's an wen a come 'ome me 'ouse was in a teribul state—yer shud've seen it.' Michael was baffled and, trying to contain my laughter, I suggested he should try a different approach. He knew that Cathy had been robbed eight times and that she was still in debt to the Electricity Board for the money stolen from the meters in the first three robberies. Couldn't he just explain what had happened, then ask Cathy if it was true? It could be managed if she only had to answer 'Yes'.

Desmond and Michael were determined to persevere and we went through 'Take three', 'Take four', and finally 'Take five'. By this time I was helpless with laughter and the camera crew was grinning.

'You've met your match, Michael!' I called.

'It's awrite fer you,' called Cathy. 'Laffin' yer 'ed off!' She was seeing the funny side of it now and was shaking with laughter.

Desmond told me, 'We'll have to use subtitles.' I said I'd stay with Cathy for a few minutes to make sure she wasn't overexcited by it all, but I need not have bothered for she had had a ball. As I left the flat I found Michael waiting for me, a huge grin on his face.

'I'm used to interviewing intellectuals, Joan,' he said, 'but I've never enjoyed an interview as much as I did that one.'

The filming in Liverpool was soon finished and Desmond was more than pleased with the way it had gone. He was concerned about the editing of the film because many of the scenes would have to be cut. Many hours of filming would have to be pruned down to only fifty minutes, which meant cutting out all or part of some of the interviews.

In three days' time I would be seeing him, Mandy, Michael and the crew again as they were joining us in Blackpool to complete the filming. By now we were all good friends and I was looking forward to seeing them at the Wembley Hotel. It was time for a holiday.

Because all the victims were strangers to each other there was at first a strained atmosphere when we gathered in the hotel lounge. We had been shown to our rooms and had unpacked. Now we had assembled to wait for the tea we had ordered. I was trying to involve them all in conversation when the hotel owners, Dilys and Gordon, brought in the tea. That was all it took to break the ice. Within ten minutes you would have thought they were all old friends. I began to relax myself as I sat back and listened to snippets of conversation. I could hear 'I used to live near there', or 'Do you know Mrs So and So? I used to go to school with her.' And then from someone else, 'Fancy you knowing our Mary, isn't it a small world?' By the time Desmond and the gang arrived the next morning we were like one big happy family. Sally Wilson was amusing us with her never-ending stream of jokes and no one seemed offended, although some of them were a bit naughty. For a woman of ninety she was incredible.

We were all sitting in the sun lounge being entertained by Sally when I saw Desmond pass the window with the others. I went out to meet them and exchange greetings. I warned them about Sally's jokes, but said I didn't want to break things up because they were all enjoying themselves so much. 'I'm sorry if any of you are offended, but I'm not going to spoil their fun.'

'Don't worry about that,' Michael said and made straight for the lounge to look for Sally, while Desmond and I sat quietly in a corner to discuss where and what to film. Desmond suggested hiring three horse-drawn carriages, which are a famous feature of Blackpool, and I thought it was a fantastic idea. We were still deep in discussion when, twenty minutes later, Michael Dean rolled out of the lounge, clutching his stomach, tears rolling down his face.

'I couldn't take any more. She's unbelievable. She just reels the jokes off one after another.'

While Desmond went off to order the open carriages, I made sure the ladies were wrapped up warmly to protect them from the sea breezes and then they were helped into the carriages where there were warm blankets to put over their legs. As we set off the pleasure on the faces of the elderly women was a joy to behold. The camera crew ran alongside, while holidaymakers watched the proceedings curiously. The ladies were waving their hands like the Queen does, and thoroughly enjoyed themselves. It made them feel important and gave them back a little of their dignity.

Back at the hotel, Desmond bought them all a stiff drink to warm them up, and when they'd settled down after the excitement, Michael was ready to interview them.

'It was lovely to go to bed last night and not be frightened of every sound,' Maggie told him, and it was while Michael was interviewing Christine that Desmond got an idea for the title of the programme. When Michael asked her why she thought the elderly were picked on by the thugs, she said, 'Because the old can't run fast enough.'

Desmond whispered to me, 'That's it! That's the title.'

Before the television people left we all went outside to take souvenir snapshots, and it was here that Michael shed the last of his reserve. He was standing with his arm round Sally, his six-foot frame bent to match her four-foot-eight frailty, and I heard her say quietly, 'I wish you were my grandson.'

'And I wish you were my grandma,' he told her. We watched as he took the folded newspaper from under his arm, flung it high in the air and said, 'Oh, blow it!' Arms outstretched, he took hold of Sally and waltzed her round the hotel forecourt, much to the amusement of the passers-by. Then it was time to say goodbye. I felt a little sad as we waved off Desmond and the gang because I had grown fond of them all. Still, I had been assured that I would be hearing from them very soon, so it wasn't a last farewell. The programme was not due to be screened until some time in October, which was almost five months away, but Desmond said there was a lot of work to be done on it before then and

305

he would have to be in touch many times.

After having the film crew with me for almost a week, then the holiday in Blackpool which was such a roaring success, it was almost an anti-climax to settle back into my normal routine. However, after a few days I was so involved in trying to sort out victims' problems that everything else took second place.

Four years before, when I'd first started visiting victims, I'd had occasion to ring the DHSS to ask them to help an elderly person who had been left penniless after a robbery, and since then had rung them many times. I never queried it when they said it would be three days before they could send a visitor though to my mind there was something wrong when an elderly person was going to be left without money for food or heating for so long. I accepted the three-day wait because I didn't think there was anything I could do about it, until the day I finally lost my temper.

CHAPTER FOURTEEN

I had been given the name of a new victim by the police, and when I arrived at his home, found him and his wife, both in their eighties, in a very distressed state. Their home had been burgled while they were asleep and every penny they owned had been stolen—two weeks' rent money due that day, electricity money also due that day, and Mrs Platt's housekeeping money. When I suggested to Mr Platt that the DHSS might help he shook his head and said he had just come back from them and they could not do anything.

'But they must give you some help,' I protested. 'How else are you going to pay your bills?'

'They told me I'd have to pay an extra pound a week to make up the two weeks' rent,' the tearful eighty-one-year-old told me, 'and they said I'll have to get in touch with the electricity people and see if they'll let me pay that off at a pound a week too.' While he was talking, his wife was sobbing quietly and I could feel a lump in my own throat. 'I told them we couldn't afford to pay an extra pound a week from our pensions,' he went on, 'but they said there was nothing they could do.'

Four years of anger and frustration came to a head inside me. How dare society not only fail to protect its elderly from thugs, but also to help them when they were robbed?

'You'd be short of money for a year to pay off those arrears,' I exploded.

'I told them that,' he insisted. 'I told them that I'd worked until I was seventy-eight and have never asked for anything in my life . . .' By this time he was crying so much he couldn't carry on.

'Don't upset yourself, love,' I urged. 'We'll sort something out.'

He wiped his eyes on the back of his hands. 'I'm sorry. I started crying in the Social Security office and I was so ashamed I had to leave.'

I could never bear to see old people cry. Now, seeing these two lovely people so distressed caused something in me to snap. I found the phone number of the nearest DHSS office and rang them, asking for the person who'd dealt with the Platts. When I was put through I said firmly, 'I'm in the home of Mr and Mrs Platt and I'm ringing to

307

confirm the story he's just told me. It seems he asked you for help to pay his bills because his money was stolen during a robbery, and you have refused to help.'

'We can't help him,' came the reply.

'Pensioners only get enough to live on,' I pointed out. 'They don't have extra to replace money that's been stolen from them.'

'I'm sorry but—'

I interrupted the voice, 'All right, dear, I'm not going to argue with you, I only rang up to confirm the story. I suggest you buy the *Echo* on the way home and read what I think of your attitude towards people in distress.'

'Wait a moment, Mrs Jonker,' the voice requested. I could hear murmurs at the other end of the phone, then a more mature voice said, 'Can I help you, Mrs Jonker?'

'It doesn't matter,' I told him. 'I only rang to confirm that you have refused to help Mr Platt. As I told your colleague, buy a paper on the way home and read what I think of your attitude to elderly victims.'

'Mrs Jonker, I do sympathize but we cannot possibly help everyone who comes to us.'

'I'm not asking you to help everyone, just two elderly people who, through no fault of their own, cannot pay their bills.' By now I was past worrying about the social niceties. 'When will people realize that victims are not just anybody but special people who are frightened and distressed and need help?'

'All right, Mrs Jonker.' The voice sounded sympathetic. 'I promise to send a visitor to see Mr Platt and we'll see what we can do.'

The next morning he rang to say that the visitor

had been and had promised to help. The next day he rang again; they had received a Girocheque covering most of the stolen money.

'How can I thank you?' he asked. 'If it hadn't been for you, I don't know what we would have done.' Which left me wondering about all the other elderly people left penniless like the Platts who didn't have someone with a big mouth to plead their case.

*   *   *

It was four years now since I'd knocked on Albert Smith's door, and in that time I had met, and helped, over four thousand victims living in areas across Merseyside. I was working five days a week, and doubt if a day passed when I didn't shed tears.

What saddened me most was that the vast majority of victims I met were in their seventies and eighties, and quite a few in their nineties. Many of them told me they wished they were dead because there was no pleasure for them in life now, nothing to live for. These were people who had contributed all their lives to making this a good country to live in, to building a strong society, admired the world over for its justice. They'd left us well-built homes, roads, schools and hospitals, and brought their children up to live without greed or envy and to show compassion for their neighbours. Yet when these people needed help there was no one there for them, not even official recognition of their plight or the injustice of it. It was plain to me, a very ordinary housewife and mother, that unless the younger generation were taught that if they committed a crime they would be punished, then our society would soon become lawless and out of control. I couldn't believe there were so many penal reformers in this country making it their life's work to stop criminals being punished when I knew their innocent victims had no rights whatsoever.

I aired my views as loudly and as often as I could, and have to say the support I received from the media and the general public was brilliant, particularly the *Liverpool Echo* and Radio Merseyside who were always ready to listen and to help raise money. It was only knowing that there were so many people out there who did care what was happening that kept me going. They were generous in their donations of money, clothing and bedding, and with offers to help in any way they could.

I was ringing three police stations now every morning for referrals, and it was hard going. Some days it could be four victims, sometimes seven or eight, and I was working alone because with Stasia's having no car it was impossible for her to travel across the city. Public transport wasn't reliable enough. But she was always there to help with the parties that many people in pubs and clubs organized for our charity, or on coach trips. And I had many willing helpers in the victims themselves. They wanted to get involved and I thought they would be helped by being given a purpose in life and feeling useful. So any day I thought I was going to be hard pushed getting all the visits in, I would ring someone in the area and they would visit for me.

The Victims of Violence charity was running very smoothly now, and had gained the support and respect of many people. There were some nights I was dog-tired by the time I climbed the stairs to bed, but I was so dedicated to helping victims even my darling husband couldn't talk me into packing it in. We had a volunteer to keep our accounts for us now, which was a great help. Her name was Jeanette Edge, a lovely young woman full of compassion for the elderly people she'd seen me with on television shows and in the newspapers. She worked in an insurance office in the city. Once a week I'd meet her and pass over details of the week's expenditure with the relevant receipts. Olive Fairman was still keeping a record of all the victims, which was also a great help. I would ring her every night with the particulars of the victims I had just visited, and the next morning she would be at her typewriter, bringing the files up-to-date.

I have to admit that I was fiercely protective of the charity and watched over it like a mother hen. I had heard of too many charities that had been found wanting, and was determined that there would never be any scandal attached to the VOV.

Charles Oxley had been concerned since the organization was set up that I was using my own money to fund it so I now agreed to take three pounds a week towards petrol costs. Outgoings were very low, the only money spent being on stationery, stamps and phone calls, plus the donations we gave to those in need and bunches of flowers for victims who were in hospital. The many parties we held for the elderly victims were in pubs, clubs or restaurants, generously funded by donations from regular customers. And, believe me, they were much appreciated. It was often said to me that many of the people I helped were having

311

more outings now than they'd ever had in their lives before, and had more friends too. Their gratitude and humility was the cause of many of my tears.

*   *   *

The VOV had never received a grant from any official body and I now decided to try my luck. They would never have a better cause than to help prevent the elderly from becoming victims. So I wrote to Trevor Jones, Leader of Liverpool City Council, requesting a meeting. I had a reply within two days stating a date when he would be available to see me. When the time came I found him very sympathetic to my request for a grant to fit burglar alarms in the homes of certain people who had been the target of thieves many times. It was to be a pilot scheme, and it would be monitored so that if we were successful we could ask Government to make more money available to widen the scheme. Trevor Jones asked me to put my request in writing so it could go before the relevant committee. I did this as soon as I got home, and in my letter stated that if my application for a grant were successful, I would prefer the money to be paid through Social Services rather than VOV.

Within a few weeks I heard that our application had been successful, and that £8,000 was being made available through Social Services for installing burglar alarms. The police and local housing manager were asked to co-operate, and at a meeting of all parties involved an area was selected for the pilot scheme, and a firm specializing in burglar alarms asked to give advice

312

and estimates.

All was going well. With an engineer I had visited all the tenants of the houses and flats involved in the scheme, and explained what was happening. Then I contacted the local Residents Committee. Obviously the help of the local community was needed to make the scheme work, for if a burglar alarm went off someone would need to respond. Each block of flats would need only one main unit and we had asked that one person should house that unit in his or her flat. It had been estimated that the cost of the electricity used would only be about ten pence per week but I knew only too well how elderly people worry about paying their bills. Eventually I contacted the housing manager to ask if the alarms could be wired into the council's main electrical supply and, as the amount involved was so small, he agreed to this being done.

Then two days later one of the men from Social Services who was involved in the scheme rang me to say that he had been contacted by the Toxteth Community Council who said that the money for the pilot scheme should have been paid to them. It was their area and they should be involved, they claimed, not me. I blew my top completely at this. Why were these people not just glad someone was trying to help people in their area? They had not thought of the scheme themselves, but now that someone else had and it was going smoothly, they wanted the money to be paid over to them. The man from Social Services agreed with me.

'The scheme can't possibly be passed over to them,' he told me. 'You applied for the grant and it was awarded to you, although it is administered through us. However,' he sounded hesitant, 'they have asked for a meeting with us about it and I'm afraid we'll have to attend.'

If I was angry before, I was now furious. 'Who the hell do they think they are?' I exploded. 'I've worked in that area every day for the last four years. What have they done for it?'

'There's something else,' he said. 'I'm afraid they have stipulated that they don't want you at the meeting.'

'You know why, don't you?' I said angrily. 'I would tell them to get lost and you can't.'

The officer from Social Services promised that my interests would be protected at the meeting and assured me that he would let me know what happened. As it was, I didn't need to be told officially because the meeting was open to residents and one of the victims I had helped rang to tell me what had gone on. She was disgusted at what they had said about me, but assured me they didn't get away with it. She promised to send me a copy of the letter they had all been given and it arrived the next morning. It turned out to be more or less what I expected. The line that stood out read, 'Mrs Joan Jonker was not present at the meeting, at the request of the Toxteth Community Council, because of her extreme political views . . .' It was the same old story; because I didn't share their views on the punishment of offenders, I was labelled a 'right-wing reactionary'. They had the mistaken idea that if they threw enough mud, some of it would stick.

Although they didn't win their fight to have the grant money transferred to them, they had done their best to scupper the whole scheme. They may not have got what they wanted but they had managed to sour the whole idea as far as I was concerned because I knew that so long as I was involved, the whole scheme would be in jeopardy due to lack of co-operation from the Community Council. I could have worked in harmony with the residents, who were effusive in their gratitude, but I knew this self-appointed body would not allow it, so I decided to take a back seat for the sake of what was a good idea and in order to help the victims. And the sad fact is, I have never been to a political meeting in my life, and never been a member of any party. Before starting my charity work, I gave little thought to politicians. After four years of seeing daily injustices I had in fact, with the exception of a few, lost all respect for them.

*   *   *

Ever since I first started visiting victims, it had been obvious to me that the lack of recognition of their needs was nothing short of a national scandal. There was no one to whom they could go for help, sympathy or understanding. The injustice of the whole set-up was brought home forcibly in the case of two young boys who were murdered.

On the radio one Sunday morning I heard of the two boys, aged eleven, who had been found on a rubbish tip badly beaten up. One had died during the night and doctors were fighting to save the life of the other. I had the address of the dead boy and, although I hesitated before visiting his family as I had no wish to intrude upon their private grief, I did feel I should ask if they needed any practical help. Had I felt at all unwelcome I would have left

315

at once, but I soon realized that my visit was appreciated. Little John was the eldest of the three children of John and Barbara Greenwood, and their grief at losing him was heartbreaking to see. It was difficult not to cry myself as they showed me photographs of their son, a handsome, healthy boy who had gone out to play one Saturday afternoon. It was the last time they saw him alive.

'Has anyone been to see you?' I asked Barbara, who was nursing her young daughter.

'Who do you mean?'

'Anyone from the authorities, to see if you need anything?'

Barbara shook her head then said, 'We had a letter from the DHSS this morning.' She took an envelope from the mantelpiece and handed it to me. Unable to believe my eyes, I had to read the letter twice to take it in. It said: 'Dear Mrs Greenwood, We are sorry to hear of the death of your son. Will you kindly return the Family Allowance book for adjustment . . .'

I looked at Barbara's grief-stricken face. 'My God! How heartless can you get?'

'My sister rang the DHSS to ask if we could draw this week's money, but they refused. We needed the money this week with so many expenses. I would have given it back to them, but they said I had to return the book without drawing this week's payment.'

As I drove home my mind was in turmoil, trying to understand a society that could treat people like the Greenwoods in this callous way. The whole system was cock-eyed. The next day I heard on the radio that John's friend, Gary Miller, had lost his fight for life so I rang Barbara to ask if she thought the Millers would like me to visit them. She suggested I should call at her house the next day and she would take me to them.

Alma and Ron Miller were, like the Greenwoods, an ordinary working-class couple. Devastated by the murder of their son, they were unable to understand why anyone deliberately should have killed him. Alma was very bitter, eaten up with hatred for the person who had taken her son from her. I encouraged her to talk about Gary, hoping that it would help, and she told me later that it had, for the tragedy was threatening her sanity.

It was two weeks before the police would release the bodies for burial and the two families decided on a double funeral because they felt the boys who had been such good friends in life should be buried side by side. Neither family had money set aside for funeral expenses because, as they said, 'Who expects an eleven-year-old to die?' I suggested that the DHSS might help. At first they said they would, but later they changed their minds. Ron Miller, who was unable to work, was on an invalidity pension and was given £30 towards the funeral expenses, but the Greenwoods were given nothing. Local people, who had been horrified by the murders, started collections in shops, at John's work, in pubs and door-to-door. The families were grateful for the donations, but the funeral and the headstones for the graves came to £800 each and the families could not raise that sort of money. In desperation, the Greenwoods were forced to surrender insurance policies, which lost them a lot of money, and the Millers had to borrow from a loan company.

Seeing the further misery and distress caused to the two families on top of what they had had to suffer because of the murders made me more determined than ever to try and do something about it. I rang Graham Page and asked for a meeting with him at the House of Commons to discuss ways of fighting these injustices. We met two days later and, after listening to my emotionally charged complaints, Graham suggested setting up a small committee of MPs to fight for the rights of victims. We decided to invite David Alton, a Liberal, and Eric Ogden, a Socialist, to join our committee, and both agreed.

A meeting was arranged in the House of Commons, and on the train journey down to London I made a list of the points I wanted to discuss. Later, in a small conference room, I put forward my proposals. I outlined specific cases and the response from the MPs was heartening. Two of the proposals, which received immediate agreement, were funeral expenses to be paid to murder victims' families and emergency financial help for pensioners.

*　　　*　　　*

Since the filming of the Man Alive programme, I'd had several phone calls from Desmond Lapsley telling me of his progress in editing the film. He told me how hard it was to cut any of it out because it was all so good, and he felt like crying every time some of it hit the cutting-room floor. He was certain it was going to make a marvellous programme and said I would be pleased with the finished product when it was transmitted. During one conversation, he told me I would be hearing from a reporter from the *Radio Times*, who wanted to interview me.

'You mean, I'm going to be in the magazine?' I asked excitedly.

'You're going to be famous,' Desmond laughed.

A few days later he rang again, and I could tell from his voice that something had gone wrong. For months I had been looking forward to the screening of his programme, and now Desmond was telling me it might never be shown. The government-funded National Association of Victims Support Schemes, which was setting up branches all over the country, had been invited to benefit from the public reaction which Desmond was sure would follow the transmission of the programme, but had declined. Not only that, they were lobbying against the programme being screened.

'They can't have it stopped, can they?' I asked him.

'They're certainly trying, Joan.' Desmond sounded weary. 'Age Concern is objecting, too.'

'But why?' I asked. 'You'd think they would be as keen as I am to let everyone know what's happening to old people.'

'They claim it will frighten them,' he told me. 'They say we're exaggerating and things aren't really that bad.'

'How can we exaggerate?' I was getting angry now. 'These people are real. Their injuries are real and people should see them.'

'Well, I invited one of the NAVSS representatives along to a preview and suggested that as the film was finished we couldn't invite

319

them to take part, but that if they wished, I could seek permission to give their name and phone numbers at the end so that any victim who wished to contact them could do so. I'm afraid they declined, though.'

'What about your boss?' I asked.

'He feels the same way as I do, but they've gone over his head with the complaints, so we'll just have to wait and see what happens.'

Desmond sounded determined, which gave me hope, but when I put the phone down I sat for a while going over the conversation in my mind. I just could not understand why two organizations supposed to be concerned with the welfare of elderly people should want to hide from the general public what was happening to those very people. Surely you don't solve a problem by brushing it under the carpet? It must be brought out into the open. To me it all seemed very strange. The next few days were worrying ones for me until Desmond rang to say that the programme would go ahead as planned on 7 October. He sounded happy and excited now that his worries were over.

The week before the screening was one of the busiest and most exciting of my life. On the Wednesday I was invited to the BBC for the press showing and, seated with critics from the major newspapers, watched the results of months of hard work by Desmond and Mandy. The programme was brilliantly produced, showing the victims as I wanted them to be seen by the public. Their age, frailty and vulnerability, together with the stories of how they were violently attacked, couldn't fail to move viewers unless they were made of stone. I lost the fight against tears and found them flowing freely. Desmond had done his homework well and gave statistics which both surprised and angered me. The most memorable one was that for every pound spent on the offender, only one penny was spent on the victim. My own part in the programme was extensive—it was, after all, based on the work of our organization—but I was more interested in the parts with which I was not familiar. These included interviews with the police and MPs.

When the programme ended, I had to wipe my eyes before turning to Desmond, who was looking at me enquiringly.

'Well?' he asked.

'Absolutely marvellous,' I gulped. 'Weren't my old people lovely?'

All the members of the press were deeply moved by what they had seen and were vocal in their praise of Desmond for a well-produced film, and of me for the way in which I had helped victims.

'What impresses me,' Desmond told them, 'is that Joan, a middle-class housewife, has devoted her life to helping working-class people.'

I interrupted quickly, 'Desmond, I'm not middle-class. I was born working-class and I'm proud of it. I am at home with these people, they're my own class.'

Desmond smiled at the reporters. 'All right, she's working-class.'

I knew in my heart that the film was exceptionally good. Desmond had handled the subject with honesty and sincerity. Nothing was exaggerated; everything was shown just as it had happened. The critics were of the same opinion and predicted it would have a great impact on the viewers. I prayed they were right.

The following day I had to make the journey to London again, this time for a Memorial Service for Sir William Butlin at the Church of St Martin's-in-the-Fields, to which Lady Butlin had thoughtfully sent me an invitation. Taking my seat in the church, I looked round with great interest at all the people I had only seen before on the television screen. Ted Rogers sat next but one to me, while in the row behind I could see Frank Carson. Eric Morecambe, Jimmy Saville and Hughie Green were just a few of the famous faces I also spotted. The church was filled to capacity with people who had come to pay tribute to the man who had brought happiness to so many. I knew I would never forget his kindness to me.

It was ten o'clock when I left home the next morning and my first call was to the newsagent's to buy a copy of the *Radio Times*. Sitting in the car, I turned over the pages until I came to a headline which made my blood run cold. Staring me in the face were the words 'Saint Joan of Merseyside'. Oh, my God, I thought, what have they done to me? I thought at once of what my friends would say. I could see them laughing their heads off and teasing me unmercifully. On the other hand, those who disagreed with my outspoken views would have a field day with this.

The article itself was good, if spoilt for me by the title. I needed to know what people's reaction would be so I called in on Stasia before I went to my first police referral. When she opened the door, grinning all over her face, I knew she had already seen the article. Within minutes we were both convulsed with laughter as I started to see the funny side of it. Shaking her head as she wiped her eyes, Stasia squeaked, 'Saint Joan!'

'In future you will kneel in my presence,' I joked.

For the next few days I had to put up with plenty of leg pulling, but I managed to laugh it off because by now I could see the funny side of it myself.

*   *   *

It wasn't long before I found myself sitting in front of the television with Tony waiting for the screening of 'The Old Can't Run Fast Enough', and my stomach was churning with nerves. I had a strong urge to leave the room on any excuse, washing my hair or having a bath, anything which meant I wouldn't have to watch. But once I saw how well my friends were coming over, I began to relax. Desmond showed only the true facts and these spoke for themselves. When it was all over I looked across at Tony.

'Well?' I asked.

'Excellent,' he said. 'One of the best documentaries I've ever seen.'

'I'm going to ring him and tell him so,' I said, running to the phone.

When I reached Desmond I found that he had been watching the programme with some of his studio colleagues. For months they had been pulling his leg because he had talked so much about Liverpool; now they could understand why. They had all been deeply moved by the stories and Desmond said that if the general public reacted in the same way there would be a massive response to the programme.

'Could you come down to London?' he asked. 'Radio London want you on the Robbie Vincent

Show tomorrow.' Here we go again, I thought, another day away from home. Still, publicity was what I wanted so I agreed to meet Desmond and Mandy at the studios the next day. Afterwards they both took me to lunch. Desmond had copies of all the national dailies and was surprised that I hadn't read the critics' reviews. Not being used to this kind of publicity, it hadn't occurred to me to look at them. He was grinning from ear to ear as he read each one and passed them on to me. They all praised the programme and I was delighted for Desmond. One critic said the film was so good that its producer should be on someone's short list for an award.

If I had thought that week was hard work, it was nothing compared to what was to come. It started the day after that trip to London with constant phone calls. The phone never stopped ringing and the postman was delivering stacks of letters every day. I would be only halfway through answering one pile when another delivery would arrive. Desmond and Mandy were also being inundated with letters and calls from people who wanted to contact me. They were surprised too by the number of requests they received from schools and various organizations for videos of the programme.

I managed to keep on top of the correspondence by writing until midnight each night, but when the BBC forwarded the mail they had received I was really snowed under. Many of the letters enclosed cheques and this entailed more work. My colleagues all offered to help with the answering but, rightly or wrongly, I felt that if someone took the trouble to write to me I should write back personally.

I received over a thousand letters offering support and donations amounting to £8,000. Praise was high for the programme maker and the victims, and the fact that at last the truth was being told about how badly people like this were neglected. I plodded through mountains of mail, answering every letter myself, but it was deeply satisfying to know that so many people cared enough to write.

CHAPTER FIFTEEN

One of the letters passed on to me from the BBC was from Chantal d'Ortez, the daughter of Moira Lister, the actress. Chantal said that she and her sister, Christabel, had watched the television programme about victims and been greatly moved by it. They very much wanted to do something constructive to help. When I rang Chantal we discussed ways in which she, with the help of her mother and sister, could do something to bring happiness to those they had seen on the programme. Moira Lister had suggested that about twenty victims could be brought to London for the day. She would cook a meal for them herself, in her home, and then take them to a show in the West End.

I was absolutely delighted with the idea and knew all the victims in the programme would jump at the chance of going to London and meeting Moira Lister. It was a marvellous, generous offer, and Chantal said they would like to do it as a Christmas treat for the elderly people. As Christmas was only about seven weeks away, I knew we would have to move quickly.

And so we did. In the next few days I visited all the victims who'd taken part in the programme, and to say they were over the moon with the invitation would indeed be an understatement. While I was organizing things my end, Chantal, with her mother and sister, had wasted no time and everything had been attended to, including the show. Seats had been booked for *My Fair Lady*, with Dame Anna Neagle and Tony Britton. I was still receiving a heavy mail bag after the Man Alive programme, and was really exhausted by trying to answer all the letters. So the invitation from Moira Lister was a real tonic. I found myself feeling less tired as I looked forward to what I knew would be an unforgettable day for me, but even more so for the twenty elderly people who were beginning to find there were people who cared.

Desmond Lapsley rang me a few days after Chantal and I had finalized arrangements, and I was full of excitement as I told him about it. He was very interested and pleased for me and the victims. 'Wouldn't it make a marvellous follow-up programme?' he said.

I gasped. 'D'you think it's possible?'

'I don't know,' he answered, 'but I'll certainly try.' With that he hung up, leaving me more excited than ever.

I spent the next two days visiting the twenty victims to let them know what was happening, and to make sure they were all right. I didn't tell them of Desmond's hopes about televising the day out because I thought they had enough excitement to be going on with. Already they were asking me what clothes they should wear. I told them anything comfortable would do, I knew they didn't have the money to splash out on new clothes. Besides, I loved them just as they were, and knew people in London would too.

A few days later, when I answered the phone and heard the excitement in Desmond's voice, I knew right away that he'd been able to persuade the studio bosses that another good programme could be made from our day out in London. After seeing their plight in 'The Old Can't Run Fast Enough', how wonderful to see the same people laughing and happy.

'Do you think Moira Lister would allow the cameras into her home?' Desmond asked.

'I really don't know. Wouldn't it be best if I gave you Chantal's phone number and then you can ring her yourself?'

After passing the phone number over, I had to sit back and wait for the result. It came two days later when Desmond told me: 'Moira has agreed to let the cameras in, I'm happy to say, and I'm working out the London arrangements with her. I'll be coming to Liverpool with the team the day before so we can film some of the victims preparing for the big day. Then we can travel down on the train with you.'

He chuckled. 'They're pulling my leg again in the studio, saying I can't wait to get back to Liverpool.'

'Tell them you've got good taste,' I laughed, 'and they don't know what they're missing.'

*   *   *

The next few weeks flew by and soon it was the

night before the big day. I had made arrangements for the film crew to visit just two victims, and had chosen Ethel and Sally because they were so natural in front of the cameras. I met up with Desmond, Mandy and the cameramen in Ethel's house, and words could not describe the look of happiness on her face as she sat and had her hair put in rollers. Her clothes were all laid out ready for next morning when her son, Jack, was coming in to help her. I doubted very much if she would get any sleep that night, her spirits were too high.

We went from Ethel's to Sally's where we were treated to a selection of her best jokes. I parted from the crew outside Sally's house as they were going to a hotel in Liverpool, while I was only a fifteen-minute drive from my home and family. We agreed to meet up at Lime Street station the next morning.

I made sure I got to the station early, as some people were coming by taxi and others were being brought by relatives or friends. A coach had been reserved for us on the train, and although the day was only starting we were all beginning to feel like royalty because the station staff were expecting us and we received the VIP treatment. Once we were in our seats, the film crew began recording all the interesting or humorous moments as the train carried us on our way. I had bought a huge greetings card to give to Moira Lister and her family, and on the journey took it around for everyone to sign. I had also bought two small vases as a thank-you gift.

When we arrived at Euston, a wheelchair was provided for Ethel to take her to the waiting coach. All the other passengers from the train stood watching as the cameras followed our progress from the station. The victims smiled, basking in the feeling that for one day in their lives they were important people

The drive through London was a treat in itself as many of the old people had never been to London before. We could hear those who had pointing out the sights to their neighbours. The roads were heavy with traffic and I knew Desmond was worried about the tight schedule so when we pulled up outside Moira Lister's house, I hopped off the coach first to gee people along and keep an eye on those who had trouble walking. The first one I helped off the coach was Fred Chapman, eighty-two years old, who had been mugged several times because he was such an easy target. As he stood on the pavement, the excitement got to him and he started to shake. He couldn't move for shaking, and I knew that until we could calm his nerves he wouldn't be able to walk. I called to Stasia to ask her to see everyone off the coach safely, then I took Fred's arm and soothed him.

'Take it easy, Fred,' I said softly, 'there's no hurry.'

After a minute he was able to walk slowly, although still shaking badly. The others had waited for us and stood back to allow me to walk him into Moira's hall where the actress was waiting to greet us. When Fred saw her, he got so excited we had to stop again to try and get his shaking under control. He was so embarrassed at Moira seeing him like that he began to cry and looked at her sadly as though apologizing.

Immediately she walked towards him with arms outstretched. Fred tried to talk to her, but not a word would come. Moira took hold of his hand and when I looked at her she was crying. I was having great difficulty in keeping my own tears in check, too. 'Don't cry, Moira,' I said, 'otherwise you'll start me off.'

'Oh, dear,' she said, 'I promised myself I wouldn't cry, and here I am crying with the first one.'

Fred would have been happy to stand there for ever gazing at the glamorous actress, but I was conscious of the need to keep to a timetable. 'Come along, Fred, let Moira say hello to all the other people.'

There was general confusion until we were seated around the five dining tables that were set out. Then I could hear gasps of admiration as everyone sat looking at the beautiful decorations and the glittering chandeliers, a sight they would never forget.

Moira Lister and her two daughters were beautiful with the peaches and cream complexion that most women envy. It wasn't only their looks I admired, though, it was their friendliness and compassion. They made my friends feel so welcome and at ease.

I could see Desmond looking at his watch, concern on his face. I knew we were running behind schedule because it had taken longer to get to the coach from the train than had been allowed for, but when you are with a group of elderly people, some of whom can only walk very slowly, it's difficult to time everything to the minute.

Moira disappeared into the kitchen with Christabel and a friend, while Chantal walked around the tables to see if everyone was happy and comfortable. That they were was quite evident from the looks on their faces and the light in their eyes. I nearly had the skirt pulled off me several times as a hand would seize it to bring something to my attention. There were nudges and whispers as my friends admired the beautifully laid tables, decorated with Christmas crackers and presents. Each table I stopped at had its own pet attraction. 'Have you seen the golden chairs, girl?' Or, 'Isn't that painting marvellous?' Or, 'I never thought I'd see anything like this in my life.'

Moira had cooked the meal herself, a chicken recipe of her own, and I helped her daughters and friend serve it. My heart warmed to our hostess as I saw her standing with a huge pan in front of her, a ladle in her hand, filling the plates that were passed to her. And after the excellent dinner came a delicious sweet followed by glasses of sherry.

The victims were revelling in it all and would have been happy to stay for ever. They were unaware that poor Desmond was nearly tearing his hair out with worry about a schedule gone completely haywire.

I tried to hurry things along when the meal was over and asked Sally and Fred to present Moira and her daughters with the thank-you card and the vases. There were tears in everyone's eyes as little Sally, four foot eight or thereabouts and without a tooth in her head, handed the card over and said in her quiet voice, 'This is from all of us to thank you for a lovely day.' I don't think Fred got a word out as he handed the vases over, he was too full up with emotion to speak.

Moira and her daughters were obviously touched by the appearance of the victims—their frailty and vulnerability. I had seen them so many times, and hundreds more like them, that I was used to it. What was making me tearful now was pride. I felt so proud of these old people who took one thing after another in their stride, able to cope with anything that came their way. Looking at them now, you would think they often spent a day in the home and company of a famous film star.

Some of them had eagerly opened their Christmas presents because there were few times in their life now that they received nice surprises. Most of them, though, were taking them home unopened so they had something left of the day to look forward to. I quickly explained that they must now move as fast as possible. A visit to the loo, don their coats and then make their way to the coach. Although this was done with as much speed as could be expected, we were running later than ever. Instead of making up some of the lost time we were actually losing more.

The London streets were heavy with traffic, and although the coach driver was urged to get to the theatre as quickly as possible, he would have needed wings to overtake the buses and cars that were forced to crawl along.

When we eventually arrived at the Adelphi Theatre the manager was there to greet us but had obviously been concerned about our late arrival. After a warm welcome to everyone, he led us down the aisle of the theatre as though we were VIPs. Our seats were near the front so that everyone would have a clear view of the stage. One whispered comment I heard was, 'Eh, did you see the price of these seats? They cost eight pounds fifty each.'

The recipient of this information gasped in disbelief. Eight pounds fifty pence was more than she received each week to pay her rent, gas, coal, clothing and food.

The lights went down, the orchestra started to play, and the curtains rose on the first scene of *My Fair Lady*. Suddenly a large cardboard box was placed on my knee and Moira Lister, who was sitting in front of me, turned and asked if I would distribute the boxes of chocolates that the box contained. More whispers from my party, then, 'I'm not opening mine, I'm saving it to show my neighbours.'

It was a marvellous show and I thoroughly enjoyed the singing, the beautiful costumes and the humour. Looking along the row I could see the expressions of wonder and happiness on the faces of my elderly friends. This day had to be the most memorable of their lives.

When the show was over, Tony Britton came to the front of the stage and explained that the television cameras had been filming the show for a BBC programme. He then explained about the victims and how they came to be there. He asked if the audience would stay in their seats for a while because the film crew had asked for an encore of laughter and applause, and he would be grateful if people would co-operate and stay in their seats for just a few extra minutes. Not one person moved, and we were treated to some jokes from Tony which summoned up the necessary mirth the film crew were looking for. From the response of the audience it seemed every person in that huge theatre wanted to be part of the experience and to show the victims a truly wonderful night.

Another surprise lay in store for them when a further container with twenty boxes of chocolates inside was put on my knee. Apparently someone, a man or a woman I would never know, had been deeply moved by the whole story of the victims and the kindness being shown by Moira Lister and family, Tony Britton and the theatre management and staff. So moved, they had ordered the chocolates to be sent over with their best wishes but no name.

I have to say that being a very emotional person, I had spent most of the day wanting to cry. I am not ashamed of the way I am; I had cried with the victims when they were in pain and suffering heartache, and now I was crying for the joy I could see on their faces. I thought the day couldn't have been more perfect, but I was wrong. We were told not to leave our seats until the rush of people leaving was over as we had been invited backstage where tea had been laid on for us. We walked in file behind Moira and her daughters, and there to greet us was Tony Britton and the star who had played Eliza Doolittle. I remember thinking that many faces wouldn't be washed for a few days after receiving a kiss from the very handsome Tony. He apologized for not being outside the theatre to greet us. He had waited twenty minutes then had to leave to dress for the show.

When Dame Anna Neagle came in there were gasps of admiration. She wore the beautiful gown she'd worn in the show and looked so lovely and regal I can only liken her to a Dresden doll. With Tony Britton, Dame Anna went around every victim to talk to them. Both were distressed by the stories they heard, and both offered to help in any way they could.

Another nice surprise, and an indication of how hard everyone had worked to make this day so perfect was when Alfred Doolittle, complete with binman's costume, came round and presented each visitor with a bunch of violets. He presented them so beautifully, bowing to each one as he passed the flowers over with a flourish. I looked across at Moira Lister and thought how generous she and her family were, and how hard they'd worked to organize a day such as this.

All good things must come to an end, unfortunately, and Desmond was concerned that we should get to the station in good time to catch the train. He didn't look as panic-stricken, though, now the day was drawing to a close and everything, apart from our being late at the theatre, had gone to plan. In fact Desmond has a ready smile, and it had been much in evidence since we had taken our seats and the show had begun. He knew it was safe to sit back and enjoy himself. As for the victims, they had enjoyed every minute since they were picked up that morning, and they didn't want the day to end. But what wonderful memories they would have.

'Come on, folks,' I said, 'we'll miss the train if we don't put a move on. And I don't fancy giving any of you a piggy-back all the way to Liverpool.'

Reluctantly, goodbyes were said and kisses exchanged before we left the theatre to join the coach waiting outside. Moira Lister had had to leave before we boarded the coach, and Christabel and her friend were the ones shaking hands with each person as they boarded the coach. The genuine gratitude of the victims was very moving, and Christabel was having problems trying to keep the tears back. Sally Wilson, who was last in the queue, was the final straw for both Christabel and myself. With her little hand-knitted woolly hat perched on the top of her head, she looked up at Christabel, took her hand, and said, 'Thank yer mam for me, will yer? It's been lovely.'

Wiping the tears away, Christabel asked, 'Can I adopt her?'

'Everyone wants to adopt Sally, I'm afraid,' I told her. 'I would love to adopt her myself.'

Finally seated, we all turned to wave to Christabel and her friend, and the camera crew who had been with us all day. They had finished with us now. Only Desmond and Mandy were left, and once we were on the train we would be on our own.

I walked to the back of the coach when we moved away from the theatre, and Desmond called me over. 'I don't know how you are going to get around this,' he said, 'but these were found under a seat in the theatre after the show was over.'

I opened the small square box he handed to me, and there, looking up at me it seemed, was a set of false teeth.

When I glanced at Desmond it was to see him shaking with laughter. 'It's going to be embarrassing for you having to ask who's lost their false teeth.'

'Not at all,' I told him, straightening the smile on my face. 'Watch this.'

I walked to the front of the coach, turned around, and in a loud voice called, 'Can I have your attention for a moment, folks? I want you all to give me a great big smile, then I'll tell you what it's

336

for.'

Walking the length of the coach, searching the faces to either side of the aisle, I couldn't see anyone looking any different from usual. There were some who never wore their false teeth, like Sally and Fred, and others who only wore them when they were going out. By the time I'd reached the back of the coach I was still none the wiser, and could see Desmond and Mandy convulsed with laughter. I turned again, and looking the length of the coach saw them all turned in my direction with curiosity written on their faces.

'I thought I could do this without embarrassing anyone,' I said, 'but you're such a crafty lot I can't keep up with you. Now,' I lifted the teeth out of the box with a hankie, 'who do these belong to?'

Laughter exploded and I saw that Scouse sense of humour living up to its reputation. Like myself they could see the funny side—a day out with film stars, treated like royalty by everyone, all wearing their best clothes and on their best behaviour, and someone loses their false teeth! It really was funny, but here was I with someone's teeth in my hand.

However, it seemed they didn't belong to anyone in our party because everyone denied ownership. And I knew it wasn't that they didn't like claiming the teeth because they weren't such snobs and certainly wouldn't lie to me. So the teeth I had in my hand belonged to a total stranger, and there was little I could do to find that person. I put the teeth back in the box and said to Desmond, 'Some poor soul will be looking for these.'

'They weren't found until after the theatre emptied,' he told me. 'The cleaners found them. There was plenty of time for the owner to miss them and make enquiries. They must have rolled to the front because they were under the seats our party sat in.'

'Well, I haven't time to do anything with them,' I told him, 'and I can't take them home with me.' So, without further ado, I put them on the luggage rack and joined in the laughter at the thought of the look on the face of the person who found them.

There was a mad scramble when we got to the station with Stasia and me seeing to those who couldn't board the train without assistance. And Desmond and Mandy, God love them, stayed and helped—and laughed—until the train pulled slowly out of the station. There were a few tears then as we waved to them through the window.

You would have thought the victims, aged seventy-eight to ninety, would have been dead tired after such a long and exciting day, but to hear them talking on the train journey home, it sounded as though they were just setting off. Stasia looked tired, I was absolutely worn out, but they seemed to have a lot of mileage left and I'm sure they could have gone through the whole experience again.

What a day it had been, though, and I mentally thanked everyone who had contributed to making it possible, particularly Moira Lister and her daughters, Chantal and Christabel. They had seen the victims in 'The Old Can't Run Fast Enough', heard their heartbreaking stories, and in their compassion had decided to help. I will never forget them for that.

A week later I received letters from Dame Anna Neagle and Tony Britton. Both contained cheques and both offered help any time I needed it.

'Wouldn't It Be Loverly' was screened on New

Year's Day, and my friends and I were able to relive that marvellous outing all over again. There was a very good response from people all over the country, and I had a particularly heavy mail for several weeks after it. I answered all the letters myself because I didn't want to send a standard letter to each writer. I believed that if a person had taken the trouble to write to me, then it should be no trouble to reply. I was very protective of Victims of Violence, determined that nothing should ever sully its name. It was my baby, and I watched over it like a mother hen.

CHAPTER SIXTEEN

1981

My two sisters and their husbands moved to Southport when they retired, and because we had always been a close family Tony and I decided to follow them and take my mother and father with us. My parents were getting on in years now, and because they had been wonderful to us, making our home one of love, warmth and laughter, there was no way I would move twenty miles away from them. They had given me a good life, and now, when they were in their late-eighties, I wanted to repay them for the love they'd given unstintingly through my whole life. My sisters said if we moved there, they would help care for our parents so I wouldn't have to stop my work with victims.

My sisters had been in Southport for only a few months when they rang to say they knew of a very nice house for sale, with large rooms and plenty of

339

space for Marsie and Pop—the pet names for our parents. We drove out to see the house and fell in love with it. So, our house went on the market and was snapped up by a friend in two days, and four weeks later we were scraping the paper off the walls in our new home. There was a niggling doubt in my mind because of the extra distance I would have to travel every day to the inner-city areas, but it was a small price to pay to be near the family.

We had been settled in the house for three months when I received a phone call one night from a probation officer called Bob Beckwith, to ask if I would be prepared to visit Hindley Borstal and talk to a group of boys there. I was stunned at first because I thought every probation officer on Merseyside, and beyond, knew my views on their lenient attitude towards offenders. 'Mr Beckwith, you do know what I think about probation officers,' I said.

'Yes, I know, Mrs Jonker, but I think the boys may be interested in what you have to say. We've tried everything else—let's try your way.'

'As long as you know what you're letting yourself in for,' I laughed. 'I see the victims of these boys, and so have strong views on the subject. And I don't water my views down for anyone. But if you think it will do any good, then I'll come.'

So I made arrangements to meet him one night the following week, in a pub car park about halfway between our homes. I would leave my car there and travel to Hindley Borstal in Bob Beckwith's.

I had no idea what he looked like, but he had said he would recognize me from the television programmes and the local papers. So on the night I sat in my car until he approached me. Bob

340

Beckwith was a middle-aged man, pipe-smoking and very comfortable to be with. As he drove, he told me that some of the parents of the boys in borstal couldn't care less what happened to them. It was his job, or part of it, to make sure the lads had somewhere to go when they were released from Hindley, but this was frequently made difficult by parents who wouldn't co-operate and were openly hostile. I found myself warming to him as I sympathized with the hopelessness he must feel at the lack of help given to him.

'What would you like me to talk about?' I asked.

'Just tell them about some of the victims you've met,' he told me.

'I'm afraid I can't talk about victims without saying what I think of the people who commit the crimes.' I knew this wouldn't go down well, but my feelings on crime and punishment were so strong I had no intention of watering them down. To me that would be making light of the sufferings of victims just to make life easy for the offenders. In other words, telling them what they wanted to hear. Well, that wasn't on as far as I was concerned. Being at the sharp end of crime, I knew that unless the offenders were punished, even shamed, for their crimes, then our society would become lawless. Already crime figures were rising rapidly, and would continue to do so while criminals knew they wouldn't be punished, no matter what they did. 'I'm sorry, Bob, but you've got your job and I've got mine. And that is to stop decent people becoming victims, and allowing them to walk the streets without fear.'

'Couldn't you, just this once, talk about victims without mentioning offenders?'

'I'm sorry,' I told him, 'I'm not made that way. I don't prepare beforehand what I'm going to talk about, I just open my mouth and out it comes. There is so much wrong in our society, so much injustice, I could go on talking for days without even thinking about it. It's because I've seen hundreds of innocent people suffering. You haven't.'

Bob was silent and I knew he wasn't happy about the prospect of me criticizing offenders inside a prison. It was also beginning to dawn on me that perhaps I had been unwise to accept the invitation. The alternative, which would please Bob and probably go down well with the inmates, was something I would not contemplate. I had never betrayed my principles to win popularity, and I wasn't going to start now.

I had never been in a prison before and was nervous as Bob parked his car outside the high walls. I knew Hindley Borstal was a maximum security unit and expected the necessary precautions we would encounter, such as the turning of large keys, the clanging of gates, the vetting by prison officers, the peepholes and the bolts on the doors being shot. What I had not expected was the pervasive air of gloom and cheerlessness. I could feel my spirits drooping as we walked along corridors between walls of a depressing colour from which the paint was peeling.

By the time we got to the room where I was to meet the boys, I had reached the conclusion I was completely crazy and asked myself how I'd come to let myself in for such a mad scheme.

'Would you like a cup of tea?' Bob asked, waving

me to a chair behind a table which faced a couple of rows of chairs.

'Please,' I answered, not knowing whether it was the cold, the atmosphere or my nerves that were making me shake.

'If you sit at that table, the boys will be coming in soon.'

Left alone in the room I glanced around, and was just thinking how sad it was for young people to be imprisoned in a place like this, when three boys came in. The first only looked about twelve years of age and this shocked me. Dear God, I thought, he's only a child.

He swaggered towards me. 'Who are you, missus?'

'Mind your own business,' I answered, not wanting to get involved in conversation with him.

'Come on, missus,' he insisted, 'who are yer?' He might only look twelve, but I knew he must be over sixteen to be in borstal.

'Mind your own business, love, and sit down,' I told him.

Other boys were drifting in and I could hear one saying, 'I bet she's a magistrate.'

One thought he knew the answer to finding out who I was. 'Who pays yer wages?'

'I don't get any wages,' I told him.

'Who pays yer, then?'

'No one pays me.' I knew this could go on for some time so I said, 'Look, Mr Beckwith will be here soon, and then you'll find out who I am.'

When Bob arrived with my tea there were twenty boys sitting in front of me. Handing me my cup, Bob introduced me to a gentleman who had come into the room with him. I was too nervous to take in his name, but he was a probation officer at the prison and was to sit in on my talk to the boys.

I warmed my hands around the cup and listened as Bob introduced me. Many of the lads had seen me on television so they knew of the work I was involved in. It was only then I realized I hadn't even thought about what I was going to say to them. I searched my mind for inspiration and suddenly remembered I had some of my photographs with me. Groping in my bag, I brought out the first one that came to hand. Looking down, I found it was of Sally.

'So I want you to listen to what Mrs Jonker has to say,' Bob Beckwith concluded, and took his seat beside me.

Twenty pair of eyes were fixed on me. I smiled and said, 'Hi.' Then, breathing deeply, I thought, Here goes!

'Before I start,' I said, 'I want you to know that I am just an ordinary working-class housewife, like your mam or your grandma. I have no qualifications or degrees. I was educated at the same sort of council school you were educated at. And now I am going to tell you a little story, a true one, and I want you to listen and tell me if I am wrong, or if I say anything that is not true.'

I looked around their faces and knew they were interested. Whether they would remain interested or whether what I had to say would alienate them, I had no way of knowing.

I held Sally's photograph up. Leaning forward, I moved my arm from side to side. 'Can you all see?' I asked.

'I'd break the feller's legs that did that.' This from a boy on one of the front seats.

'Precisely,' I said, making sure each lad could see the extent of Sally's injuries.

'That's bloody awful.' This from another boy.

'Well, my little story is about this lady,' I told them. 'Her name is Sally, she is eighty-nine years old, four foot eight in height, and weighs roughly six and a half stone. She lives in Kirkby—I bet some of you come from there.' I looked around to see several heads nodding.

'Don't forget to tell me if I go wrong, OK?' I knew I had their attention now, and as I looked at their young faces I also knew I wanted to get through to them.

'Sally had been to the shops one day,' I started, 'and on her way home, one of you—I don't know why you are in here, but you've all been bad so we'll pretend that one of you is the person who mugged Sally—one of you decided to steal her bag. Now Sally didn't want to let go of her bag, so she was pulled to the ground, dragged along, and these are the injuries she received. There was three pounds in Sally's bag, so you went to the pub that night with your mates and bought a few pints. Unfortunately, someone had seen you attacking Sally so the next morning a policeman knocks on your door. Now, this is where I want you to tell me if I go wrong—will you do that?'

They all said 'Yeh' in unison.

'From the time that policeman knocks on your door, you are entitled to legal aid, a probation officer, a social worker and a solicitor. And if you are found guilty we pay to keep you in here, and we pay the cost of the court case. Am I right so far?' I asked, and waited for their heads to nod before going on.

345

'Well, we'll go back to Sally now because she is still lying on the ground. You see, there is no help for Sally. That three pounds you stole was all the money she had for food and heating so she had to go cold and hungry until her next pension day. No probation officer or social worker came to see if she needed help because, you see, Sally has no rights.'

'That's not bloody right,' called one boy in anger.

'I know it's not bloody right,' I said, 'and Sally knows it's not bloody right. But unfortunately no one seems to care.'

From then on my heart was warmed by the gut reaction to the injustice of Sally's case that those boys showed. They all joined in, asking what they could do to change things. They even suggested signing a petition and sending it to the Government.

'What can you do?' one lad asked. 'One woman on her own can't do anything.'

'Well,' I told him, 'I have a big mouth, and if you joined me there would be two of us. Of course, there is another way to help,' I dared to say, 'and that is to stop mugging old ladies.'

There was a strong reaction to that—most of the boys called out that they didn't do such things.

'You probably know boys that do, though,' I said. 'You could try and stop them.'

The boys were allowed one cigarette at these weekly debates, and Bob Beckwith had warned me on the drive there that my audience would probably walk out once they were given that cigarette. He said it was only the cigarette that brought them, and I wasn't to be upset if they left

346

because that's what they did every week, regardless of who the speaker was.

As the cigarettes were being handed around, I realized I had quite enjoyed myself, and felt this hour had been more constructive than many of the meetings I had been invited to speak at. I enjoyed speaking and was always well received, but I was usually preaching to the converted. Here, it was different. I knew what I had said to the boys had made an impression, and although I was not naive enough to think I could convert them all, it would have been worth the effort if I had got through to just a couple.

Their cigarettes were lit now, and the boys were sitting forward, waiting for me to carry on. 'What I am going to say now will surprise you, but it is how I feel and I've always had the courage to stick by my convictions. So I have to say I have little respect for people who make excuses for criminals. It is rude of me, after Mr Beckwith was kind enough to invite me here, but I have to say that probation officers are generally among those people.'

There were loud laughs and sniggers from the boys, and I held my hand up, saying in a loud voice, 'Don't laugh! The only reason I say I have no respect for them is because they have made excuses for you, and to my mind there is no excuse for committing a crime.

'Just take a look at each other. You are all nice-looking boys and will one day marry and have children. Is this the society you want for your families? Where if you are strong and violent you survive, but if you are old or handicapped there is nothing for you? Is that really what you want—to live in a jungle?'

As I listened to the boys protesting that it wasn't what they wanted, I knew that my visit to this borstal was having an effect on my own feelings towards offenders. Was it their fault they were in here—or was it society's for not teaching them right from wrong? There were some boys in this group who would never be rehabilitated, and would spend their lives in and out of penal institutions—after all, there has always been a criminal element in our society, and always will be. But until the last few years, I had never before known anyone from the working class to steal from the working class. It just wasn't done. Surely, for those who could be rehabilitated, borstal was not the place to do it. People who break the law have got to be punished but, for certain crimes, I strongly believe physical punishment administered quickly and humanely, without a custodial sentence, would be more of a deterrent.

To those who say corporal punishment is barbaric and degrading, I would answer that it is not as degrading as sending someone to such a soul-destroying place as a borstal, where they are rubbing shoulders with hardened criminals who teach them the tricks of the trade, and are far more likely to re-offend when their sentence is served. A smack on the bottom is usually enough to teach a small child right from wrong—would it not have the same effect on a grown-up if the smack was harder? The cane was used in the school I went to, and when it was administered it had the effect it was meant to have—it deterred the offender from being naughty again. To my knowledge, none of the lads who went to the same school as me ended up becoming criminals. And to those who use the words barbaric and degrading when referring to punishment, I would ask is it not degrading for an elderly woman to be pushed to the ground and have her belongings stolen? Is it not barbaric for an elderly man who was once a proud, brave soldier to be reduced to being kicked by thugs because he is too old and frail to defend himself? Is it not degrading for a woman to be raped? Or the wife of a violent husband to be regularly beaten black and blue, in front of her crying children?

I shook my head to clear it of these thoughts, and looked at the boys facing me. Then I asked them a question that I knew I would get a straight answer to. 'What would you do if someone stole something belonging to you?'

One boy shouted, 'I'd beat him up.' Another said, 'I'd give him a bloody good hiding.'

'Belt him one,' came from another.

'Is that what you do in here if anyone steals from you? You punish them?'

The answer to that was a very definite 'Yes' from all of them.

When Bob said it was time to end the meeting it was obvious that the boys were as disappointed as I was. These youngsters could have been my own sons, except my children were brought up with love and taught right from wrong. Had these lads been brought up to respect other people and their property they wouldn't be in prison. So what had gone wrong? Was it parents who didn't care what they got up to as long as it didn't interfere with their own lives? Or was it the television shows that churned out scenes of sex and violence and bad language?

'Will you come again?' I was asked over and over

again by the boys surrounding the table. And when Mr Beckwith tried to get them to leave, they asked him, 'Can she come again?'

Finally the last one left and Bob came towards me, rubbing his hands. 'That was absolutely marvellous,' he told me. 'The boys have never sat all the way through a talk before. They usually get their cigarette then drift out one by one. They have never become involved before or joined in a discussion. They have all asked if you'll come back again, and one boy who is in here for bag snatching said as he was going out, "I'll have to stop doing that".'

'I've enjoyed myself, too,' I told him. 'I feel as though I haven't wasted my time.'

'Will you come back again?' he asked. 'Could I put your name down on the list of speakers?'

'I'm sorry, Bob, but I just don't have time. I spend my days visiting victims, contacting the necessary authorities for them, filling in criminal injuries compensation forms, and then I get dozens of requests to be a guest speaker. I hardly see anything of my husband and family, and it's not fair. I wouldn't mind coming back here for you, but not for anyone else.'

On the way home Bob was telling me how he would like to open a small factory to give some of the boys work when they came out of prison. He was convinced some of them would make good citizens if they had a job and could keep out of trouble. His idea was to open a workshop and employ six ex-offenders and six boys off the dole queue. He knew he could get hold of some machinery, but couldn't get the premises. As I listened, I thought that here was a good man. He was sincere, genuinely cared for the boys and wanted to help.

*   *   *

I was at this time liaising with three police divisions, and my days were hectic. Although my family tried to slow me down, it wasn't as easy as that. Once you start something, you can't just throw your hands in the air one day and say you've had enough. I might not have righted any of the wrongs in society, but I was certainly letting people know about those wrongs. The statistics were rising, the crimes becoming more violent, but it appeared that while I could see it and was concerned, those elected members of Parliament who asked for our vote so as to represent us, either didn't see or didn't want to. They promised the earth before an election, then you didn't see them until the next one came around. If it hadn't been for the support I was receiving from ordinary people, newspapers and radio, I would have given up long ago.

*   *   *

A few months after my visit to Hindley Borstal, I was invited back again. This time the appearance of the place wasn't such a shock and I wasn't alarmed by all the precautions before we were admitted. Bob Beckwith told me the meeting would be in another, larger room, and took me to it. Twenty boys were there and some of their faces were familiar. Once again the prison probation officer joined Bob and myself at the table.

The room was noisy and I could sense a difference in the atmosphere. Some of the boys were sitting with their feet propped up on tables and although I expected them to sit up properly when Mr Beckwith arrived, they didn't move. I couldn't put my finger on the reason why I was beginning to feel apprehensive, but there seemed to be tension in the air.

It was difficult to speak to the boys as freely as I had on my first visit because some of them had already heard what I did for victims and it took me a while to get into my stride. I was conscious all the time of an undercurrent, as though a plot had been hatched and the players were just waiting for their cue. Anticipating that something was about to happen, I started to study the boys in front of me. All of them were listening, but I could see many were ill at ease and avoided my eye. Then one boy started to stand out from the rest. He sat, chair tilted back, with his feet on the table and an insolent smirk on his face. Two others, both strangers to me, were sitting near him, grinning. These are the ones, I thought, and wondered what they had in store for me.

After I'd finished speaking, I didn't have long to wait before the ringleader proved my fears right. He was an attractive boy, slim, with fair hair and startling blue eyes. He lost no time, and showed no respect, in telling me that he couldn't care less about victims. If he wanted money—if his mates were going to the pub and he had no cash—then he would go out and steal it. With an arrogance I had never before seen in one so young, he said he was only interested in himself, and didn't care what happened to anyone else. 'I'll look after Number

One,' he said, pointing his finger at his chest. His two friends, while not as bold as him, joined in. It was obvious they were drawing courage from him, and also wanted to be as tough as him. They too said they would rob anyone if they wanted money.

By this time my nerves were completely shattered. Part of me wondered why the two probation officers allowed such a complete lack of respect to go unchecked, and the other part wondered how to cut this threesome down to size. For I had no intention of letting three hooligans get the better of me.

'You are so greedy,' I said, 'that you would go out and rob an old person of their pension just so you can go to the pub with your friends?'

'Well,' one sneered, 'you can't go to the pub without money.'

'You are very brave to rob old people,' I said. 'You must be very proud of yourself.'

'If I want money, then I'll get money.' The blond ringleader tipped his chair back. 'I'm only interested in Number One.'

I looked around at the other seventeen boys and saw most of them were sitting with their heads bowed as though they didn't want to get involved with the troublemakers. For their sake, and for my own pride, I had to take those three down a peg or two.

'You,' I said, pointing to the ringleader, 'with the big mouth. I've got a bigger mouth than you'll ever have, but the difference between me and you is that you're a loser.'

The chair banged on the floor as he suddenly righted it. The expression on his face told me he didn't like what I'd said one little bit. 'What d'you mean, I'm a loser?'

'You're in here, aren't you?' I was as angry as him now. 'I'm not. I can go home, but you can't. You will always be a loser, spending your life in and out of jail.' I could see the look of surprise on his face and the heads of other boys being lifted as they looked over to where he sat. I wanted to show them that the bully doesn't always win and I was now getting into my stride. 'Now, let's talk about Number One,' I said. 'You're going to be very clever and look after Number One.'

'I'll look after myself,' he growled. 'Nobody will ever get the better of me.'

'OK, Number One,' I said, my fists curled on the table in front of me. 'You will get married one day, I suppose, and then there will be two of you. Then you will probably have children, say one or two. That means we have Number One, Two, Three and Four.'

'I'll look after my family,' he said. 'Nobody will ever dare touch them.'

'Well, you are going to be a very busy person,' I told him. 'You will have to go to the shops with your wife, take your children to school, stay with them there, play with them, never let them out of your sight. Because the minute your wife and children go out on their own they stand the same chance as everyone else of being murdered, raped or mugged by someone just like Number One. There will always be thugs like you out there waiting to choose their victim. Don't ever forget that.'

I wasn't sorry when Bob said it was time to bring the meeting to a close. My nerves were thoroughly frayed. I had more than held my own with the three bully boys, but I didn't think it should have been necessary. Surely a prisoner should show respect for prison officers and visitors. I couldn't believe they were allowed to sit there, as bold as brass, and say they intended to commit more crimes when they were released. I thought the whole meeting had been a shambles, but was greatly cheered when some boys I had met on my last visit came over to talk to me. Most of them were ashamed that the meeting had been spoiled by the troublesome three and were at great pains to tell me they were in prison for fighting and not robbing elderly people. This was not strictly true as I knew a couple of them were in for bag snatching, but when they said they were never going to get into trouble again, I hoped that at least some of them meant it.

Even the ringleader, who for looks would be a son any mother would be proud of, came over to talk. But looking into his face I could see his blue eyes were as cold as steel, and would wager that here was a young man who would one day be a serious criminal.

*   *   *

I visited the courtrooms now and again, when I had time, and would spend an hour listening to how our justice system worked. I got to know many of the court clerks, and I was always made welcome by them. They heartily agreed with my outspoken views and told me of the lack of satisfaction they now found in their job. Many had worked there for years, and were disgusted at the way some young offenders swaggered in and out, grinning because they'd had a solicitor who got them off. They were noisy and showed a total lack of respect for the building itself, the clerks, and even the magistrates or judges.

One day I was so angry at the way a trial was being conducted, I almost walked out in disgust, having seen a solicitor continuously making excuses for the person he was representing. The youth sat there in court with a grin on his face the whole time while the solicitor came out with such lame excuses I could feel my blood boil. His client came from a bad home, the family were split up, he didn't get on with his mother, he was sorry about breaking into the old lady's house and he wouldn't do it again. All the same lame platitudes were trotted out and I wondered at the nerve of the man defending the young thug sitting with a smirk on his face. There was no one there to say how his elderly victim was—what effect the break-in had had on her. Whether the money he'd stolen was all she'd had to live on. It appeared so one-sided to me, I couldn't believe that the country I'd always been so proud of was allowing justice to be made a mockery of in this way.

I sighed with despair and hopelessness, and was about to leave the courtroom when I saw the solicitor turn and lift his thumb to his client, giving a broad wink. A signal of victory for the young thug, brought about by a solicitor being paid by legal aid. In other words, the taxpayers' money was keeping the young thief from being punished, and allowing him to sprawl on a chair in the courtroom, that sickening smirk on his face.

CHAPTER SEVENTEEN

When Bob Beckwith rang to invite me to Hindley for a third visit, I mentioned that I hadn't thought the last one went down very well. But he said, 'I thought it was a great success.'

'If that was a success, I would hate to see a failure.'

'It's not the three troublemakers you have to look at but the other seventeen boys. You got through to them, and that's the main thing. If you only get through to a couple, then it's well worth the effort.'

So, once again, I found myself at Hindley Borstal. But after settling down in front of the boys I knew from the atmosphere that this visit would be more fruitful. They were all polite, well-behaved lads, and seemed interested in my tales of the victims and my views. One boy's face was very familiar. He had been there on each of my three visits. As I no longer felt like a stranger in the borstal, I would talk to individual boys about their homes, their families, and their hopes. This particular boy, when I asked why he was still there, told me he was in for four years. He was the quiet, well-spoken sort, and I felt sorry for him because he didn't seem to belong there. When I asked Bob Beckwith about him, he said he came from a very good home and his parents were heartbroken. He had never been in trouble before and apparently insisted he wasn't guilty of the crime for which he had been imprisoned. I felt sorry for his parents, and thought what a sad old world it was.

On this occasion I spent some time talking to the boys about their idea of punishment. I told them if they were my boys I would give them a good hiding rather than see them in a place like Hindley. And they all said they would prefer the hiding.

'Forget I've come here to lecture you,' I said, 'pretend I'm your mam and tell me what your feelings are. Anything you want to get off your chest, you can tell me because I've got no axe to grind.'

I was told some very interesting things by these young boys who were, after all, only the product of a corrupt and greedy society. One young lad sounded dejected when he told me, 'I'm a better criminal now than when I came in here. I know how to enter a house without leaving any clues, how to disconnect a burglar alarm and not leave any fingerprints.'

This from a seventeen-year-old boy who wasn't bragging, merely telling me that being in prison wasn't a cure or a deterrent.

I started to talk about the elderly people I visited. Told the boys of their sense of humour, and the way they could still raise a laugh even when they were in pain after being attacked. How they'd had to struggle years ago when there was no money around. How many of them had lived through two world wars, and how neighbours used to help each other out. I told the boys they could learn from the experiences of the older generation. Many of the boys were from the Lancashire area and we appreciated each other's sense of humour. So I told them about an elderly lady who had been referred to me by the police. Her name was Kitty and she was ninety years of age, had no family and lived alone. She woke up one night to find three men in her bedroom going through her wardrobe and drawers. They didn't steal much, Kitty didn't have much to steal, just an electric kettle and toaster which she had recently bought from someone's catalogue and would have to carry on paying for even though she no longer had them.

'But those men terrified Kitty,' I told the boys. 'She was found wandering the streets in the middle of the night because she was too afraid to stay in her own house. When I called on her she was still crying and shaking with fear. Through her tears she told me of the fright she'd got when she opened her eyes and saw those three men in her bedroom . . .'

Every lad was hanging on to my words, and I prayed I was getting the picture through to them. 'I couldn't get her to stop crying, and feared Kitty would never again go to bed and sleep in peace. And as I had never left a victim without a smile on their face, even though they might have been in pain, I was determined to put one on Kitty's face. So, while I was sitting with my arm around her shoulders, I whispered in her ear, "You know, the one ambition in my life is to have two men in my bedroom. You have three and you're still moaning." It took a while for it to work, but my gamble paid off and Kitty eventually started to laugh. It was a tearful laugh, but a laugh nonetheless.'

The boys were laughing and guffawing. I could only hope that from then on they would start seeing elderly people not as a race apart, but as people they could respect and learn from—and enjoy the learning.

That visit to Hindley Borstal was to be my last

because I was getting involved in so many things I didn't know whether I was coming or going, and had to draw a line somewhere. I was trying to fit too many things into a day, not liking to refuse when I was asked to speak at a meeting and such like. And I was meeting more families of murder victims, which is really heart-breaking.

Murder is so final, there is nothing you can say to them to give them hope; no one can bring their loved one back. The best I could do was to listen to them, help them out financially where the organization could afford it, and cry with them. Murder was becoming commonplace now, with barely a day going by without my reading a report in the paper about some innocent person's life being taken. I really did despair, and wonder what was going to happen if the powers that be didn't bring in effective deterrents.

Then, one day, I was so sickened by an article in the paper about an elderly lady in the London area being murdered, I got really angry. It seemed the thugs weren't satisfied with killing her, they had jumped up and down on her body, breaking every single bone in her body and face. I was in tears as I read it. What a dreadful way for one so old to end her life, tortured and terrified. I was so angry I sent a telegram to Margaret Thatcher to say the Government was responsible for the murder as they were far too lenient with criminals.

I received a telegram in reply the next day. It merely said that she had passed my telegram to William Whitelaw, the then Home Secretary, to deal with. This made me even more angry because I knew nothing would come of it, and that old lady's murder was just another statistic to them. So

I sent off another telegram to Margaret Thatcher, saying she had wasted her time because William Whitelaw was totally ineffectual. Now I might have misquoted a word or two here because it is a long time ago, but I can assure you that somewhere in the bowels of a Government department my two telegrams are gathering dust. And when people ask me each year why I'm not in the New Year's honours list, I have to explain that criticizing any politician does not exactly make you popular.

*   *   *

I received a phone call early one evening from Peter Hodgson, a prison officer at Wymott Prison in Leyland, inviting me to visit the prison to talk to the officers. I accepted, as long as it was an afternoon visit and I could still ring the four police stations I was now receiving referrals from. Apart from that, I didn't like driving to a strange place in the dark because I'm notorious for getting lost. I have no sense of direction and usually manage to lose my bearings at least once a day. But Peter gave me very clear instructions on how to get there and I found myself driving into the prison car park having had a clear run. I was congratulating myself as I locked the car door and taking note of the well-kept grass verges around the very modern prison building.

I was met by Peter and taken on a guided tour. It was a far cry from what I imagined the older prisons to look like. We ended up in the dining room where the prisoners were queuing with their trays for what looked like a very appetizing meal. From there I was taken to meet some of the other officers, and it was then I found out the reason for my being invited. They wanted to know more about the work I was doing with victims, and to offer their help. We discussed several possibilities—decorating for elderly people, perhaps—and then I had an idea.

'It would be too far for you to travel to actively help the old people, but do the prisoners have a workshop where they make things?' I asked.

It was Peter who asked, 'What sort of things?'

'We have a Christmas party every year for about fifty people,' I told him, 'and I wondered if they could make things we could give as presents?'

The prison officers came up with several ideas, then Peter suddenly said, 'Why don't you hold a party here?'

I laughed. 'You're not serious, are you?'

'Why not? We could supply the food, the prisoners could serve at the tables, and we've got several lads who could put some entertainment on.'

At first the idea seemed crazy to me, but all the officers seemed eager and their enthusiasm was so infectious I began to see what a marvellous idea it was. The victims would have a good party without me having to worry, and it would do the prisoners good, perhaps, to see how old and frail the victims of crime were. It might just prick a few consciences.

I met the Governor before I left, and it was arranged that Peter would set the wheels in motion. I had to tell him how many people I would be taking and sort out a coach to bring them and take them back home again. As I drove away from the prison I was smiling at the idea of a Victims of Violence party in a prison. It had to be unique. Heaven knows what my elderly friends would think

362

of the idea.

As the time drew nearer, I made a list of people to ask, which wasn't easy when I'd met hundreds who would qualify for the party. I tried to be fair and choose those who had no family at all and would be alone over the Christmas holiday. I had also been offered twenty food hampers by a well-wisher, so that meant if I took fifty people to the party and gave out twenty hampers, I would be helping seventy old folk.

With that sorted out in my head, I set about visiting the fifty people on my party list. At every house where I called the reaction was the same. First a look of surprise and amazement. Then laughter because they thought I was pulling their leg. When they realized I was serious it was a case of, 'I'll go anywhere with you, Joan, even prison.'

During an interview with a reporter from a small local paper, I casually mentioned the party at Wymott Prison. Little did I know that when the article appeared it would bring so much interest from the media. National newspapers and television companies contacted me, and the Prison Governor was inundated with requests to allow reporters to attend the occasion. He must have rued the day he ever met me because of all the trouble he was put to in turning down requests as 'not in the best interests of the prisoners'.

The day arrived, and when people had settled down in their seats on the coach, I could hear laughter and jokes. 'Ay, they won't keep us in, will they?' This from Kitty. Then from Sally, 'I don't mind if they keep me in as long as the men are good-looking.' Aggie wanted to know, 'Will they frisk us before letting us in?'

Stasia was sitting next to me when the coach was waved through the prison gates. She turned to me and said, 'My God! The places you get me into.'

There were prison officers waiting to help the elderly off the coach, up the steps and along a corridor to the room where tables were all set out for the party. With balloons and decorations it looked very festive, and not a bit like a prison. As soon as everyone was seated some prisoners brought round a very welcome cup of tea, while one sat on the stage strumming a guitar and singing.

For a while the atmosphere was strained as the old folk were not sure if they should speak to the prisoners but when second cups of tea were offered, smiles began to appear. By the time the food was served the atmosphere was quite relaxed with the prisoners fussing over the victims, making sure they had plenty to eat, pulling crackers with them and laughing when paper hats were put on heads and fell down over their eyes. It was a warm and pleasant atmosphere.

When the meal was over and the tables cleared, the singing started. The prisoners on the stage were playing guitars and singing all the old songs. One woman, Nellie, asked if they could dance and I could see heads nodding as if to say they too would like to dance. Now it may seem odd that women of eighty-five should want to dance, but they have more energy and enthusiasm than I have. They can leave me standing.

I was watching them dance as I walked across the room to talk to the Governor and his wife, and the Chaplain, who had been going around making sure all the guests were enjoying themselves. We were laughing at their antics when the Governor said, 'Would you make sure they don't ask the prisoners to dance, Mrs Jonker? It's not allowed.'

I went round telling the ladies, but at one table an eighty-five-year-old said, 'Aren't you mean? I've got my eye on the one singing.'

I bent down to kiss her and said, 'Well, you'll just have to deny yourself the pleasure or we'll all be thrown out.'

Noticing one of the ladies looked distressed I went to see what was wrong and found she was feeling ill. The Governor's wife saw me helping her to the toilet and came over to offer assistance. After ten minutes, when the elderly lady was beginning to look and feel better, the Governor's wife suggested I should return to the others and she would stay with Mrs Watson until she was fit enough to go back to the festivities.

Thinking how kind everyone was, I made my way back to the party room. Long before I reached it I could hear the music and singing. It was so loud it sounded more like a pop concert for thousands than a small party for elderly people. As I pushed the door open I froze in my tracks, my smile fading. On the floor, dancing with the prisoners, were several of my charges, while on the stage, horror of horrors, were three more, arms around the men, singing with gusto at the top of their voices 'You'll Never Walk Alone'.

I didn't know whether to dash on to the floor and separate them, or jump on the stage, or just run away and hide. I looked over to see the Governor surveying the scene and ran across to him, gasping, 'I'm sorry. I did tell them, but you can see what's happened!'

Halfway through my apology I suddenly realised he was smiling. 'Don't worry, Mrs Jonker,' he said. 'It's all right. They're enjoying themselves.'

I knew it must have been a tense time for him and the prison officers, watching over the proceedings. It was the first time such a party had taken place and if anything had gone wrong, perhaps an unfortunate remark from one of the victims, there could have been trouble and the Governor would have had to take responsibility. But I had had no doubts that the party would be a success, because I knew my elderly charges would break down any barriers with their simple, straightforward friendliness. They had certainly won my love, respect and admiration.

The party had probably been good for both sides, and I think the Governor and officers were very pleased with the way it had gone. For me the best thing was that the prisoners could see first-hand the vulnerability of these victims as well as their courage and spirit.

Everyone had been given a free raffle ticket on arrival, and at the end of the party the draw was made. It turned out there was a prize for everyone, all donated by the officers, and the prisoners joined in the clapping and cheering as each person went up to receive a prize. When it was time to leave the Governor, officers and prisoners lined up to shake hands with the guests, pleased that they had enjoyed themselves. Everyone had worked hard to make the party a success, and I think we had all learned something from it.

On the way home I was walking down the aisle of the coach, chatting to everyone about how well the party had gone, when Sally waved me to come closer. 'I just want to tell you, girl, that I'm glad I got mugged because I wouldn't have met you otherwise. You've shown me more in life than I've ever seen before.'

The people in the seats in front and behind heard what Sally said, and they agreed and added their gratitude for what I had done for them. I could feel myself filling up, and sniffing the tears back, said, 'Don't be daft, it's been my pleasure. And don't forget, when you get a treat, I get one as well. So there's method in my madness.'

I hurried along the aisle to the seat next to Stasia. I was too full to speak. Those people didn't owe me a thing. I was part of a society that owed them the right to live in their homes and walk the streets in safety. It owed them the right to be able to keep themselves warm and well fed. Most of all it owed them the right to retain their dignity and pride.

* * *

I took it easy for the two days after the party, just visiting the new victims referred to me by the police. Then came the day when the twenty hampers had to be picked up and delivered to the homes of the victims on my list. I knew I would never be able to cope with delivering the heavy hampers on my own because many of the victims lived in flats up flights of stairs, so I contacted two men who were staunch supporters of VOV and they agreed to take seven each. I would only have six to deliver. When Christmas Eve dawned I thanked my lucky stars I'd been able to get help because it was cold, the wind was bitter, and to cap it all it started to snow.

The hampers I was delivering were all to addresses in the Toxteth area, and as I battled against the wind and snow to the block of flats where Maggie Matthews lived, I really didn't feel in the Christmas spirit. I staggered up the flight of concrete stairs, my fingers nearly dropping off with cold, and wondered what on earth was in the hampers to make them so heavy. I was relieved when the door was opened quickly and I was able to put the heavy box down on the table.

'Ah, you look blue with cold, girl,' Maggie said, 'and your clothes and hair are wet with the snow. You shouldn't have come out in this weather.'

'I haven't got many to do, Maggie, because I've got some friends helping me out.' I held my hands to the fire. 'I know I shouldn't do this 'cos I'll get chilblains, but, oh, it feels good.'

'I've got the kettle on, girl, so you can have a nice hot cup of tea.'

I was feeling in a much better frame of mind with a cup of tea in my hand. I could see Maggie eyeing the hamper and said, 'I'm a nosy beggar, Maggie, so open it up and let's see what's inside.'

The box was very thick cardboard and Maggie couldn't get it open. With the help of a large dangerous-looking knife, I went to work prising the lid up. Then I stepped back and watched as Maggie took the goodies out and put them on the table. Her eyes were like saucers because there was enough food in that hamper to last her a week. There was a decent-sized chicken, tin of ham, fruit, cakes, box of chocolates, potatoes, veg, biscuits, tins of fruit and a small Christmas cake. Seeing the pleasure on Maggie's thin, lined face, and knowing she wouldn't go short of food over the holiday, suddenly brought a glow to my whole heart and body. Knowing that another nineteen people were going to have the same expression on their face as they opened their hampers made me so happy I could have faced a blizzard, never mind a few snowflakes. But Maggie was so overcome she began to cry.

I put my arms around her and said, 'Don't start me off, Maggie, 'cos if I cry and then go out in the snow, the tears will become icicles. And the hampers were donated by a very kind businessman who I'm sure expected them to bring happiness, not tears. So give me a kiss before I go about my business, and promise me you'll have a nice Christmas and eat all that food in the hamper. I'll be in to see you after the holiday.' I got as far as the door, then turned with a smile on my face. 'Unless, of course, I get so drunk I'll have a hangover for a week. And you never know—stranger things have happened at sea.'

CHAPTER EIGHTEEN

1981

Sunday morning was always a lazy time when I looked forward to sitting with my husband and reading the papers, Tony one end of the dining table, me the other, and Philip sitting on an easy chair listening to the radio.

It was the hourly news bulletin that caught my attention. I lifted my head to listen. The newsreader was telling of an armed robbery at a building society in Southport on Saturday. Two members of staff had been badly injured and were in hospital. No names were given, of the victims or the building society.

'Did you hear that, love?' I asked. 'Armed robbers in Southport.'

Tony nodded. 'It surprises me because most building societies close at one o'clock on a Saturday, and the streets are crowded with shoppers. You wouldn't expect anyone to point a gun at the staff when there are hundreds of people passing the premises all the time.'

'I'll have to try and find out some details,' I said. 'But I can't ring the local police station because I don't have a referral arrangement with them. Even though they know me it would be more than they dare do to give out information. Besides, if the two women are seriously injured they wouldn't want me getting involved.'

So I heard nothing more about the incident until Thursday morning. I had just put the phone down after ringing the four police divisions I liaised with, and had made a note of the victims they'd referred to me. I was pushing my chair away from the table when the phone rang. The caller said she was a Sister at the local hospital and was ringing about a patient who was causing them some concern. It was one of the two women who were badly injured in the armed robbery at the building society, and she was so traumatized she wasn't responding to doctors or nursing staff. She was refusing to speak or even look at anybody. 'I have discussed this with my colleagues, and we wondered if you would come in and see her?' the Sister asked. 'We know of your work with victims of crime and thought you

370

may be able to get through to her. We really are most concerned about her.'

I glanced down at the list in my hand. Six victims across the city, plus travelling time. 'I'll certainly come in to see her, but I'm afraid it won't be before mid-afternoon as I have other calls I must make.'

'That's fine, Mrs Jonker. If you come straight to the office on the ground floor, I'll take you to see Mrs Roberts. Perhaps you'll have more success with her than we have.'

'I can but try, dear, so I'll see you about three o'clock.'

The first two calls were practically identical. The women, both in their late-seventies, had been coming back from the shops the day before when a youth pushed them to the ground and ran off with their bags. Fortunately, the ladies had their door keys in their pockets which saved them having to have the locks changed. But the thief had got away with what little money they had, sentimental items that they treasured, and their peace of mind.

The third call was also a bag snatch, but this time the victim was eighty-three and very small and frail. When the thug had pushed her to the ground two days before she'd fallen face forward and broken her wrist as well as receiving heavy bruising to her face. Although I'd seen thousands of elderly women who looked like her, it never ceased to sadden me. How I would like to shame the men who did this! For it wasn't only youths who were the culprits, many of the offences were committed by grown men.

The next two calls were to houses which had been burgled during the night when their elderly occupants were asleep. In both cases the victims

371

weren't hurt, but they were in their eighties, afraid and heartbroken because everything they'd had of any value had been stolen.

The last call was to a frail old lady who had allowed a man to enter her house when he said he was from the Water Board. Once in the house, the eighty-two-year-old lady was manhandled and forced into a chair while the imposter let his accomplice in. While one stood over the terrified woman, telling her if she didn't make a noise she wouldn't get hurt, his mate ransacked the house and they got away with her life savings plus trinkets and jewellery of great sentimental value. Once again I asked myself why our society was breeding cowards who wouldn't dare pick on anyone their own size. I didn't know how they could sleep at night.

*   *   *

It was exactly three o'clock when I parked the car in the hospital car park, locked the doors and made my way inside. I found the office of the Sister who had telephoned me, and soon I was walking down a corridor with her. 'I'll take you to the ward, Mrs Jonker, but don't be surprised if Mrs Roberts doesn't even acknowledge you. She hasn't spoken to anyone since she was admitted. All she does is stare into space.'

'Don't expect too much of me,' I warned as we turned into a ward. The Sister stopped at the second bed which had curtains drawn around it. Finding an opening in the curtain, she pushed me gently through, saying, 'A visitor for you, Mrs Roberts.' Then I was alone.

372

I was ill prepared for the sight that met my eyes. The young woman who was half sitting up with pillows behind her had had all her hair shaved off, and her head was covered with what looked like sticking up bits of black wire. I knew they were stitches—about a hundred of them—but was too shocked to think clearly. I took in the fact that she was a beautiful girl with fine features, at the same time noting the deep red angry mark around her neck. The mark was really deep, as though a noose had been tied around it and she'd been hung up, and she had lots of bruises and cuts also.

She didn't acknowledge my presence in any way—didn't move her eyes or head—just kept staring in front of her at the coloured curtain. I didn't know what to do. I stood there for several seconds in silence. It looked as though the person who'd caused these horrendous injuries had wanted to kill her. How must that feel to the victim? I looked at the chair at the side of the bed, and after breathing deeply and telling myself I wasn't doing any good standing there like a statue, sat down. 'I'm sorry I'm late coming,' I said, putting my bag down at the side of the chair, 'but I had half-a-dozen calls to do.'

There wasn't a flicker, not a sign that Mrs Roberts knew I was there. Her eyes never wavered. I was really struggling mentally to find the right words to catch her attention. I started talking and hoped for the best. 'I had six victims to call on today, all elderly people in their eighties, and all had been robbed and left terrified.' Still not a flicker from Mrs Roberts, but I carried on. 'I felt sorry for them all, but the last lady really got to me. Eighty-two she is, and a lovely, gentle, frail lady.

She let a man in who said he was from the Water Board. Once in, the bloke pushed her into a chair and frightened her into keeping quiet. He let another bloke in and he ransacked the house. They walked off with her life's savings and what bit of jewellery she had.'

It was then that Mrs Roberts turned her head. 'That's disgusting, that is, hurting and stealing from someone so old.'

And that is how the ice was broken and I got through to her. I asked her what her first name was because it sounded so formal calling her Mrs, and she told me it was Jean. After telling her briefly about the other victims, I said, 'Whoever did that to you, Jean, must have really intended to kill you.'

In a very quiet voice, she told me, 'He left me and the girl working with me for dead. We knew him, you see. He had to kill us so he wouldn't be caught.'

'How is the other girl?' I asked. 'Is she in this ward?'

Jean shook her head. 'No, apparently they didn't want us in the same ward. I think I heard it said that the police didn't want us together, but I could be mistaken because I don't know what's been going on.'

'So the police have caught the man?'

She nodded. 'They picked him up right away.'

I was afraid of asking too many questions in case she got upset. I kept my visit short. 'I'll come in and see you again, Jean. I don't want to tire you out or I'll have Sister on my back.' I bent to kiss her forehead. 'I'll see you soon.'

*   *   *

I intended to call at the hospital the following day to see Jean, but fate had other things in store for me. I had just come out of a house and was walking towards my car which was parked in a small lay-by a few yards away. As I put the key in the lock I looked around to check for suspicious characters hanging about, as I have done ever since being mugged. The only person I could see was an elderly lady crossing the road about twenty yards away. I could see the outline of a man behind her. A sudden movement caught my eye and I saw he had darted in front of the woman and was now practically on top of me. Another attacker, another attempt to steal my bag, another kick which sent me reeling into a wall and I felt myself falling, still holding on to the bag. Lying on the ground, I didn't have the strength to pull any more. After a few short tugs, the bag was torn from its handles and the youth ran away clutching it to his chest. Groaning with pain, I got to my feet. My side was sore where I'd been kicked, and my wrist felt as though it was broken.

The elderly lady was standing there like a statue, petrified with fright. She told me she'd thought it was a dog jumping on me and it was so quick she didn't realize what was happening. Not that she could have done anything to prevent it. The robber wanted my bag and no one was going to stop him. If she had been a man then the thief would perhaps not have taken the chance, but an elderly lady was no threat. She couldn't even tell me what the youth looked like, so there was no point in asking her to tell the police what she'd seen.

Half an hour later I was sitting in the police

station when a call came through from someone saying they had found a handbag. It turned out to be mine. Minus the money, of course. When describing my attacker to the police officer I mentioned that he looked neat and tidy, and that reminded me of the many times a victim has said to me, 'But he looked so respectable and well dressed.' Muggers can afford to be well dressed on other people's money.

*   *   *

Once again I had to ask Tony not to mention the incident to my family who would have insisted that the attack was to do with my outspokenness. I tried to make light of it in front of him but my whole body ached and my wrist was very painful. I was glad when it was time to go to bed, but it was a long time before I felt relaxed enough to sleep. I kept thinking of my attacker's leg, and how he'd raised it before kicking me. It was easy to see it wasn't the first time he'd done such a thing.

The next morning, Saturday, I was hoping for a lazy day to ease my aching bones as I didn't ring the police stations on a Saturday. But a call came from a police officer asking if I would visit an elderly couple, and although Tony said I was stupid to visit a victim so soon after being one myself, I felt I should go. I hadn't realized it would be agony changing gear with my sore wrist, though, and I groaned all the way to the victim's house.

Mr and Mrs Morris were an elderly couple living in a large old house which was well cared for on the outside and comfortable inside. I soon forgot my own troubles as they related their own terrifying experience. It wasn't the first time they'd been victims, but the night before was by far the worst. Because Mr Morris suffered badly from asthma, they occupied separate bedrooms so Mrs Morris could get some sleep. The night before my visit, Mr Morris had been woken by three masked men standing over his bed. As he struggled to sit up, they hit him over the head with a pitchfork, which they then held to his throat. His wife heard the noises, and thinking it was her husband calling to her, she rushed into his bedroom and became hysterical when she saw what was happening. Two of the men pushed her out of the room and back to her own, where they threatened her in an attempt to make her say where their money was kept. She was crying that they didn't have any money, and Mr Morris, hearing his wife's cries, tried to get up to help her, but was pushed down again with the pitchfork. It was only when the men threatened to use further violence on her husband that the terrified woman told them what they wanted to know. Having found the money, the men left the couple terrified and distressed.

'This house is far too big for you,' I said. 'Couldn't you move to a smaller one, where you'd be safer?'

'We've sold this one,' Mr Morris told me. 'We should have moved out last week but there was a hitch. We're going next week.'

'Do the people who have bought this house know what's happened?' I asked, thinking I wouldn't buy it for a big clock.

'Yes, they were here this morning. They said they have a big dog.' Mr Morris smiled. 'It's not a dog they want here—it's a bloody great lion.'

*   *   *

I hadn't told anyone about being mugged except Stasia until the following Wednesday when I had a phone call from Les Almond of the Men's Voluntary Service. He was talking about the increase in crime, and I mentioned casually what had happened to me. I thought nothing more of my conversation until the next morning when Val Woan from the *Echo* rang to ask how I was.

'I'm fine, Val, why do you ask?'

'I found a curious note on my desk this morning,' she told me. 'It says, "If they'll mug Joan Jonker, after all she does to help victims, then they'll mug anyone".'

I didn't answer, and after a few seconds Val asked, 'Have you been mugged?'

'Well, yes,' I admitted. 'It was last week, but I didn't want anyone to know because I haven't told my family. My mum and dad worry about me.'

'You can tell me,' she coaxed.

When I had given her all the details, I said, 'But I don't want you to report it, Val, for two reasons. First it would upset my family, and second it happens to so many people, why should I get publicity?'

'But it's news, Joan,' Val insisted, 'because of the work you do with victims.'

'It was just an incident, and I don't want you to report it,' I repeated.

'We'll see,' was all she would say. Then, half an hour later, she rang back.

'Sorry, Joan, but you're on the front page.'

'Oh, no!' I groaned.

378

The front page of the *Echo* that night carried a large photograph of mc underneath headlines which read: VICTIMS' CHAMPION MUGGED. I didn't even have time to read the article before the phone calls started. Members of my family, my friends and well-wishers. Most national newspapers carried the story the next day and I had calls from Lady Butlin, Desmond Lapsley and Geoffrey Levy of the *Daily Express*.

* * *

Our case files were growing daily and now numbered well over four thousand. I had filled in hundreds of claims for compensation for criminal injuries and represented victims many times at appeal hearings when I'd thought the offer they'd received didn't reflect their suffering. I'd always found the three board members who heard the cases friendly and fair. I'm happy to say I had never lost a case.

One day, however, I arrived at the court only to refuse to represent the person I had helped claim compensation.

It wasn't often I took a dislike to anyone, but this particular woman, Elsie Morrison, had rung mc one night and said she'd been attacked by a group of girls, had hurt her leg and now wasn't able to walk without an aid. The voice at the other end of the phone was slurred, and I had the feeling the person had been drinking. But it wasn't for me to judge so I arranged to meet her the next day at a certain time, at a destination in Liverpool. I arrived on time. The woman was waiting and hobbled towards the car. Her story was that she had always been lame in one leg and the girls who'd attacked her had been making fun of her before pushing her to the ground and hurting the leg she had a problem with.

I sat with her in the car and after asking Elsie Morrison all the details, filled in the form and told her I would send it off and the reply would come to Victims of Violence. I would contact her as soon as I heard anything, but warned it could take six to twelve months. That she was a bully was obvious for her voice was harsh and loud and every other word was a swear word. I was glad when she got out of the car and I was able to drive on to my next call. It was a few weeks later that I heard from her again. She rang one night about ten o'clock and asked if I would give her some money and she would pay it back out of the compensation money. She had obviously been drinking and her language was foul. I cut short the conversation and told her I didn't have any money, and even if I did I wouldn't lend it to her. I also asked her not to call my home again at that time of night, and said I would let her know when there was news from the CICB. I heard from her several times after that, and each time she was pleading poverty and complaining about not being able to walk without a stick. I had taken a real dislike to the woman and didn't trust her so I never entered into any conversation and was as brief as possible.

Then, after a few months, a letter came from the CICB turning down the application. I rang Elsie Morrison right away and arranged to meet her at the same place as last time so she could read the letter for herself. When she got into my car she was in a really bad temper, saying she was always picked on and made fun of because of her limp. 'You can appeal if you think you've been badly treated,' I said. 'All you have to do is write to the address on the letter and give your reasons for wanting to appeal.'

'I can't write proper, why can't you do it?' Here was a woman who obviously didn't know the meaning of the words 'please' or 'thank you'.

'Why can't you write?' I asked. 'You know your reasons for wanting to appeal, it would be better for you to put them down on paper than me.'

There was such a change in the woman's attitude then my mouth dropped in surprise. Gone was the loud, strident voice and in its place came a wheedling tone. 'I didn't go to school much, Joan, because the kids used to make fun of me game leg. They used to shout names after me and I'd end up crying and running home to me mam.'

For some reason I just could not believe a word this woman was saying, but it was more than I dare do to reveal to her my feelings. I didn't want her to go around telling people that Joan Jonker refused to help her. She was definitely the type to cause trouble if crossed.

'I'll appeal against the decision for you, but you'll have to convince the panel of judges you're entitled to compensation.'

She was all sweetness and light then. 'I'll treat yer when the money comes through.'

'You needn't bother,' I said, leaning across her and opening the car door. 'I don't get paid for what I do, nor do I let people treat me. Now I must leave you, I have a lot more calls to do. I'll call you when I hear any news.'

A few weeks later I had a letter from the CICB,

381

giving me a date for the appeal hearing. I passed the date on to Elsie Morrison and arranged to meet her in the Liverpool Crown Court building where the CICB held their hearings. I gave our names in to the clerk who sat outside the courtroom and he entered them on his list. Then I went to sit beside the woman I both disliked and distrusted. She was in a very good mood, sensing money which would no doubt be spent on drink. She never stopped talking about what she would say to the judges if they turned her down, and the more she spoke the more I could see the bully in her.

I could keep quiet no longer. 'I don't think you were attacked at all, were you?'

That took the smile off her face. 'What d'yer mean? Of course I was attacked, I told yer. A gang of girls was making fun of me and they were pushing me about and I fell over.'

I shook my head. 'No, Elsie, the truth is you'd been drinking and *you* picked a fight with the girls.' I had no idea what made me say that, I just knew she was lying. 'You started the fight and were crafty enough to report it to the police as an attack so you could claim.'

She looked around her to make sure no one could hear. 'Well, so what? It won't do you no harm if I get some money. After all, it's not coming out of your purse, why should you worry? And I've told yer, I'll treat yer out of the money.' Every other word was a swear word and I'd had enough.

'Excuse me a minute.' I stood up and walked over to the clerk. 'Would you tell the panel that I refuse to represent Miss Morrison, please? Make my apologies, but I can't on principle go ahead with it.'

He looked interested. 'Will you wait here while I have a word with them?' He was back in a matter of minutes to say the board members had said if that was how I felt then of course I shouldn't represent Miss Morrison. But they asked if I would be kind enough to sit in court while she gave her reasons for the appeal. I would not be required to speak. I agreed, of course.

There were very few words exchanged between myself and the so-called victim before we were called into court. One of the panel smiled and waved me to sit down. 'We would like you to stay, Mrs Jonker, but you won't be called upon to speak.'

I've heard some sob stories in my life, but the performance Elsie Morrison put on in that courtroom was worthy of an Oscar. She told how she'd been picked on since she was old enough to walk. Peg-leg Pete, she was called, and Hop-along Cassidy was another name shouted after her. And she even managed a catch in her voice when she described the dreadful life she'd led as a cripple taunted by everyone. As she pleaded for sympathy I was shaking my head and tutting. I could not see this rather large, tough lady allowing anyone to make fun of her. I bet she'd given more belts than she'd received.

When she had finished telling her tale in a whining voice, she was told to sit down while they decided what their verdict was. They didn't take long. The spokesman said that the panel was not quite satisfied with Miss Morrison's version of what happened when she was allegedly attacked and would therefore not find in her favour on that account. But because she had suffered through her lameness, they had decided to allow her the lowest compensation available, the sum of £200.

Now £200 to someone who liked her drink probably seemed a fortune and she was delighted. The member seated in the middle told her, 'Go to the gentleman at the desk outside and he will arrange payment for you. Mrs Jonker, we would like you to stay back for a few minutes.'

The four of us watched Elsie Morrison walking towards the door. I almost burst out laughing when halfway across the room she realized she was walking perfectly well, and suddenly developed a very decided limp. After all, she didn't have the money in her hand yet.

When the door closed I turned to face the three smiling board members. The end one said, 'So, you think we've been misled, Mrs Jonker?'

I nodded. 'You have been well and truly had, gentlemen. Every word out of her mouth was a lie. I have never trusted her, and while we were sitting outside I told her I didn't believe she'd been a victim at all, that she was probably the one who had attacked the girls. She admitted I was right, but asked why I should worry when it wasn't my money she was asking for. That did it for me, I couldn't be party to a lie. I'm sorry about that, gentlemen, and I apologize.'

The three men were laughing. 'Mrs Jonker,' the middle one said, 'you are like a breath of fresh air in this room and we admire your honesty. It's not often someone like you comes along. Most victims come to the appeal hearing with a solicitor whose job is to fight to get as much money as they can. We thank you, and wish you well in the fine work you do.'

I have never heard of, or set eyes on, Elsie Morrison since—nor do I wish to.

*   *   *

The Criminal Injuries Compensation Board has strict guidelines to follow, and I can understand that. But I don't always agree with them. For instance, a young man of twenty-five is attacked and has two front teeth knocked out. Now he will receive far more in compensation than a man of fifty would be offered. My argument at an appeal hearing into a case like this was that an attack on a fifty-year-old was in fact more serious because of his age. His physical and mental scars would take longer to heal—if they ever did. Fortunately I was able to put forward a good argument and the fifty-year-old in question was given an increased offer.

Where I do find the Board clearly at fault is in not providing enough compensation in the case of a murder victim. Grieving families are offered pathetically small amounts which don't even cover the cost of the funeral, and the bitter feeling that society has set a very low price on their loved one causes additional suffering.

One example of how an offer of compensation can bring extra heartache is the case of the two eleven-year-old boys who were murdered. Alma Miller rang me one day and I could hear the bitterness in her voice.

'My son's life was worth one hundred and eighty-four pounds,' she said. 'That's what I've been offered by the Criminal Injuries Board, and I've worked it out at thirty pounds a leg—'

I interrupted because I could tell she was at breaking point. 'Don't get distressed, Alma, we'll appeal against it.'

'I don't want their money. They can keep it if that's all they think my son's life was worth.'

Poor Alma, my heart went out to her. She had loved her son so much and was nearly out of her mind. He had been murdered and she would never see him again—it was all too much for her mind to cope with. And to be offered £184 in compensation for a young life was an insult, the last straw. 'We'll appeal, Alma,' I repeated. 'I'll call tomorrow and write a letter refusing the offer. Has Barbara been offered that too?'

'Yes, she feels the same,' Alma said, bitterly.

'Ask her to stay in tomorrow, I'll be there by ten o'clock. We can write down our reasons for refusing the offer and ask for an appeal hearing. I'll write the letter with you and post it in the nearest pillar box.'

After refusing the offer, we had to wait months before being given a date for the appeal hearing, but the day eventually arrived and, although the two husbands came along, it was only necessary for the two mothers to appear before the Tribunal. Alma went in first with me, so bitter and angry that she had every intention of telling them exactly what she thought, and asking how they would feel if it was their son who'd been murdered. But she was treated with such kindness and sympathy her anger disappeared. It was the first time anyone in authority had shown her this consideration and it knocked the fight out of her. A new offer of £680 was made, and although it was still unrealistic, the Board members went to great lengths to explain that they had to work within the guidelines and this was the most they could offer.

Barbara was offered the same amount for the loss of her son, but although, God knows, the two families needed the money, it was not that so much as justice they were after. The consideration finally shown to them by the board members meant a lot.

*   *   *

One day I had six victims to visit, one of them a ninety-five-year-old called Archibald (what a marvellous name!) who had been robbed by conmen. He turned out to be a marvellous person, too. He lived alone and was determined it was going to stay that way. A year previously his house had been decorated by a group of youths from one of the centres in the area. Being old, Archibald didn't have a clear idea of where the boys came from; he was just happy to have his home decorated. A few months later two youths conned their way into his house and stole his wallet. Naturally, Archibald didn't connect the robbery with the decorators, so, a few weeks later, when two youths called and told him they were part of the group who had decorated his house and were calling to see how he was, he let them in. Half an hour later they left with his new wallet. He couldn't tell the police where they were from because he didn't know. He was deeply confused.

The day before I had been given his name by the police, Archibald had been to the shops where he was approached by two young men. One had a little girl with him, and they chatted to the old man as if they knew him. An hour after he arrived home, he answered a knock on the door and it was the same two young men who said they'd called to see if he needed anything doing. They had been there about ten minutes when there was another knock at the door and one of the visitors jumped up to answer it. A third man walked in, walked straight over to Archibald's jacket which was on the back of a chair, put his hand in the pocket and drew out the wallet. Not a word was spoken as he walked out, wallet in hand, without either of the other two men making any effort to stop him. Archibald tried to go after him, but the other two men stood in his way. Pretending they didn't know the thief, they left the old man confused and distressed. It would seem that before the third man arrived on cue, the other two were to find out where he kept his wallet and pass the information on at the front door.

I rang the police station and asked the detective if they were aware of the connection between the decorators and the robberies. They said they were now, and that they were hoping to catch the culprits. I didn't make any further enquiries about the outcome because I felt that I shouldn't be involved with the apprehension or punishment of offenders. I did hope, however, that the culprits were caught, because to steal from someone of ninety-five is a despicable crime. To steal from someone of ninety-five four times goes beyond being cruel and heartless, it is a sign of someone with no capacity for kindness, compassion or respect. Because one thing Archibald did deserve was respect for having lived to such a good age. He'd fought in the First World War and was still able to cope in his own home. A man of pride and dignity. No thug should be allowed to spoil whatever time Archibald had left.

But to say this to them would only bring sneers. They wouldn't understand what being respectable was. Wouldn't understand that the people they were stealing from had worked all their lives while they, the scourge of our society, wouldn't know what an honest day's work was. The best way to punish such heartless cowards is to shame them in front of everybody else. Let them be known for what they are, and let them feel the anger and contempt of their friends and neighbours.

CHAPTER NINETEEN

1984

One of the most distressing things about visiting victims was having to leave them upset and afraid. If they lived alone with no one to talk to or sympathize with them, I always felt guilty as I walked down the path waving goodbye. I felt I shouldn't be leaving them and in the beginning I wanted to take them home with me. But I was now visiting so many I couldn't take them all home. I used to say to them, 'If I ever get enough money, I'll buy a big house and you can all live together.'

The years had gone by, but I often thought of that big house and wished I had the money to make it possible. Lady Butlin had kept up the donations that Sir William had started and the people of Merseyside were very generous in helping financially with all the schemes I had planned over the years, but, as soon as the money came in, it went out again. I believe that when someone donates money to help victims, it should be used to do just that and not left in the bank to gather interest or paid out in wages. I regularly gave donations to victims who were left penniless after a robbery, and twice a year for the past two years had taken a coachload on a five-day holiday to a small hotel in Blackpool. Even though it meant my being away from home for those five days, I felt it was worth it to see people enjoying themselves. So the dream I had of opening a house to give shelter to those afraid to stay in their own homes remained a dream. Until one Saturday morning when Tony and I were reading the papers.

He had his head bent over the national newspaper while I was reading a local one. I had read it from front to back while my husband was only halfway through his. So I began at the beginning again and slowly turned the pages, hoping to come across an article I had missed. As I turned one page I felt a quickening of interest. It was a full-page advertisement for an auction of houses in the Liverpool area. My eyes went straight away to two properties in Deane Road, a place I was familiar with. The houses there were terraced Victorian dwellings with a small garden in front. I had driven down the road many times and had noticed that while many of the properties looked neglected, these were the type of large houses that would be ideal for what I had in mind.

I didn't mention it to Tony because I knew he would be dead against it, thinking I was overdoing things as it was. But I made a note of the auctioneer's phone number, and also the solicitor's printed under the two houses in Deane Road which were to be auctioned the following week. And then

I had to contain my excitement over the weekend.

*   *   *

Monday morning saw me flying around as usual, making beds, dusting and preparing an evening meal. Then I rang the four police stations I dealt with and took down the details of my calls for the day. That done, I sat for a while by the telephone talking myself into phoning the auctioneer's. Finally, after taking a deep breath, I dialled the number. A man answered the phone. 'Good morning,' I said, 'I saw in the paper on Saturday that there were two houses in Deane Read being auctioned this week, and wondered if you could tell me what the reserve price is on those properties?'

'I couldn't tell you that!' The voice at the other end of the line sounded surprised. 'We don't give the reserve price out, that wouldn't make sense. If you're interested you'll have to come to the auction and see how the bidding goes.'

Feeling as stupid as the man probably thought I was, I thanked him and replaced the receiver. I sat still for several minutes, thought it over, then redialled the number. The same man answered the phone and before he had time to speak, I said, 'I just rang you regarding two houses in Deane Road which are up for auction this week. Before you say anything I'd be grateful if you would listen to what I have to say. Then, if you still feel you can't tell me the reserve price, I will understand. My name is Joan Jonker, Chairman of the Victims of Violence Organization, and my interest in one of those houses is to turn it into a shelter for elderly victims of crime. A place of safety for them to come to

391

after they've been robbed or mugged, where they could stay until they felt able to go back to their own home.'

The quiet voice at the other end of the line said, 'Mrs Jonker, the reserve price is eleven thousand pounds and we have not had this conversation.' With that, I heard him replace the receiver before I could thank him. Then, because I felt luck was on my side, I dialled the solicitor's number and told him the same story. He too was very kind, and said he would ring his client and try to arrange a meeting for me to view the houses.

'I would be grateful if you could do it this morning, as soon as possible,' I said, with my fingers crossed and hoping I wasn't pushing my luck. 'You see, I have several calls to make and I will be out of the house most of the day.'

'I will try and get back to you within the next ten minutes,' he said. 'If I don't, it will be because I haven't been able to contact my client.'

He rang me back. 'My client is a Mrs Coates, and she'll meet you at number sixteen Deane Road at ten o'clock tomorrow morning. I wish you the best of luck, Mrs Jonker.'

What I should have done then, of course, was ring the rest of the committee to tell them what I was up to. But I decided to wait until I had something more definite to tell them. After all, I might just be chasing a dream.

*   *   *

I pulled up outside sixteen Deane Road the following morning to see a woman about to put a key in the front door. I smiled at her as I walked up the path. 'Both on time!'

She smiled back, then seemed to narrow her eyes. 'Aren't you Joan Jonker?'

'Yes.' I nodded my head. 'And that is why I'm interested in the house—I would like it as a shelter for elderly victims.'

We were still standing on the top step when Mrs Coates said, 'Oh, I'd like you to have it. You're doing such marvellous work.' She pushed the front door open and I followed her into the hall.

'Mrs Coates, what I would like and what I can have are two different things. I'd love to have a house for the reason I've given you, but I must be honest with you and tell you we don't have that much money available and it may take some time to raise more.'

'I'll wait for it,' she said promptly. 'I really want you to have this house, and I'll drop the price five hundred pounds as my contribution to the charity.'

'You are very kind, and I appreciate it. But in all honesty I think you should let the auction go ahead and, if you can get your price for it, then let it go. It could take me a while to raise the money.'

She shook her head. 'No, the house will be taken out of the auction as soon as I can get to a phone. I want you to have it, and even if it takes two years for you to raise the money I am quite prepared to wait. But I have two houses in this road, would you like to see the other one before you make up your mind?'

'Of all the houses I've lived in, Mrs Coates, I've never bought one that didn't feel like home to me. You probably think I'm daft, but there are houses that make you feel welcome and others that you know would never feel like home. This one I know would be a lucky house for me and the victims who would come for shelter. But I believe you should give yourself time to think things through. You're putting a lot of faith in me, and I can't make any promises as to how long it will take.'

'I will wait as long as it takes.' She was very determined. 'Now come and look around the rooms and see what you think. It needs some work doing on it, but I'm sure you'd get plenty of help with that.'

It was a large double-fronted house with two sitting rooms, six bedrooms, a dining room, kitchen and bathroom. There was also a small stockroom on the ground floor which, in my mind, I earmarked for a downstairs toilet for those elderly people who would find difficulty in climbing the stairs. I had a good feeling about the house, which was light, airy and friendly, and knew in my heart that this was the place I'd been dreaming of for years.

After we had been right through the house, I promised Mrs Coates I would contact her as soon as I found out if the purchase was possible. Once again she repeated that she was willing to wait for as long as it took. All I had to do now was contact the committee. There was a spring in my step as I walked to my car. By hook or by crook the Victims of Violence organization would be the proud owners of that house, even if it meant me going round with the begging bowl.

I met up with three of our committee members two days later in Liverpool. I was expecting opposition because of the financial burden involved not only in buying the house but in its upkeep. But the opposition was not as strong as I'd expected; everyone seemed keen and excited about the idea. 'Where will the money come from?' asked Michael Bancroft, our accountant.

'If we can raise five thousand, I think Mrs Coates will wait for the rest. She said she's prepared to wait for as long as it takes.'

Jeanette, our treasurer, asked, 'How are we going to raise the money?'

'We'll have to work hard at it,' I said. 'It's something I've always wanted, a shelter for old people to stay in for a few days, or weeks, until they get over their distress and their homes are made safe.'

'You'll get it,' said George Downey. 'I've got every faith in you.'

'Not just me,' I told him, 'you'll all have to get stuck in.'

So it was agreed that we should put all our energy into raising the money to secure the first Victims of Violence Shelter in the country.

*　　　*　　　*

The next four months of my life were a nightmare. Although we didn't yet own the house Mrs Coates agreed we could start work on it straightaway, and I coaxed, pleaded and argued with workmen and authorities alike as I tried to have work done on the shelter free or at a reduced price. As with a lot of old houses, once you start doing work you find a lot more than you first thought. A group of boys from the Manpower Services Training Scheme came to do the decorating but found there was much more to it than just painting and papering walls. They were a great bunch and seemed to enjoy the work. Between visits to new victims each day I would call into the house and find them covered in dust and dirt as they ripped out old cupboards and fireplaces. I had hoped we could have the house open in two months but the festive season came and went, the house still looking as though a bomb had hit it.

I coaxed clubs to hold charity nights for us, and cajoled local singers and comedians into entertaining. I will never forget how generous they were with their time. The *Liverpool Echo* gave me plenty of publicity and money started to come in from all directions. On top of that, I spent every evening by the phone, ringing friends or writing to charitable trusts asking for donations. Jeanette and I had a list which we divided between us to share the work of writing letters. The money was coming in quite quickly, but instead of being able to bank it towards the £5,000 I had promised Mrs Coates, a lot of it was going on materials for repairs and modernization.

I would fall into bed every night, too tired to sleep, wondering if I wasn't being too ambitious and taking on more than I could reasonably cope with. But I've always had a stubborn streak, and was determined that the shelter would open and the £5,000 be paid come hell or high water. Gradually the money coming in overtook that being paid out, and the bank balance began to look healthy. Cheques were arriving from local organizations, and charity groups were having raffles, coffee mornings and jumble sales to raise cash. There was a great deal of interest in the project from press and radio, and many offers of support and help.

As the boys finished each room I could see it all taking shape, and mentally pictured how the finished house would look. Although I had enough on my plate, I realized I would have to start thinking about furniture sooner or later. All the bedrooms were decorated in bright sunny colours and curtains, all donated, hung at the windows.

By the end of January we had raised the £5,000 and had enough money left in the bank to finish all the jobs in the house except the fire prevention work which the City Planning Department had advised was necessary. We would have to worry about that when the house was opened. To do it now would mean months of delay. To raise the £5,000 plus had been hard going, and thanks must go to all the ordinary men and women who saw the need to help victims and gave so willingly and generously. Without them it could never have been done.

*   *   *

I was deluged with work when a researcher from Yorkshire Television rang me to say that Jimmy Young was doing a series of programmes for the network. Each of the six would deal with a topical subject, one of which was to be victims of violence. I was told they would like me to take three victims with me, but I asked some questions of my own before agreeing. One was about the length of the programme because it was a long trip to Leeds and I had to know whether it was worthwhile. I was so busy I couldn't afford to lose valuable time if it wasn't going to be a long programme, but I was promised that I would have time to air my views.

The series was due to start the following week and my subject was scheduled for one of the first two programmes. I was asked to find three victims, and the researcher told me I would be contacted when the date was definitely set.

Because it was mid-winter and the weather was cold I decided to ask three younger victims to come with me. Jean Roberts was my first choice because she was very articulate. I had kept up my visits to her while she was in hospital and after she was allowed home. The armed robbery had had a dreadful effect on her. She wouldn't allow anyone near her, and would crouch in a corner if there was a knock on the door. Even the window cleaner she'd had since she moved in wasn't allowed into the house. Her wounds had healed, the stitches been taken out of her head, and her hair had slowly grown back. But six months after the incident she was still too afraid to return to work. Her colleague hadn't been so badly injured, even though the armed robber thought he had left them both for dead, and was ready to go back to work in the building society. And the reason these two young women were put through such a terrifying ordeal is beyond belief.

The man who'd carried out the attack had opened an account in the building society the day before with £10. He told the manager that he had a very large sum of money coming to him in the near future and would deposit it in the building society. The manager suggested to the staff they should treat him with courtesy as he could become an important client. So when he put in an appearance on the Saturday morning the two women were polite and didn't question him when he took a seat and said he was waiting for someone. He was still sitting when it was time for the branch to close, but the women didn't pester him to leave. They were behind a safety door and had no idea they were in danger. Eventually, though, Jean's colleague Ann told him it was time to close the shop as it appeared his friend wasn't going to turn up. Then the man put on an act of feeling faint and asked for a glass of water. One woman got the glass of water, and her colleague opened the safety door just enough to allow her through, then closed it again. The woman left him with the glass then slipped back again behind the safety door. They were curious about why he was just sitting there, and also eager to get home. But while they cursed him silently for the inconvenience, they never for one second thought of him as anything other than a well-dressed, respectable customer.

After a further five minutes, however, the man must have sensed their impatience and walked to the side door, holding out the glass. The women exchanged glances. They had been warned never to open that door for anyone. But it was either open the door or insult the man by telling him to leave the glass on the chair or floor. So Jean opened the door slightly, just enough for her colleague to put her hand through the opening.

That was all the man needed. Before either woman could stop him, he'd pushed the door open and was standing with them behind the counters where he lost no time in closing the door again and drawing a gun from his pocket. That was when the nightmare began for the two women. He ordered them into the back so anybody glancing through the window wouldn't see what was going on. They

399

were put in separate rooms and had their hands tied behind their back. Neither knew what was happening to the other as the man with the gun walked between the two rooms, hitting them repeatedly with the gun. When he was out of the room, Jean wondered what was happening to her colleague—indeed, what was going to happen to both of them? The man was like someone demented, talking to himself as he walked back and forth, addressing them in words that made no sense. This went on for well over an hour, and as time passed the attacker became more agitated. Each woman felt at the back of her mind that he wouldn't let them live. Jean was lying on the floor, blood trickling down her face, beginning to drift in and out of consciousness. She saw in a daze that he had taken what looked like a piece of string from his pocket. She felt him putting it around her neck and pulling it tighter until in the end she couldn't breathe and blacked out.

In the other room, Ann stopped breathing when she heard his footsteps, and after listening for a while the man was satisfied she was dead and went back to where Jean was lying in a pool of blood. He stood over the body for a while, then, satisfied she too was dead, he went to finish what he'd set out to do, and that was steal whatever money was in the tills.

And the reason for this? He'd lied to his girlfriend about his job, telling her he earned far more than he did. She began to pester him for an engagement ring, wouldn't let up, so the Saturday before he'd taken her to a jeweller's in Lord Street where she had chosen an expensive ring. He asked the assistant to put it away for them until the following Saturday, even though he knew he had no way of getting the money. Then he thought up the idea of starting an account at this particular building society. It had all gone as planned. The two women were dead so they couldn't point the finger at him. He left the building society and walked along to the jeweller's where he'd arranged to meet his girlfriend, paying for the ring with the stolen money. But it wasn't long on her finger because Ann managed to crawl to where Jean was lying and raised the alarm. What kind of a man would cause such fear, pain and suffering, just to give his girlfriend a ring so she would think he was well-off?

So Jean was my first choice to come on the Jimmy Young programme, and my second was Karen, whose brother had been murdered eighteen months previously. Both were roughly the same age, attractive young women. At first they were nervous at the thought of appearing, and being asked to speak on television, but when I assured them they didn't have to speak if they didn't feel up to it, they both agreed to come with me. I decided to make no decision about the third guest until I knew the exact date of the programme.

When the researcher rang me the following week it was with the news that since I was concerned about the length of the programme they had decided to leave the subject of victims of violence until the end of the series when they were to have a couple of forty-five-minute slots. I assured him I had organized the victims and he promised that I would be given three weeks' notice of the programme date.

Work on the shelter was nearing completion now, and to hurry everyone along I chose a date for the opening: 29 February. We still had no furniture, and with twelve rooms to furnish that was a frightening thought. So I rang Billy Butler, a DJ on Radio Merseyside, and asked for his help. Would he ask his listeners if they had any spare furniture or anything else needed to make a house into a home? Billy, a very likeable and popular man, sounded so sincere that the next morning when he broadcast his appeal he had me looking around my own house for things to donate!

Three days after that I had had one hundred and thirty calls offering everything from three-piece suites and bedroom furniture down to glasses and cutlery. I could hardly cope with the number of offers, what with making notes of names and addresses and what they had to donate, and then arranging to have it collected. Within a week I had enough to completely furnish the house not only with necessities but with luxuries like a colour television, fridge-freezer, washing machine, cooker, vases, pictures, and stacks of bedding and crockery, right down to needles and thread. I was absolutely overwhelmed by the public's generosity and eagerness to help. When I rang Billy to tell him of the marvellous response, I said, 'The whole world must listen to your programme because they all rang me.' He was delighted, and the next morning I heard him say that once again the people of Merseyside had shown how kind and generous they were when asked to help.

With only a few days to go before the opening, I

literally had to push the boys out so that I could start sorting carpets. We had been given dozens, but as the rooms were all large I was afraid they wouldn't fit. I was keen for the house to be just right for the opening because I had invited so many important people. Lady Butlin was coming over from Jersey, the Lord Lieutenant, Wing Commander Sir Kenneth and Lady Stoddart, the Assistant Chief Constable and his wife, a representative from Social Services, and of course, most importantly, some victims. I'd die of humiliation if they arrived and the house wasn't ready.

I'd called at a house a few weeks before in answer to a phone call from a young woman who said she had plenty of time to spare and would like to help in the shelter. Her name was Rosemary, and she was an absolute angel during those last few weeks. She followed the workers around, brushing and scrubbing after them. I could never have managed without her. When she agreed to act as warden in the house until we got sorted out, I could have kissed her. There were small jobs to be finished off during the last week and, although we had sorted the furniture out for each room, we couldn't lay carpets while the workmen were still tramping through the house.

It was the Saturday before we were due to open that we were finally able to unroll the carpets and try them for size. I was so tired and worried, I thought I'd never smile again. Jeanette and her husband Tom were there to help, also Rosemary and Karen. And my beloved husband, of course. We managed to fit out all the bedrooms, and when we were finished we stood back to admire our handiwork. Now that the furniture was in, and frilly bedspreads arranged, the rooms looked bright and cosy. Earlier in the week Rosemary had cleaned all the windows, hung the curtains and even put pictures on the walls.

Satisfied that upstairs was ready, we trooped down for a warming cup of tea before tackling the downstairs rooms. It was freezing cold in the house with doors and windows open to dispel paint fumes, and we needed hot drinks to stop us from shivering. We split up then; Jeanette and her husband went to buy the floor covering for the kitchen, Tony started to lay a carpet in one of the sitting rooms, and Karen, Rosemary and I started in the other. We worked until three o'clock, tired, dirty and dishevelled. Jeanette and Tom had to leave then, but they had finished the kitchen and dining room and were pleased with themselves. The rest of us weren't so happy, though, because the two sitting rooms were big rooms and the carpets were small and only covered the centre. I was so disappointed I felt like crying.

'They don't look too bad,' Karen said, trying to cheer me up.

'They spoil the whole effect.' I refused to be comforted.

'Well, you can't do anything about it now,' Rosemary said. 'You'll have to leave everything until Monday.'

'If I had enough money on me I'd go out and buy a carpet, but I gave Jeanette nearly all the cash I had to buy covering for the kitchen and dining room.'

Karen looked at her watch. 'I'll have to go, Joan, 'cos I'm meeting Billy. Will you be all right? I don't like leaving you like this.'

'You go,' I told her. 'We won't stay long, 'cos there's not much more we can do.'

When Karen had left we surveyed the rooms again. I said, 'It's no good, I won't sleep tonight worrying about it. I wonder how much money I've got left?' A search revealed the grand total of £41. 'That's all I've got. Get your coat on, Rosemary, and we'll see what we can come up with.'

Tony measured one of the sitting rooms. 'It needs thirty square yards.' I knew my money wouldn't stretch to that, but after taking a deep breath, I said, 'Come on, Rosemary, there's no harm in trying.'

It was raining heavily as she hurried down the path after me. We got into the car and she asked, 'Where are we going?'

'There's a carpet shop in Townsend Lane that I pass nearly every day, I'll try there.'

When we reached the shop, Rosemary shook her head. 'You'll not get a carpet to fit that room for forty-one pounds.'

'Perhaps not, but at least I will have tried.' We walked into the shop and I smiled at the woman behind the counter as I handed her one of my visiting cards. 'Would you listen to a tale of woe, please?' She grinned and nodded, so I carried on. 'My name is Joan Jonker of the Victims of Violence Organization.' I explained briefly about the shelter being opened on Wednesday and how desperate we were to finish at least one room tonight. 'I want about thirty square yards of carpet, but I only have forty-one pounds on me. Would you let me walk out of the shop tonight with the carpet and trust me to bring the rest of the money on

405

Monday?'

There was sympathy and understanding in the woman's smile. 'I'll ask Mr Longstaff, he's in the back.' She took my card with her, leaving Rosemary looking at me in sheer disbelief. She'd heard me being bossy in the last few weeks, but this request was more than she'd thought even I had the nerve for. But I had helped at least seven thousand victims in my time, and that wouldn't have been possible if I'd been too proud to beg for help.

The assistant returned, smiling. 'Mr Longstaff said you can take the carpet with you and you can have it for forty-one pounds. That will be his contribution towards the shelter.'

After choosing a carpet with a beige background patterned with autumn-coloured flowers, I had to wait for it to be cut, and spent the time expressing my gratitude and pleasure. I was like a child with a new toy as the salesman carried the carpet out to my car. Thank goodness it was a hatchback or we would have had to wait until Monday to have it delivered, and that would have meant a weekend of worry for me.

Tony helped us carry the carpet up the path, then he worked like mad to fit and cut. It was finished by six o'clock and we stood there, tired and dirty, looking at a room which was completely transformed by the warm colours. How grateful I was to Mr Longstaff for his support and kindness.

*　　　*　　　*

I didn't go to the shelter on the Sunday because I was too tired to face any more work. But I rang Rosemary who had moved some of her own stuff in

406

and was living there now. The telephone had been installed free by British Telecom after I'd asked them for help. I had become good at asking people for something for nothing and, although I sometimes felt embarrassed, consoled myself with the thought that if I didn't, the shelter would never open.

Rosemary sounded bright and breezy over the phone, saying she was still washing and polishing. 'But, I've got to say, the hall and stairs look scruffy against that new carpet.'

This gave me food for thought. At nine o'clock on Monday morning I was on the phone to ask Mr Longstaff if he would send someone out to measure up the second sitting room, hall and stairs, and give me an estimate for carpeting them to match the one I'd got from him on the Saturday. I've never known anyone work so quickly. Monday afternoon saw the fitters leaving, having laid the new carpets. Mr Longstaff only charged me £130 for all the carpet plus fitting. He is just one of the many people I've had cause to be grateful to. My native city might not always have a good name but it's been proved to me thousands of times over that its people are the most generous and caring in the world.

Wednesday finally arrived and I met Lady Butlin at her hotel and took her across to Radio Merseyside for an interview. Afterwards George Downey drove us to the shelter. On the drive I was hoping that everything was ready for the arrival of the guests. I needn't have worried. Rosemary had everything under control and the house looked lovely. I was so happy I couldn't keep the smile off my face. Many of the guests had arrived, been

407

introduced to each other, and suddenly the house had that 'lived-in' feeling, with the sound of voices raised in conversation and laughter. I had invited a group of the boys who had worked on the house and also twelve elderly victims. They were very quiet at first, overawed by the sight of the Lord Lieutenant, and the Assistant Chief Constable in his very impressive uniform. On being introduced to Lady Butlin they didn't know whether to shake hands or curtsy, but she is so down to earth it wasn't long before they were chatting away with her.

I was dashing from one room to another making sure that everyone had something to eat and drink and no one was left out. I kept blessing Rosemary for the little touches that made the house look like a home. Books were arranged on bookshelves, ornaments graced the tops of tables, and there were flowers and plants everywhere. It was a source of amazement to everyone that, apart from the carpets, we hadn't had to buy anything. It had all been donated, even the glasses we were drinking from.

In the midst of all the excitement the media arrived in full force. A Granada TV crew came first, and while they were setting up cameras in one of the lounges the BBC crew arrived. I was trying to help them get organized, talking to reporters and feeling guilty about a journalist from Radio Merseyside who was waiting in the dining room for an interview. I would usually have been nervous being interviewed with so many people watching, but today I was on cloud nine—so happy and so proud that I forgot to worry. Everything had gone so smoothly, the shelter looked beautiful, and my dream had come true. I was in seventh heaven.

I had booked a dinner for eighteen of the guests at the Holiday Inn Hotel, paid for by one of my more affluent supporters. From there we went to Ernie Mack's Montrose Club to finish off a wonderful day by being entertained by singers and comedians who gave their services free.

It was now nine years since I'd knocked on the door of the first victim, and during that time there had been many proud moments, like when I won Merseysider of the Month and was presented with a huge ceramic cup and saucer by the Crown Foods Company. And then I was chosen as Merseysider of the Year, and presented with a tea service on a silver tray and £1,000 in cash. I kept the tea service as a memento, the money went to the charity. When the *Echo* asked its readers to nominate someone they thought should have been in the New Year's honours list, I was very proud to be nominated and have the medal, with my name on, in my bedroom drawer, nestling on a bed of silk in a velvet box.

There have been other nominations since for the people of Merseyside and the media have been good to me. It is they who helped me fulfil this dream, the opening of the first shelter in the country for victims of crime and violence.

CHAPTER TWENTY

The week after the shelter opened, one of the police referrals I received was to a woman whose bedroom had been set on fire by burglars. Her name was Martha, and she was seventy-five years of age. Her bedding, furniture and clothes were ruined, and the smell of burning made it impossible for her to stay in her flat. So she came to us until the council had repaired and redecorated her home. She was the first victim to make use of the shelter, and Rosemary looked after her so well Martha didn't want to go back to her flat when the work had been completed. But our committee members had ruled that the shelter was to be used only as a temporary refuge for those in desperate need. So Martha went back to her flat, but afterwards was a regular visitor to the shelter and would call in a few times a week for a cup of tea and a chat with Rosemary or myself, as I called in every day while out on my rounds.

Then one night I had a phone call from Ann West, very distressed because it had been reported in a newspaper that Lady Longford had joined forces with her husband in calling for the release of Myra Hindley. Ann wanted me to write to the Home Secretary, Leon Brittan, requesting a meeting, and asked if I would go along with her if he agreed.

'I'll write to him tonight,' I promised, 'and as soon as I get a reply I'll ring you.'

'I hope it's soon,' Ann said. 'I want to see him before Hindley's appeal goes before the Parole Board.'

I had just put the phone down when it rang again. It was the researcher from Yorkshire TV to say the programme on victims was scheduled for Saturday, only three days off. He asked if my three guests were ready, and I told him there was no problem there. Then I asked for further details on the format of the programme. There was to be an invited audience, Jimmy Young was the presenter, and on the platform would be Leon Brittan, the Home Secretary. As soon as I heard that, I remembered my conversation with Ann West just minutes before. She wanted an interview with the Home Secretary. Why not let it take place on television for the whole nation to hear?

'I've just been talking to Ann West,' I said. 'Could I bring her as one of my guests?'

'Ann West?' The researcher sounded puzzled.

'Her daughter was one of the Moors Murders victims.'

'Would she come?' he asked, becoming interested.

'I'll ask her and let you know. If she won't, then I'll get another victim.'

I rang Ann right away and explained the situation. She didn't hesitate. 'I'll come,' she said at once. 'Isn't it funny that it's worked out this way, almost as if fate had taken a hand?'

I rang the researcher back, and after telling him that Ann would come, asked if he would make sure she was given a chance to speak. He promised to do all he could.

I made arrangements with Jean and Karen to meet them at the station on the Saturday morning, having already asked Ann to join the train at Manchester. Everything went like clockwork and the four of us arrived at the studios in plenty of time. We were shown to the hospitality room, and it was as we were helping ourselves to some food that Ann leaned towards me and said, 'That's Jimmy Boyle. What's he doing here?' I followed her gaze and saw him sitting with a group of people and, like

411

her, wondered why he was there. It was supposed to be a programme about victims of violence. When I asked the researcher, I was told he was a member of the audience. I introduced my three friends, and briefly, with their help, told their stories. I asked if Ann was going to be allowed to speak to the Home Secretary and was promised she could.

Ann was clearly in a state; her face was white and she was trembling. 'I don't think I'll be able to speak,' she said, 'I'll be too nervous.'

'You'll be all right,' I assured her. 'Just tell him what you've told me about all your suffering over the years.'

'I don't think I can,' she whispered, 'I'll be too frightened.'

'You've told Jean and Karen how you feel,' I reminded her. 'What difference does it make telling the Home Secretary? And remember, you may never get a chance like this again.'

I tried to make it sound so ordinary, as if appearing on television and speaking to the Home Secretary was an everyday occurrence. How easy it was for me to talk. My young daughter, a mere child, hadn't been tortured and made to do terrible things before being brutally murdered by Hindley and Brady. I couldn't begin to know how Ann had suffered every day since Hindley had lured her little girl into the hands of not one but two evil, depraved monsters. I have always said that Hindley was the more evil of the two because no normal woman could bear to stand by and listen to a child crying for her mam while being subjected to the most horrific acts of degradation. Ann West had heard those tapes, heard her daughter's cry to be

412

allowed to go home, and her young voice pleading for them not to take her clothes off again. Ann had told me once that she would hear her cry until the day she died. In my opinion, Hindley and Brady should not have been allowed to live. And for those who would say I was inhuman and barbaric, I would answer that we all have a choice in life: to break the law or live within it. The victim isn't asked if they want to be raped, burgled, mugged or murdered, they have no choice. So any criminal who goes out with the intention of breaking the law should do so in the knowledge that they will be punished according to the seriousness of the crime they commit, whether it is greed for money, sexual satisfaction or political gain.

There was movement in the huge television studio now as we were all being transported to an old church a few miles away. If we were given a reason for this, I cannot remember what it was. When we arrived at the church, Ann and I were asked to sit at the far end of the front row of audience seats, while Jean and Karen, to their relief, were seated five rows back. There were two lots of six tiers with ten people in each tier. Jimmy Boyle was seated at the opposite end of the front row.

Jimmy Young introduced the programme, then Leon Brittan spoke for ten minutes, telling us of the Government's determination to punish offenders realistically and saying that plans were being made for more prisons.

Then Jimmy Boyle was asked to speak, and out came the phrases I had heard so many times over the years. We shouldn't put people in prison, he said, we should rehabilitate them. Like two other

413

people in the audience he was now working with ex-offenders, and the three of them thought they knew all the answers. Not a word about the increase in crime, not a word about the victims of it. I bet the word 'victim' never even entered their heads.

When asked about my work with victims, I told them of my first visit to Albert Smith and how he'd been left badly injured by an attack. Since then, I said, I had met and helped thousands of victims. None had been offered help by any authority, nor had they received justice.

Then Jimmy Young introduced Ann, and there was dead silence.

'Mr Brittan, my little girl was murdered by Ian Brady and Myra Hindley.' Her voice was so low that it was difficult to hear and the entire audience was leaning forward, straining to catch her words. 'I want to ask you, Mr Home Secretary . . .' Ann stopped, her voice too choked to carry on. I was holding her hand and could feel her trembling.

'I'll ask him for you,' I said, feeling a rush of pity for the woman who had suffered more than any mother should have to.

'No, let Ann ask him herself,' Jimmy Young said.

Ann's face was wet with tears as she swallowed and continued, 'I would like you to assure me, Mr Home Secretary, that Myra Hindley will never be paroled. I'm serving my life sentence—there's no parole for me. She has Lord Longford and Jimmy Boyle's wife to help her.' She glanced across to where Boyle sat. 'I have no one. I would like your assurance that she will never be released.'

There was absolute silence. The audience all seemed to have their head bowed. I think everyone was too overcome with emotion even to breathe.

Then Leon Brittan spoke, and the tone of his voice revealed that he too had been deeply affected. 'Mrs West, neither I nor my predecessors have yet done what you don't want us to do. That is the only answer I can give on a programme of this sort.'

I thought this answer to Ann's question was the best he could give, and I appreciated it. Ann nodded her head as though she too was satisfied.

The camera was now on Jimmy Young, and although he opened his mouth to speak, no words came out. He bowed his head for a few seconds and when he looked up I could see he too was deeply affected. He raised his hand saying, 'Sorry.' Then he carried on asking questions, but even the anti-punishment lobby was subdued. After witnessing Ann's heartbreaking suffering no one was in the mood for scoring points.

But Jimmy Boyle was speaking again, and I wondered how he had the nerve. He'd been serving a prison sentence when he was befriended by a prison visitor, a titled lady. They eventually married and now he seemed to think he was respectable and his crimes forgotten. I wondered if criminals ever gave any thought to their victims?

My own thoughts were interrupted when I heard Jimmy Boyle saying, 'Putting a person in prison only takes away their sense of responsibility.'

This was more than I could take. 'What a stupid thing to say!' I stood up and shouted. 'If they had any sense of responsibility they wouldn't be in prison in the first place.'

One woman there ran a home for ex-offenders, and she told the Home Secretary that if he would give them more money they could help more people. My God, I thought, I have to go round with a begging bowl to help the victims of these offenders she's talking about.

At the end of the programme Jimmy Young came over to kiss Ann and wish her well. I was told by the studio staff he had been even more deeply affected by her plea to Leon Brittan than we, or the viewers, suspected. After he left, I took Ann across to meet the Home Secretary. They spoke for a few minutes and I was touched by his obvious compassion. I could hear Jimmy Boyle and his cronies talking and laughing, and was stung into saying, 'I opened a shelter for victims of violence last week, Mr Brittan, and had to raise the money for it by donations from the public. While the likes of Jimmy Boyle can get money for hostels for offenders, there's nothing for the victims.' I didn't really expect an answer because I'd put him on the spot, but he nodded as though he understood and sympathized.

On the train journey home, Jean and Karen said how glad they were to have been seated so far back and not asked to speak. But they'd both been affected by Ann, and thought she'd been brave to speak out. Jean has two children, and said she didn't know what she'd do if one of them was murdered.

While the three women were talking, I was thinking that it had been another programme that produced no solutions. It had been very fair and completely unbiased, but it wouldn't change anything. Only those in power could do that, but they were still listening to the do-gooders who thought bad people could be turned good if you

416

were nice enough to them. Like a Good Samaritan who saw an old lady being mugged and started to run—only instead of running to the old lady, he ran after the offender to offer him help. These totally misguided people are in the minority, but they have had the ear of successive Governments. They haven't a clue what life is like outside their own little world, but think they know it all. And, unfortunately, we are all suffering for it. There are even some judges and magistrates who turn on its head the old maxim 'crime doesn't pay', by dishing out sentences that are neither just nor a deterrent.

For instance a twenty-one-year-old man convicted of a horrific sexual assault on a two-year-old child was given a twelve-month suspended sentence. The judge said he had already served the equivalent of six months in custody, and the victim, the judge had been told, would suffer no long-term physical or mental consequences. After saying that, he went on to add that the offender needed help. 'I accept in your favour that this was a momentary impulse and completely out of character, but it remains a horrific offence.'

So 'horrific' did the judge consider the offence to be that he let that man walk free from the court. The little girl had been left bleeding profusely and needed an operation to stitch her wounds—who, in God's name, was qualified to say she would suffer no long-term physical or mental consequences? Who was able to guarantee that she wouldn't suffer nightmares for the rest of her life, or that she would ever trust a man again? I have known similar cases where a sexual assault on a child has ruined their lives. Even when that child became a woman, in many cases she never enjoyed a normal, happy

417

sex-life with the man she married.

A prime example of the sentence being no more severe no matter how many crimes were committed was that of Edie Booker. She lived alone, and one night woke to find three men at the side of her bed. One of them had a stout piece of wood in his hand, and Edie was beaten with the stick as she lay there terrified and unable to move.

When the men finally left with all her money and jewellery, Edie rang the police. Within half an hour the thieves were picked up. I kept in touch with Edie, and through her found out that the offenders were due in court on a certain day. Fortunately there was no need for the victim to attend, the police had told her, and this was a relief as Edie dreaded the prospect. I asked her to ring me if she was told how the court case went. It was a few days after the trial that she did, and then I was as angry as she. The oldest of the men charged was twenty-three, and he was up on forty-three charges. His sentence was three years' imprisonment. With good behaviour and a sympathetic probation officer to appeal on his behalf, he would probably be paroled in half that time. His sentence would be over well before Edie's who would never forget that night of horror.

Such a lenient sentence cannot begin to reflect the misery and suffering of forty-three innocent victims, and if he took money and valuables from each house he burgled he would have lived well by his activities. Was a short stay in prison, with no money worries and three good square meals a day, going to deter him from committing further offences when he was freed? Is there such a thing as justice?

I was dashing out one Friday morning, got as far as the front door and the phone rang. I was in two minds as to whether to answer it then thought I'd better as it might be important. So with my bag under my arm, and keys to the house and car in my hand, I hurried back to the dining room. The caller introduced himself as George Howarth, a councillor and magistrate from Knowsley. He said there was a conference the following day at Manchester University, and as they had been let down at the last minute by one of the speakers, he would be very grateful if I would stand in for her. I grinned, wondering if he realized what a back-handed compliment he was paying me. I declined the honour, saying I didn't see much of my family and Saturday was one day I liked to keep free.

'You would be doing us a great favour, Mrs Jonker, and as you would be our first speaker you could be away in an hour, I promise you.'

'Mr Howarth, I would never find Manchester University, I'm notorious for getting lost. Is there no one else you can ask?'

'I'm working today so I don't have much opportunity.' He again coaxed, 'I would meet you somewhere and you could follow my car. Please, be a gem and help me out.'

Calling myself a sucker for punishment, I began to give in. 'As long as I'm only there for an hour then I'll come. But where shall I meet you, and what is the conference about?'

'I'll fill you in on all the details when I meet you.'

Mr Howarth then went on to describe in detail where I should come off the motorway and where we could meet on the outskirts of Manchester. I was scribbling down the instructions as he spoke, and as they sounded fairly easy to follow I promised to meet him at eight-thirty the following morning and bade him good day. Then it was a rush for me to make up for lost time on a day when I had the names of five victims to visit.

*　　　*　　　*

Saturday morning at 7.30 the sun was already shining and I was happy as I drove along the motorway. I took the exit I had written down, came to the large island Mr Howarth had told me of, and thinking how clever I was to have come so far with no problems, drove around the island and came off at the third turning. I expected to see a green car waiting twenty yards past the island, but didn't worry when there was no sign of it. I was early and he'd be along any minute. But after ten minutes I began to feel uneasy because I was supposed to be the first speaker at nine o'clock and still had no idea what this conference was about. Another five minutes passed and I was concerned enough to stop a man and ask if I was on the right road for Manchester University. He shook his head and told me I'd have to go back to the island and come off at the second exit, which was the main road in to Manchester.

I did as the man directed and was surprised by the number of vehicles on the road. So after driving for ten minutes at quite a slow rate, I decided to turn off to my left and ask for help. I did this three times, each time coming on to a one-way system where it was impossible to stop and ask for directions. By this time I was a nervous wreck. I should have been on the platform at the conference, and my mouth was dry as I began to panic. I thought about giving up and going home, but decided that even if I was late, I'd let them see I had made the effort. I drew up at a set of lights which were on red, and noticed a bread van pull up beside me. I wound my window down and waved to attract the attention of the woman passenger in the van. When she turned to me I said quickly, 'Can you help me, please? I've been lost for an hour, haven't a clue where I am, and I should have been at the University an hour ago.'

The lights turned to green and the woman, after a few words with the driver, said, 'Follow us, we'll take you there.'

So it was, I arrived at the hall over half an hour late, a nervous wreck and dying for a drink. However, when I pushed open the door and entered the foyer, I was immediately approached by five or six men. 'Who is the man with the green car who was supposed to meet me?' I asked.

Instead of an answer, I felt my elbow being cupped and was shepherded through double doors into a large hall. 'Will you go straight on to the platform, Mrs Jonker? We had to put another speaker on at nine o'clock when you didn't turn up.'

I tried to pull my arm free. 'I can't go straight on to the platform, my mouth is dry and I need a drink.'

'As soon as you've finished speaking there'll be a drink ready for you.' As I had never met George

Howarth, I didn't know if it was he who marched me down the aisle to steps at the bottom of the platform, and then gently but firmly pushed me up them before walking back down the aisle. I stood at one end of the very large stage, feeling bewildered. I could see a man seated at a table at the far end, his head bent over a stack of papers, so I made my way towards him. He looked up briefly and handed me a microphone. 'We're running very late, Mrs Jonker, so if you can start.'

With the microphone in my hand, I looked down at his bowed head then turned my eyes to the audience. There were four hundred people there, all gazing up at me, and I hadn't a clue what I was supposed to be doing here. Then my apprehension gave way to anger. This was ridiculous! I faced the audience, and with the microphone close to my mouth, I said, 'Blow this for a joke! I've been lost for an hour in Manchester, and a bread van brought me here. My mouth is dry, I'd like a drink, and I need to go to the toilet.'

Laughter erupted in the hall and I could see smiles on all the faces. 'And that's not all,' I told them, 'I haven't a clue who you are or what I'm supposed to be talking about.'

The man at the table raised his head. 'They're magistrates, Mrs Jonker, and we would like you to talk for half an hour.'

I wasn't a bit happy with the situation and wasn't about to let him off lightly. 'Tell me when you've had enough then, because I can go on for twenty-four hours.'

There was more laughter in the hall and I could imagine the audience thinking they were in for some fun—some light relief. How wrong they were.

I had been complaining for years about judges and magistrates being too lenient with offenders. Well, now I had the chance to tell them about the victims. 'So, you're magistrates, eh? Well, perhaps you can answer a few questions for me. For instance, how dare you pass sentence on an offender when you have no idea of the dreadful consequences of his or her crime?' There were no smiles on the faces now, but I was more interested in justice than in being popular. 'You don't see the old lady, or old man, who has been beaten and robbed of what little money they have. You don't see them cower when a knock comes on the door, or sitting with no fire in the grate because some thug has taken all their money and they have no one to turn to. You don't see their sadness at the loss of their dignity and pride. And until you see this, how can you possibly know what punishment should be meted out to the offender who stands before you, all neat and tidy and looking as though butter wouldn't melt in his mouth? With the right solicitor or probation officer to plead his case, you will probably let him off lightly. If only it was the same for the victims! If there was someone to plead their case then the scales of justice might be even. Unfortunately, victims don't have that luxury.'

There was absolute silence in the hall and I could see the set expressions of those in the audience. But so far no one had interrupted, and at least I was getting off my chest all the anger, sadness and frustration that had built up over the last nine years. 'When you have an offender before you, and a report from either the probation service or a solicitor, giving excuses and promising the offender will in future stay on the straight and

423

narrow, before you pass sentence demand to have a report on the victim of his crime and how they have been affected. I have seen thousands of victims, with black eyes, broken bones and broken spirits, and I wonder what is happening to our society. And as a mother and grandmother, I know that if a child isn't punished when it does wrong then they will think it's all right to be naughty. That, I believe, is only common sense. If we carry on being so lenient with wrongdoers, then in a few years we will have a lawless society where elderly people will have to live behind high walls to be protected from the thugs.'

I thought I had said all I could say without repeating myself. And whatever the views of the magistrates, I wouldn't take a word back. Turning to the man in the chair, I said, 'I think my time is up. And I'm dying for a cup of tea.'

The applause from the audience started off quietly, then suddenly all the magistrates were on their feet. One man held a ten-pound note high and said, 'Mrs Jonker is like a breath of fresh air in this room, and I would like her to put this towards her funds.'

Then a woman stood up and also waved a ten-pound note. 'She is saying what we all know is right but haven't the guts to say. I'll match his donation.'

George Howarth came on to the stage, introduced himself formally and took my arm. 'Come and have a drink now, Mrs Jonker, there's refreshments being served.'

But so many of the magistrates had gathered around me, asking questions and saying how their hands were tied when it came to sentencing, that it was fifteen minutes before I was being led towards some double doors. Standing in the middle, hands on hips, was the Chief Constable, Kenneth Oxford. 'Well, I've heard you speaking many times before, Joan, but today you surpassed yourself.'

I grinned. 'Ah, well, you see, Joan got herself in a temper this morning.'

'Unfortunately for me,' Mr Oxford said, 'I have to follow you, and that's not going to be easy. I think I'll head for home.'

'Well, I won't be here to hear what you have to say because I promised my husband I'd be home to make the dinner. So, after a much-needed drink, I'm off.'

'I'm afraid you won't be able to go for a while, Mrs Jonker,' George Howarth said. 'You see, they've had a collection and you'll have to stay until it's counted and checked.'

'In that case, Mr Oxford, I'll stay and listen to you. In fact, I'll sit on the front row and cheer you on.'

An hour later I was presented with the grand sum of £1,000—the money donated by the magistrates. I was so grateful for it and for the warm reception given to me, I asked and received permission to interrupt the speaker for a moment to thank everyone for their courtesy, friendliness and generosity.

CHAPTER TWENTY-ONE

In the months following the opening of the shelter, life was becoming more hectic each day. People were ringing to ask if an elderly neighbour could come to us because she or he was terrified after a robbery, and the house was always busy. Rosemary was brilliant. She seemed to spend her life making cups of tea and hugging people, and always with a smile on her face. I couldn't spend much time there as I had too many calls each day so a neighbour of Rosemary's offered to work as a volunteer. Her name was Pauline, and like Rosemary she was marvellous with the elderly people. I had good reason to be grateful to them because I was rushed off my feet.

So on the day I received a letter from Merseyside Police Headquarters saying they had received notice from the Government that in future every victim of crime must receive a visit, regardless of the type of crime, I shook my head in disbelief. What the government minister was asking was impossible. There were tens of thousands of crimes committed across the country every single day, some petty, some serious. There was no way I could visit every victim in the four areas where I liaised with the police. The way it worked now, with the police referring only those they thought most in need of help, was sensible and practical. This latest ruling was typical of some faceless person sitting in a comfortable government office who hadn't a clue what life was really like. And I bet he wouldn't get off his chair in that comfortable office and try visiting a victim himself, either! Words are cheap, particularly when you have no idea what you're talking about.

I put the letter down on the table. I thought I was doing a good job, and wasn't going to change the way I worked for someone who had nothing

426

better to do than come up with such a hare-brained scheme. So without further ado I took out one of our headed sheets and began to write. When the letter was finished, I addressed the envelope to the Chief Constable. The contents were brief. I told him it was an impossible task to visit every single victim, and if I couldn't do a worthwhile job then, although reluctant to do so, I would rather relinquish the referral system I had with the four police divisions. But I reserved the right to visit any victim, in any area of Merseyside, if asked to do so by a victim or a member of their family.

I knew I would still be run off my feet visiting because I was so well known everyone associated me with victims. The only thing which bothered me was that the police referrals would now be passed over to one of the nationwide government-funded organizations which operated in the areas of Merseyside I didn't cover. Never once had I heard them raise their voices in anger at the way victims were treated. I reckon they were afraid of biting the hand that fed them. You take the money and you dance to the tune.

Well, Victims of Violence had always been independent of any national organization and was never afraid to speak out. I was noted for being a very outspoken critic of the way society, in the shape of the authorities, ignored the blatant injustices suffered by innocent people who never harmed anyone in their lives. I deliberately turned away other organizations who wanted to be associated with us because I didn't want anyone I wasn't sure of to speak as though what they were saying was Victims of Violence policy. I watched over the charity with the eyes of a hawk and the

427

love of a mother hen. We were a well-respected organization, and I knew I could trust those helping us in any capacity. I also knew that every penny donated to us went towards the purpose for which it was generously given—to help victims of crime.

It was important to me that Victims of Violence kept its independence so we could speak out about the injustices we saw every day. I was the main voice of the organization and could say what I thought without having to worry about how others viewed me. I was answerable to no one except my colleagues, the people whose generous support allowed us to keep going, and last but by no means least, to the victims who needed help. I had never let red tape stand in my way—much to the despair of many council officers—but everything I did was to help those refused help from any other source, and to whom a visit, and a kiss and a cuddle, meant a lot.

David Mellor was a government minister when he visited our shelter in Deane Road. There were about ten elderly victims there that day, and, credit where it's due, he was friendly with everyone, chatting and asking how they came to be there. There was one lady there, eighty years of age, who had been blind from birth. Her name was Flo, and she was an easy target for thugs who were constantly breaking into her house and robbing her. The last time they had used force on her and left her badly bruised, terrified and upset because they had taken her money and items that were of sentimental value. She'd come to the shelter for a few days until the council made her front door safe.

I had explained to David Mellor why she was

428

there, and he began to speak to her. Because she was blind, and her hearing wasn't good, I could see she couldn't hear him. 'David, she's blind. She can't see you and can't hear properly. Will you bend down to her, please?' And I'll never forget the way he dropped to his knees and took her hand while asking her questions. There are not many government ministers who would do that!

When he had finished speaking to Flo, David got to his feet and straightened the crease in his trousers. With a grin on his face, he said, 'I was told before I came that you don't believe in red tape. They were right.'

I feigned surprise. 'What is red tape, David?'

*   *   *

I picked the post up from the mat one morning and my mouth gaped when I saw the top letter was from Buckingham Palace. What on earth could it be? They don't put you in the Tower of London for speaking out, surely. I hurried through to the dining room to get a knife as I didn't want to tear open the envelope. I could feel my heart thumping as I read that I was being invited, with a guest, to a garden party at the Palace. As a woman, the first thing I thought of was clothes. What do people wear to a Buckingham Palace garden party? I had plenty of clothes, but couldn't visualize anything in my wardrobe that would fit the bill. I folded the letter and put it in my bag to take to the shelter and show the girls and the ladies staying there. I knew I'd get my leg pulled, but it would be worth it to see the looks on those elderly faces when they saw the Buckingham Palace address. Things like that didn't

429

happen to people they knew. They didn't happen to me, either, and to be honest I'm not really partial to posh dos. I also wondered what Tony's reaction would be because he's far more shy than I am.

But when my family found out they were delighted. The fact that I was considering not accepting the invitation horrified them. So it was a new outfit for me, with a posh hat, but my husband refused to buy a new suit for the sake of a couple of hours when he had several hanging in the wardrobe which would serve any occasion.

Once we were sorted, we put our clothes away until the two weeks before our London trip had passed. They flew by. Before we knew it we were standing in line outside a gate at Buckingham Palace, handing over the invitation cards and being directed to the right path. There was certainly a variety of clothes on show, and a variety of accents in the voices passing by. The rich young men with their top hat and tails, and their rather loud, confident voices, seemed to be perfectly at home there, as though it was an annual event for them. The ladies were very well dressed to match their menfolk, and they too oozed confidence as they made their way to the refreshment marquee.

Tony and I walked around the gardens first, and they really are beautiful. We stood by the lake, admiring the trees nearby and the well-kept lawn. But to see the whole of the gardens would take hours, and we were both hungry as we'd had little time for breakfast with having to catch an early train from Lime Street, so we walked slowly back to where the huge marquee stood. Long trestle tables covered in linen cloths ran the full length of the tent, and on the tables there were plates of sandwiches and cakes. There were plenty of waiters and we were soon served with a much-appreciated cup of tea and plates filled with an array of delicacies.

It had been an honour to be invited, and an enjoyable experience for Tony and me, one of the truly memorable occasions we would long remember.

*   *   *

One Saturday morning I received a phone call from a police constable in Toxteth to say he had just been to visit an elderly victim and was very concerned for her. He apologized for disturbing me on a Saturday but said she was in such a bad state he hadn't liked leaving her and wondered if it were possible for someone from our organization to visit her that morning. There were one or two people who lived nearby that I could have asked, but because the police officer sounded so concerned I decided to go myself. It was a twenty-five-mile drive each way, which meant dinner for the family would be late, but my husband came up trumps and said he'd prepare the potatoes and veg ready to put on when I got home.

I stopped outside the address I'd been given, and after locking the car I stared up at the terraced house which stood at the end of a block with a narrow entry at one side. The front entrance was for the top flat, the side entrance for the flat I was looking for. As I walked down the entry, I could see how easy it would be for a burglar to break in. Once out of sight of anyone walking in the street, it would take a professional criminal a matter of seconds to boot the door in, and from the look of the woodwork around the lock it appeared to have been repaired many times. I sighed. The police officer had said the victim's name was Miss Pringle and she was eighty-six years of age. What a way for an elderly person to spend the last years of her life.

There was no answer to my first knock so I tried again, a little harder. Then I called her name. After a minute or so I could hear a shuffling behind the door. I lifted the letterbox. 'My name is Joan Jonker, Miss Pringle. The police asked me to call on you.'

The door was opened a few inches. All I could see was a pair of eyes filled with such fear my heart went out to her. 'The policeman that called to see you this morning gave me your name and address. You mustn't worry, I've only come to see if I can help you.'

I have seen thousands of sad cases which have reduced me to tears, but I had never before seen fear you could practically touch. This old lady was stooped with age and so thin you could knock her over with one finger. When we were in the living room I felt anger swelling up inside me. There was so little of any value in that room. It was ages before I could get a word out of her because she was so traumatized with shock she couldn't speak. Gradually, though, I managed to get her to tell me what her Christian name was. 'Miss Pringle' sounded so stiff. She told me she was called Kathy, and this was the seventh time she'd been a victim— only this time the attacker had hit her on the side of her head with a hammer which still lay on the floor. 'I can't stay here any longer,' she said, her

432

hands on the back of a chair for support. Her eyes were wide with fear and her lips quivering. 'They'll kill me next time they get in.'

'You're in a bad spot here, Kathy, you need to be in sheltered accommodation.'

'A visitor from the church comes every week, and she said she's put my name down for a flat in sheltered housing, but I can't wait for that, I've got to get out now. I can't spend another night in this place.'

I thought of the shelter. There was room there for Kathy, but I couldn't uproot her without telling anyone. It would mean leaving the flat unattended for anyone to come in, and although I thought the furniture and knick-knacks were of no worth, they must have had some sentimental value for Kathy. I couldn't take a chance on getting her to the shelter, then some evil thug getting in and setting fire to this place. I couldn't take that responsibility. 'Have you any family, Kathy, or friends you could call on until we can have you moved to a safer place?'

There were tears in her eyes when she said, 'I haven't got any family or friends. When my mother and father died, I was left all alone.'

'When is the church visitor due again? I'd really like to have a talk with her to see what the situation is.'

'She's coming on Monday morning, but I won't be here by then. I'll walk the streets before I'll stay another night in this place.'

I looked at her frail, stooped figure and wondered what on earth had happened to our society. When I was younger, like my sisters and brother, I was brought up to respect the elderly living in our street, and to help them if they needed

433

any messages. But the young thugs of today not only lack respect, they lack sympathy, understanding and compassion. They don't care who they hurt as long as they get what they want. And they are so stupid, in their own tiny minds they probably think they're big and strong when in fact they are cowards, only unfortunately nobody in authority has the guts to tell them so.

'Kathy, I can take you away on Monday to a place you will be safe. It's a lovely house where you'll have a beautiful room to yourself, be well looked after all the time.' I could see this wasn't to her liking so hurried to say, 'I can't take you now because it's more than I dare do without notifying someone who knows you. So if you can ask the church visitor to help you pack whatever personal effects you have, and any things you will need, I'll pick you up on Monday morning and take you and your budgie to a place where I know you'll be happy until your offer of sheltered accommodation comes through.'

Kathy Pringle had learned the hard way that you can't trust people. And I was a complete stranger to her, so why should she believe what I was saying? 'You won't come for me, I know you won't.'

I put my arms around her frail shoulders and kissed her. 'Kathy, I don't tell lies, sunshine. I say I'll be here on Monday morning, then I'll be here. And I'll give you one of my cards to show to the lady from the church, so she can ring me if she's in any doubt.'

When Kathy looked at my card, she seemed more at ease. 'I've seen you in the *Echo*, you help a lot of people.'

'And I'm going to help you, Kathy, you have my

434

word on that. So why don't you start looking for the things you'd like to bring with you? With the lady from the church to help you pack, you should be ready for me on Monday morning.'

I found it very difficult to leave Kathy Pringle, and I didn't do it with a clear conscience. But there was little else I could do. She didn't know the address of the church worker so I couldn't go and see her, and I certainly wasn't going to knock on the doors of any of the neighbours because I could be giving out information to the wrong sort of people. It was getting to a point where I didn't trust anyone except my family and friends and those involved in the charity. On the drive home I felt really guilty so the first thing I did when I walked through the door was to ring Rosemary and tell her about Kathy. I asked if she could fix up a bed in one of the downstairs front rooms because the old lady would never make the stairs. I knew I didn't have to ask her to make the room comfortable, Rosemary didn't need telling. After saying it would probably be lunchtime on Monday before I arrived with our new guest, I hung up and gave my darling husband a big hug of thanks for putting up with me, then set about seeing to the dinner—as a proper wife and mother should.

* * *

When I arrived back at Kathy's flat on the Monday morning it was to find the church visitor busy packing clothes, linen, a few ornaments and some photographs into an old suitcase, and a carry bag was standing near by filled with crockery wrapped carefully in newspapers. I thanked the woman from

435

the church and asked if she heard anything about Kathy's application for sheltered accommodation, would she let me know.

As for Kathy, she was walking up and down in her coat and headscarf and not listening to anything that was said to her. All she wanted was to get out of the house where she had known no happiness since the day she'd moved in. In the end I took her out to the car and sat her in the passenger seat. 'You stay there, Kathy, while I carry the bags out.'

The woman from the church had introduced herself when I arrived, but for the life of me I couldn't remember her name when I was opening the car boot to start loading and she came out of the house to say she'd have to go because she had an appointment. She promised to keep in touch but although she said goodbye to Kathy, all she got in reply was a sharp nod of the head. The old lady just wanted to be away from that house, out of the street, to somewhere she wouldn't be woken in the night to find a man bending over her with a hammer in his hand. A hammer he didn't think twice about using when Kathy tried to scream.

Thank goodness my car was a hatchback and I was able to get the case and all the bags in. Then I had to make room for Kathy's only friend—her yellow budgie in a cage.

Rosemary must have been watching for us through the window because the door was opened as I took Kathy's arm to lead her up the path. Rosemary met us halfway, and she took the other arm. 'I've been waiting for you, Kathy,' she said, 'and your room is all ready. The kettle's boiling and I'm going to spoil you 'cos you're a lovely little thing.'

In years to come, when I retire, there will be many things to look back on with pleasure and pride. The moment Kathy was led into her room at the shelter will be one of them. She stopped inside the door, her eyes wide with surprise. The room looked lovely, a far cry from the one she'd just left. It was a large room with high bay windows which gave the whole place a bright, sunny appearance, and Rosemary had done her job well. There was a fire in the grate, a plant on a table beside a rocking chair placed near the hearth, a vase of flowers on the windowsill, and against the wall behind the door was a single divan bed, with a frilly cover on to match the pillows.

It was a while before Kathy could take it in. Then she looked from Rosemary to me and asked, 'Is this for me?'

I nodded. 'Yes, sunshine, this is your room and no one can take it from you until you are offered a new flat in sheltered housing.'

Tears began to roll down her lined face, and Rosemary and I couldn't help ourselves. It ended with the three of us, huddled together in the middle of the room, crying our eyes out. It's funny how happiness can bring on the tears.

Kathy was with us for three months before a letter came for her one day. I arrived, as I did every day now we had so many people there, to be told she wanted to see me. I knocked on her door before walking in and finding her sitting with the letter in her hand. It was to say there was a flat available for her in sheltered accommodation. I thought she would be pleased, and after reading the letter said, 'That's nice for you, Kathy.'

'I don't want to go,' she said, her top lip trembling. 'I want to stay here.'

'Oh, I'm sorry, sunshine, but our rules are that we don't take anyone in on a permanent basis. Otherwise we'd be full in no time and not able to help anyone in desperate need.'

'But I couldn't look after myself now.' There was a catch in her voice. 'I couldn't go to the shops or wash my bedding! I wouldn't be able to fill a kettle.'

And as she was talking, I knew she was right. She was too old and frail to look after herself. While she might be safe from thugs in sheltered accommodation, she would still be expected to do her own housework, washing, cooking and shopping. And she wasn't capable of doing any of those things. But if I said she could stay with us, then I'd be heading for trouble with the committee. I closed my eyes and sighed. I wouldn't sleep at night if I sent this frail old lady to somewhere she wasn't looked after or happy. I would far rather face the committee than live with that on my conscience. After all, I was the one who saw the unhappiness and the sadness, they didn't.

I waved the letter. 'I'll take this, sunshine, and ring them and say you won't be taking up their offer. You can stay here, but please keep it a secret for now or you'll have me shot.'

I stood up to the committee at the next meeting, telling them I didn't see the point of having shelters to help victims if we were going to send them back home as frightened as they were when they came to us. There were no objections and Kathy stayed, followed in the next month or so by Maggie, Lizzie, Nellie, and three other elderly victims who needed the shelter and the care that Victims of Violence offered.

Everything was running smoothly when Lady Butlin rang to tell me she would be in London on business in the very near future, and if she could manage it, would make the trip up to Liverpool to see the shelter and some of the victims.

She had been so good to our charity I decided to do something special when she came. So I rang Ernie Mack at the Montrose Club and explained that I would like to have a charity night at his club with Sheila Butlin as the guest of honour. Ernie agreed, and as his contribution said there would be no charge for the use of the club. Then I contacted Ken Dodd, and because he was a patron of the charity with Lady Butlin he offered to put on a show. The next thing was to confirm the date with her, have four hundred tickets printed and coax everyone I knew to sell them. Not that I thought they wouldn't sell, because Ken Dodd's shows are always a sell-out, but I was really pushing myself to the limit here, trying to be all things to all men, and even I can't work miracles.

It was at this time that our treasurer, Jeanette Edge, told me her firm was transferring her to its office in Norwich. I was dismayed because she was a lovely person, we got on so well and she kept our accounts spot on. But it was a promotion for her so it would have been wrong not to offer genuine congratulations. Before Jeanette left we found someone who could take over the book-keeping. Her name was Lorna Cooper and she worked in an office in the city. She had heard over the radio about our shelter opening and had volunteered to spend one evening a week helping with the old

439

folk. It was ages before I got to see her because I wasn't there in the evenings, but I had many reasons to be grateful to her. Apart from that one evening a week she offered to do our books and I introduced her to the charity's accountant, Michael Bancroft. So that was one big worry off my mind.

The charity show at the Montrose was a sell-out and hugely successful. Lady Butlin had told me she would have to leave at eleven because she was expecting a phone call from her hotel in London about that time, but she was still there at midnight joining in the laughter as Ken's jokes came thick and fast.

She thoroughly enjoyed herself, and being born in Liverpool herself, said she felt at home with the quick-fire humour. As a comedian, Ken Dodd stands head and shoulders above the rest, and as a friend and charity worker he is the best.

The money raised at the show was put towards the four thousand pounds we still owed Mrs Coates. She'd never mentioned it and would probably wait longer, but because she had been so kind and trusting the debt was always at the back of my mind. I mentioned it to a reporter from the *Echo* who had come to interview me, and he said he would have words with his boss and perhaps the paper could help. Within two days I had heard that they were to start a campaign to help raise the money.

On the day I received that news, I received another phone call which was such a shock I had to sit down and ask the caller to repeat what he had said. Still not believing my ears, I heard him say I had been chosen as the winner of the Brinsworth Award, and my husband and I were invited to stay at a hotel in London for five days. We would be expected to travel down on the Thursday of the following week and take a taxi to the Drury Lane Hotel which would be our base there. On our first night we would be dining with Marge Proops whose job it had been to select the winner of the award from the thousands of nominations. We would have an escort for our time in London who would drive us everywhere and see to all our needs. The second day would be spent sightseeing and then going to a theatre in the evening. On the Saturday we were to be taken to the Royal Variety Show, where I would be presenting the Queen Mother with her bouquet as she arrived at the theatre.

By this time my head was in a daze and I wasn't taking it all in. I couldn't even remember the caller's name, even though he had introduced himself and said he worked for the *Mirror* newspaper. I asked for his phone number and said I would ring him the next morning to confirm the arrangements. After putting the phone down I just flopped in a chair, flabbergasted. A short while later I pulled myself together and started on my day's calls. The first was to the shelter to see if everything was all right and to chat to the occupants and give them their daily hug and kiss before going out on calls to new victims. I never mentioned the phone call to anyone, even though I was excited, because I felt it would sound like bragging. My Tony would be the first to hear, and I wondered what his response would be.

That day's calls were all to elderly people, and they soon brought me down to earth and forced me to put my priorities in order. One man, Jimmy, had been confronted by two young men who

441

manhandled him until he told them where his meagre savings were. At eighty-two, having worked until he had to retire at sixty-five, he'd lost his wife eight years before and still pined for her. He was thrifty with his money because that was the way he'd been brought up, and each week would put a bit by out of his pension. Now every penny had been stolen by thugs who had probably never worked a day in their lives. Oh, they had left him something—they'd left him with deep angry bruises on his arms and wrists. As he was telling me what had happened, Jimmy began to cry. Nothing upsets me more than seeing a man cry because he is no longer able to protect himself, his family or his home. The ten pounds I was able to give him would be of little consolation, but at least it would keep him in food until his next pension day.

The next two calls were on ladies in their late-seventies, and both had been the victim of a handbag snatch. They hadn't been injured, not physically anyway, but they were very shaken and tearful because their bags had contained photographs of loved ones. I had a cup of tea in each house and sat for a while until they were more calm. Then I made my way to the last call of the day—a lady I knew very well because she and her sister had been robbed many times. They lived just a few doors from each other, both lovely ladies with snow white hair who kept their houses spotlessly clean and always had the kettle on before you had time to sit down. Ada was eighty-two, the eldest of the sisters, and when I drew up outside her house I was in for a shock. In fact I was horrified to see there was a cage across the whole front window, made up of bars of strong steel. In the name of

God, I thought as I knocked on her door, have we really come down to this, where elderly people have to live behind bars while thugs rule their neighbourhoods?

'Ada, what on earth have you got those bars on the window for?' I asked as I took a seat.

'It's the only thing I can do to keep the robbers out.' She looked tired and weary. 'I've had too much, Joan, I couldn't take any more and had to do something.' And then, with her usual indomitable spirit, she said, 'I'll put the kettle on and make you a sandwich.' To refuse would only have made her feel worse. She would have fretted all night if I hadn't allowed her to treat me as a welcome visitor, as she always did.

But I was angry as I drove home. There was no need for all this heartbreak and misery, it could be stopped if only we had someone in power with the guts to do it. Why were they allowing decent people to be prisoners in their own homes while the criminals had the freedom of the streets?

*　　　*　　　*

Saturday saw my two sisters and me traipsing around the boutiques in Lord Street looking for a suitable dress to wear when meeting the Queen Mother. I stood firm on not buying an evening dress which I would probably never wear again, and eventually found a cocktail dress I fell in love with. It was in a deep purple silk, figure-hugging, with a cascade of material falling from a sequined flower at the waist. And while I was doing that, my husband was out hiring an evening suit for the occasion. When we met up at home, we were both

443

quite pleased with ourselves. Five days to go and then we'd be off to London on a once in a lifetime adventure.

I rang the *Echo* to tell them I would be away for a few days and was told the money from their campaign was starting to come in. I said I would ring them from London on Monday before we were taken to the lunch where I was to be officially presented with the Brinsworth Award by Lord Delfont on behalf of the Entertaining Artistes Benevolent Fund.

I said it was to be a once-in-a-lifetime adventure and it certainly was. Tony and I were treated to the best of everything. I have to admit to being terrified as I stood with a huge bouquet in my arms waiting for the Queen Mother to arrive, even after being told by Roy Hudd, President of the EABF, that I would outshine her Majesty—he was being very kind. My husband was standing about ten yards back from me. Unfortunately no one was allowed to take photographs. There was another woman standing at the side of me, also with a huge bouquet in her arms, and I found out later she was a resident of Brinsworth House, a home for retired artistes sponsored by the fund. I was getting more nervous by the minute and when there was a sudden hush, found myself wishing I'd practised my curtsy a bit more.

Then came a flurry of excitement and I leaned forward to see the Queen Mother walking towards me, followed by Princess Diana and Prince Charles. I was introduced to the Queen Mother by Lord Delfont, did my curtsy and then presented her with the flowers. The lady next to me stepped forward and presented Princess Diana with her bouquet, and I was delighted when the Queen Mother and the Princess stayed to chat for a while. They were both very friendly and beautifully dressed. I told them they were prettier than the flowers, and I meant it. Princess Diana was so beautiful, with bright blue eyes like saucers and skin one can only dream of. There was nothing stiff about either of the Royals, and I realized I'd been worrying for nothing. When they moved along the line, I found myself facing a smiling Prince Charles. He asked what I was there for, then after I'd told him, jokingly asked if I'd bugged the Queen Mother's bouquet. It was then I made a remark I was to remember with sadness in later years. I told Prince Charles he was very lucky with the women in his life.

The Variety Show was excellent, but Tony and I were tired after the tour of London sights the day before and the theatre in the evening. So I asked if we could have a free day on Sunday to lounge around. I was glad I had because on Monday, by the time I'd found a hairdresser's to have my hair set it was almost time for the car to pick us up and take us to the lunch. But I found a moment to ring the *Echo* to ask how the campaign had gone, and jumped for joy when I was told they had raised more than the amount we needed. It seemed everything was going well for me and the charity, and I was in a very happy mood when we walked into the huge room where tables were nicely laid out and most of the seats occupied. My jaw dropped when I saw the people sitting in those seats. So many famous faces, I didn't know where to look next. On the table next to ours sat the full cast of Last Of The Summer Wine, and Denis

445

Norden. Then I spotted Christopher Cazenove, a favourite of mine. I got a chance to have a word with him after the meal before he sprinted across the room to get an autograph for one of his children. My husband wasn't as star-struck as me, and I envied his ability to stay calm under any circumstances.

After the meal Roy Hudd spoke about the work I did with victims, and sang my praises while I blushed to the roots of my hair. Then he surprised me by telling everyone about our shelter, and how I was trying to raise four thousand pounds to clear the debt on the property. How he knew this I never found out. He went on to say that the Entertaining Artistes Benevolent Fund were going to make a donation of four thousand pounds to Victims of Violence to clear the debt.

I felt my heart miss a beat. Roy looked so happy to be making the announcement which brought smiles and nods of agreement from the hundreds of people there. I was stunned. Only a couple of hours ago I'd been told the money had been raised, and not to make the fact known would be acting a lie. I couldn't do that. So I stood up and told them that only that morning I had heard the *Liverpool Echo*, who had been campaigning to raise the money, had reached the target. There was loud applause and Roy said he was very pleased and the EABF would still be making a donation.

After that I was taken on stage for the official handing over of a beautiful carriage clock. Flash bulbs were going off like mad. I remember thanking everyone, but for once in my life I had little to say, I was too full of emotion. Then when I got back to my table, David Frost and Barry

Humphries came over to have their photograph taken with me. Very kindly I thought, David Frost said if there was ever anything he could do I just had to get in touch.

It was a truly wonderful experience, the memory of which I will treasure.

*　　*　　*

Two days later I was back in the thick of it, and rushed off my feet. There were many requests from elderly people, or their relatives, to come to the shelter, but we were full up. Some of the rooms were large enough for two single beds, but I know how elderly people value their privacy and didn't even consider doubling up. Then I heard about a house in the next street being up for sale. It was one of a pair of large Victorian semis, built originally for someone with loads of money and servants. But the area had deteriorated over the years and I heard the house had been let as bedsits to students before being put up for sale.

I drove round to the next street and stood in front of what had once been a very gracious dwelling. It was a lot bigger than the Deane Road shelter, and as it was on three floors I guessed it would take many more victims. It had a garden back and front, and space for several parked cars. So I jotted down the number of the agent and drove back to Deane Road where I phoned to ask for details. Fortunately my name was familiar to the agent, and he explained that the house had belonged to their client's mother, and had indeed been let out to students. He said the structure was sound, but inside the house would need a lot of work doing to it. While he was talking, my mind was racing. We had finished paying off Mrs Coates, and had some money in the bank. Not enough to buy a house, but enough for a deposit. Doing work on it was not a problem, nor furnishing it, because there were plenty of volunteers.

I told the agent that what I had in mind was another shelter for victims, but it would depend on what the asking price was. We could manage ten thousand, but no more. He said he would contact his client, who was a school teacher, and would get back to me. I thought I would have to wait a few days, but he rang back the same afternoon and sounded very happy when he told me the house was on the market for quite a bit more than I had offered, but because his client thought I was doing a worthwhile job, he said the charity could have it for ten thousand.

Once again I rang Billy Butler at Radio Merseyside, and instead of saying he would spread the word, I was invited to go on the programme to ask the listeners myself. My request brought quite a response. Before I left the studio the phones were going like mad with offers of everything from a fitted kitchen to beds, bedding, curtains, fridge, and goodness knows what else. And plenty of women volunteered to come and give a hand to clean the house through. The generosity of people never ceased to amaze me, and I was glad to get out of the building so I could blow my nose before the tears had a chance to show themselves.

One person to hear my radio appeal was a good supporter of ours, a Miss Mann. Her mother had left several thousand pounds to Victims of Violence in her will, and when I rang Miss Mann to thank her, I invited her down to see for herself the work we did. She was very impressed and after that often called in for a chat with the residents. After hearing the latest radio appeal, she rang to say she would donate the ten thousand to buy the house. I was stunned, and this time I didn't even try to keep the tears back.

I couldn't help much with the cleaning of Beech Street because I had victims to visit every day, criminal injuries compensation forms to fill in and send off, and also some fund-raising to do to make sure we kept money in the bank. There was no point in opening new shelters if we couldn't afford to keep them going. Anyway, it took the volunteers a month to clean the house from top to bottom, but it was worth the effort because it looked so much nicer when everything had been washed down. People had been calling with curtains and nets, lampshades, crockery and ornaments, so my job was to find a sympathetic removal man to pick up the large items. I found two nice young men who couldn't do the job for nothing as they had young families to care for, but they cut their price right down to the bone. Eight weeks from me hearing about the house, it was furnished and ready to admit anyone needing sanctuary. I'll not pretend the place was a palace, for everything in it was second-hand, but it wasn't junk, and all the rooms were bright and cosy.

Our first resident came to us a week after Beech Street opened. Her name was Ann and she was ninety years of age. Her house had been broken into several times, but on this last occasion the thug actually had his hands to her throat and threatened to strangle her if she screamed. Her niece brought

449

her to the shelter and Ann wouldn't even go back home for her belongings, but asked her niece to do it as she never wanted to see the house again.

I needed volunteers to work at the shelter during the day, and someone who would sleep over. The days were no problem because we could get staff from the Youth Opportunity Scheme—we had three from the scheme working in Deane Road. We also had a man doing community service after I'd checked with the necessary agency to make sure he wasn't violent, a drug addict or thief. I was told he was none of these and perfectly harmless. When I asked him if he would stay nights, Mike agreed because he lived with his mother and had no other commitments. Another problem solved. Mike proved invaluable when the furniture began to arrive and he and the volunteers had the rooms sorted out in no time.

Another victim moved in a few weeks after Ann. Her name was Mary and she'd lost her husband a few months before. Since his death, she'd been broken into three times. The last time, three thugs bundled her into the kitchen and threatened what they would do to her if she moved or screamed. Terrified, she stood in the kitchen, wondering what they would do to her when they found she had nothing for them to steal. They'd already taken everything of any value. Then one of the thugs burst the kitchen door open and tried to take her wedding ring from her finger. He couldn't get it off because over the sixty years she'd worn it, her fingers had grown plumper. The thug became very angry when he couldn't get the ring off, and threatened to cut her finger off. Poor Mary was put through agony before she asked him to let her put her finger under the cold water tap. Eventually the ring came off and the thug got what he wanted. Mary was left terrified, and broken-hearted. After her came Lizzie, and very soon all the rooms were taken. Like Deane Road, the atmosphere was happy and homely.

The lady who occupied the house adjoining ours in Beech Street stopped me on the path one day and said she was putting her house up for sale. She asked if I would be interested as the two houses could be knocked through, making one very large property. It was a really exciting proposition, but I had been inside her house once and knew it was very badly in need of repair. I said I would put it to the committee and asked what price she was asking. When she said fifteen thousand, I shook my head. 'No, I wouldn't pay that for it, it needs too much work doing to make it habitable.'

Several times the neighbour stopped me to ask if I'd changed my mind, and I told her she would have to come down three thousand for us to be interested. After all, every penny we had had been donated and I wasn't about to give it away. In the end, twelve thousand was agreed and a month later Victims of Violence were the proud owners of numbers five and seven Beech Street. I asked the *Echo* to do a piece on it so that those who were giving generously would know their money wasn't being wasted.

Seeing the newspaper article, a reporter from a radio programme rang to see if he could interview me in the house. I couldn't see the sense of that, not on the radio. But the reporter had more imagination and brains than me, and as we walked through the empty rooms, describing the work that

451

needed doing, our footsteps echoed on the bare wooden floor and you could hear the emptiness of the house as the young man described the bad state of the plaster, the wallpaper hanging down in strips, and cobwebs everywhere. Our voices sounded hollow and eerie to my ears, but the young reporter was very happy with the result.

He would never know that his interview was heard by a trustee of a newly formed charity, the McCarthy Foundation, founded by John McCarthy of the builders McCarthy and Stone. He was so interested in what the house was to be used for he rang to ask if he could come up from Bournemouth the following day. His visit resulted in Victims of Violence being the first charity to receive a donation from the Foundation. It was for ten thousand pounds. Six months later, after many visits from members of the Foundation's committee, including Sir Marcus Fox, it offered to buy a further two properties in Deane Road for the use of victims, if the charity ever ceased to exist the properties to be returned to the McCarthy Foundation. They were adjoining houses, like Beech Street, but while the gift was a generous one, it had a sting in its tail. The two houses were bought for around £40,000, but afterwards an architect, surveyor and builder drew up plans for the work necessary to satisfy Social Services, including everything from fire-proofing, alarm systems, lift, call systems in every room, six toilets, three bathrooms, and special equipment in the kitchen. When the specialists had worked the figures out, the whole operation would cost £175,000. I was the only fund-raiser, it was a daunting task. But it would provide at least ten

452

additional bedrooms for victims, so it was a task I was prepared to take on.

A few weeks before Christmas, I visited two elderly ladies who had been robbed of many things, the most precious being their wedding rings. I was shocked when I called to one house to find the eighty-five-year-old victim covered in bruises. The day before, she had answered a knock on the door to find two strange young men standing there. She was immediately alarmed and tried to close the door, but she was no match for two men. She was pushed into a chair and one thug kept punching her while the other searched her flat. I'll never forget her tearful voice saying, 'They didn't have to hit me, I couldn't have stopped them doing what they wanted to do.' She raised her hand. 'They stole my wedding ring. Sixty-three years it had been on my finger, since the day I got married, and those wicked lads stole it.'

I was so angry, the next morning I rang the *Echo* and asked if they would print the fact that I had recently seen three elderly ladies whose wedding rings had been stolen, and say how broken-hearted they were. And because I could still see the frightened faces of those ladies, I asked them to print that I said the thugs weren't only criminals, they were cowards.

I wasn't really expecting a response to the article, but next afternoon I had a phone call from Christopher James Jewellers in the city centre. Christopher said he would like to donate three wedding rings to the ladies, and asked would I bring them to the shop so they could choose which ones they liked. The ladies were delighted. When I took them down they were treated like royalty, and the happiness on their faces put some cheer into my heart. Every day I saw the sadness caused by the wicked people in our society, but the good people I met reminded me there were far more of them than bad, and with their help and support I would carry on doing the best I could for those most vulnerable members of society.

CHAPTER TWENTY-TWO

1991

The latest house opened in the summer of 1991. It had been hard going raising £175,000 because none of the others involved in the charity were as outgoing as myself, and while they would sell and buy tickets if I'd arranged a show or a dance to raise cash, they weren't the type to ask people for money or rattle a collecting tin. But I was lucky in as much as I had many friends and supporters who never refused to help, and the backing of the local media. I did feel guilty sometimes, asking the same people over and over for donations, but they always came up trumps. Only through their generosity has the charity been in existence for fifteen years, and over ten thousand victims of violence been helped.

John McCarthy and two other trustees from the Foundation had travelled up from Bournemouth for the opening, and as John cut the red ribbon to open the shelter officially, I think he was pleased to see the sign over the door reading McCarthy Lodge. There were plenty of dignitaries there, including several high-ranking police officers and a couple of local celebrities. And, of course, about fifteen elderly victims, some of whom would be making McCarthy Lodge their home. The girls from our old shelter in Deane Road had been offered permanent jobs and they were over the moon, even though they would be on the national minimum wage. They'd been with us for a year on the Youth Opportunity Scheme, and we knew they were kind, considerate and patient with the elderly people. Bernice Styles, who had been with us as a volunteer for several years, was offered the position of manager. She and the girls had been very busy that morning laying a spread on for the visitors and seeing we possessed enough glasses to go round. The two tables were beautifully set, the sandwiches and cakes and other dainties looking colourful and inviting, and the atmosphere was alive with pleasure and happiness in a project successfully carried out.

The shelter was lovely inside, with everything done to satisfy Social Services, even a lift. There was also a small office furnished with equipment I'd been able to coax from friends, and a staffroom. There had to be two members of staff on duty at all times, plus a cook and a cleaner. We were receiving Housing Benefit for each of the residents, but it wouldn't cover wages and upkeep. Still, that was a worry for the future. Today was a day to be celebrating although I knew that, like myself, my colleagues and the staff from our first shelter, just five doors away, were sad at having to sell that house to pay for the twelve new divans with fireproof bedding, the fireproof carpeting and curtains, etc. It hadn't been a posh house, not like McCarthy Lodge with everything new and bright, but it had been a very happy house, always full of laughter, and we would miss it. And it was the first shelter for victims of violence in the country.

*   *   *

Over the next few years we saw a change in the type of victims we were helping. The phones in both McCarthy Lodge and Beech Street were ringing constantly with victims seeking help. Many young men were now being viciously attacked, robbed and left with severe injuries. In one week I was dealing with six, all of whom had had their jaw broken and suffered other minor injuries. One thing they had all suffered was a loss of confidence because they hadn't been able to protect themselves. They weren't small, weak young men, they were mostly six footers you would have thought capable of looking after themselves. But no matter how big or strong, no one is capable of protecting themselves from a gang of thugs armed with knives and determined to rob you of any money and jewellery you have on you. I filled in compensation forms for them and carried out all the necessary correspondence. I told the victims it could take a year for their claim to be processed, but kept in touch with them in the meantime. When an offer came through, I would ring the victim the same day, and if he was satisfied with the offer would ask him to call into the office to sign the acceptance form. However, if he and I felt the offer wasn't enough for the injuries he had suffered, I would appeal and represent him at the appeal hearing. And, fingers crossed, I had always been successful at appeal hearings.

I had met the families of about forty murder

456

victims by now, and sitting with them listening to their sorrow was as heartbreaking as ever. There was nothing I could do to help, though, except in a few cases where the family had no money for a funeral, then Victims of Violence would give a donation of several hundred pounds. No one can bring a loved one back, and the finality of murder is the hardest thing to bear. All I could do was comfort and cry with them. And, while doing so, wonder how Tony and I would feel if one of our sons went out one day, happy and smiling at the thought of going to the cinema or a dance, and we never saw them again. Never had a chance to say goodbye. It really is enough to affect the sanity of any devoted mother and father. And there is no help for these people. No one in Government or any authority writes to say how sorry they are at the loss of a young life, or to ask if the family need help. Yet the murderer if caught, is humanely treated and given a probation officer and a social worker to protect their rights. And, of course, come the trial, and the help of legal aid, a solicitor and barrister will plead on his behalf. However, if the murderer isn't satisfied with his legal representation, he can ask for replacements. What sort of justice is that? When a person who has unlawfully killed another, can claim legal aid which comes out of the taxpayers' pocket, including the parents of the person he murdered! Surely to God anyone with half an ounce of intelligence and a sense of fair play can see how cock-eyed the system is?

There is a saying that there are none so blind as those who don't want to see, and I would add to that by saying there are none so deaf as those who don't want to hear. I have been shouting out now for sixteen years, on the television, in the newspapers and anywhere I am asked to speak. But while it has had an impact on people like myself who see the wrongs in society, I am just an irritation to the ones who don't want to see things as they really are. Penal reformers have been taught that the way to change criminals is to be kind to them, don't look down on them, treat them as an equal. And we've reached the state now where young thugs laugh at the police because they know they can't be touched. Never once have I ever heard a magistrate or judge ask to see the victim to get their side of the story. And they say crime doesn't pay. What a farce that is.

Another dreadful crime that we were coming into contact with more and more was armed robbery. A middle-aged lady who worked in a building society was brought by her husband to see me. One day a week before—on a day like any other day, or so she thought—she'd finished attending to one customer, and as she turned to a man she thought was another found a gun being pointed to her head. She was so traumatized she froze like a statue, unable to reach for the panic button or scream. The robber got away with a substantial amount of cash before another customer came in and raised the alarm. Although a week had passed since the incident, when she came to our shelter she was still in a state of shock. Her eyes were glazed and she had trouble telling me what happened, as though she didn't want to be reminded of the terrifying ordeal. She hadn't been to work since the robbery, wouldn't even venture outside the house until her husband coaxed her into coming to see me. At first her eyes kept going to the door all the time as though she wanted to run away from the memories which came flooding back at the mention of the gun. So I took the conversation down a different avenue.

I have always found that the best way to release the pent-up fear each victim has inside them is to get angry. So I spoke to her about some of our elderly victims, and how they had been robbed and injured. It wasn't difficult for me to sound angry for by now I'd had over ten thousand reasons to be angry. How dare some thug steal something that didn't belong to him? What right did he have to take away your money and your peace of mind? How dare a man carry a gun, knowing it will terrify any person into giving him what he wanted? Without that gun he's nothing, just a coward. But he and his family would be living the good life on his ill-gotten gains, while his victim—in this case a woman in her late-thirties—was terrified to go back to the job she'd had for years and which previously she'd enjoyed. The anger in my voice seemed to penetrate her fear and confusion and soon she was joining her husband in damning the thug, and saying she wasn't going to let him spoil her life. Because she hadn't been injured, I couldn't apply for criminal injuries for her, but I gave her a form and told her if she felt she couldn't go back to work, then she should fill it in and perhaps claim loss of earnings.

A few weeks later I received a phone call from a man in a very distressed state. His words were jumbled, but I could make out he worked in an estate agent's and that a man had come in and held a gun to his head. His voice told me he was in a

459

state of panic and I asked him to come down to our Beech Street shelter. When he arrived I took him into one of the small rooms there and one of the volunteers made him a pot of tea. I found it very difficult to get anything out of the man who appeared to be in his mid-twenties. He was totally out of his mind and his eyes were moving the whole time like a trapped animal's looking for a way of escape. The tea was poured out but left untouched on the table. I spent hours trying to calm him and draw him out of the state of shock he was in, but it wasn't easy. I didn't ask him about the ordeal but talked about things in general, hoping to ease the pressure on his mind. Where did he live? Were his family close? What was the weather like outside?

I kept on until he suddenly looked at me as though seeing me for the first time. Then I found out why he was in such a deep state of shock. He worked with a friend in the estate agent's. His friend, who I was led to believe owned the business, had slipped out for half an hour and as there were no customers the young man began to read a magazine. The next thing he knew cold steel was being pressed to his temple. He looked up to see a man with his face half-covered by a scarf, and was told that if he stayed quiet and showed the man where the money was kept then he wouldn't be hurt. The victim froze with fear and made no effort to move or speak, just nodded to a drawer behind the desk he was sitting at. There wasn't much money in it as the office had only been open a short time and business hadn't taken off yet. So the robber found little to steal, and his temper was such that if they hadn't been on a main road, with people passing all the time, he would undoubtedly have vented his anger on the young victim. As it was he fled with very little cash, but leaving behind a broken man who would be haunted by the ordeal for years.

I coaxed him into staying the night at the shelter because he wasn't fit to be left alone, and a comfortable bed was made up for him. But when I arrived the next morning I was told he had left very early after refusing breakfast, and one of the staff who had tried to persuade him to stay said he seemed disturbed and wouldn't leave his address and phone number. I've never heard from him since and I didn't try to contact him because I believed if he needed help he would ask.

* * *

I would not have been able to do everything I have without the help of Lorna Cooper, who had taken early retirement from her paid job. She was still doing our book-keeping, and attended to the staff's wage slips and income tax. She was also a great help to me with answering letters and making sure our filing system was kept up-to-date. She did all this willingly, several days a week, on a purely voluntary basis except for the few pounds she received to help with her petrol expenses. Every morning except at weekends which I now kept strictly for my family I called in to McCarthy Lodge to visit the residents. Walking through the door of the Lodge was always an uplifting experience. The place was like a palace and there was always laughter in the air. I was indeed lucky with the staff there who, under the guidance of Bernice Styles, had made it into a home from home for residents who had not known such happiness for a long time. They were warm, well-fed, cared for, and above all they were safe. No longer afraid of a sound in the night, or looking over their shoulders when they went to the shops. And this was how it should be— it was what they deserved and what they should have been able to take for granted.

It was on one of my visits to McCarthy Lodge that I received a phone call to say one of the charity's best friends and supporters, Miss Mann, was in hospital suffering from cancer. The call came from a nun, Sister Winifred, who was very close to Miss Mann. She told me I could visit her in hospital if I wished. I went the same afternoon and was shocked that there could be such a change in a person in a very short time. Although she was smiling and put a good face on, it was obvious she wasn't a well lady and it saddened me. When I rang the hospital a few days later, it was to be told Miss Mann had been transferred to the Royal Liverpool Hospital. I drove down right away, and after asking several people for directions, found the side ward Miss Mann was in. Sister Winifred was with her, but it was clear the very sick woman didn't want anyone else there so I left with tears rolling down my cheeks. Ten days later I was going with Sister Winifred to Miss Mann's funeral. She had been very good to our organization and I looked on her as a friend, but the best friend she had was Sister Winifred who cared for her in the last painful weeks of her life.

*　　　*　　　*

I still had various people from the City Council

after me regarding work they wanted doing on the Beech Street shelter. The Planning Department, architects, surveyors and Social Services were only doing their job and were never less than respectful. I understood that when a house is used for multiple occupancy one should comply with legislation regarding the safety of residents, but I couldn't pick money off trees. We had complied with McCarthy Lodge, and now must bring Beech Street up to standard. I contacted an architect and the builder we had had for McCarthy Lodge, and asked for an estimate for a complete refurbishment to comply with all the demands of Social Services. I knew the cost would be sky-high because the houses were much larger than in Deane Road, and I didn't relish the thought of another flat out fund-raising campaign. But the work was badly needed so we could take advantage of the extra bedrooms that would be created. Before I tackled the job I had a holiday due with Tony and Philip. And, believe me, I was ready for a break and some time with my husband. We may have been married for forty years but the romance and sparkle was still there. So the week we were going to spend in a cottage on the side of a mountain in Wales was just what the doctor ordered.

It was good that I came back refreshed from our holiday, otherwise I probably would have run a mile when I saw that the approximate costing for the refurbishment of numbers five and seven Beech Street was £200,000. I couldn't hope to raise that much on my own, I needed help. So I rang Arthur Johnson at the *Echo* office and asked if he would see me. We arranged an interview and I took along the file with the estimates in. After going through

463

the papers, Arthur agreed to help us raise awareness of the need for cash and to give us publicity. I left his office feeling much happier and more sure of tackling the huge undertaking I was letting myself in for. The architect and builder knew we had nowhere near the amount needed, but they agreed to start buying materials with the cash we had in the bank, and would slow down if funds were slow in coming in. Then I heard from Miss Mann's solicitors saying Victims of Violence was one of the beneficiaries in her will, and when they'd sorted her affairs out they would be sending a cheque which, the caller said, would be quite substantial and a great help in the fine work we were doing. It was several weeks before the money started coming through from the solicitors, but it totalled over £30,000 and considerably lightened the load on my shoulders. I was wishing she was there to thank with a big hug and kiss. It was such a help at a time when I really needed help. Little did I realize that there were many headaches in store for me.

Twelve months after the work began on the property we had now named Mann Lodge the houses still looked like a bomb-site. I had handed over £125,000 so far and couldn't see where it had gone. Tony came down with me one day, and as he walked from room to room, stepping over debris and shaking his head, he said from what he could see it would take another twelve months to finish and another £125,000. That finally decided me to put my foot down, and let everyone involved in the project know that dealing with a woman wasn't such a pushover. So I had row after row until the work started to take shape properly and I could see, now the two houses had been knocked into one, that it was going to be a beautiful property, a place Miss Mann would be proud to put her name to. But my problems over raising money, and worry over the work being up to standard, were far from over. I had raised, with help from the *Echo*, businesses, charitable trusts, clubs, shops, pubs, and my generous friends, the £200,000 which had been the original quote. But the house wasn't yet finished and I needed to raise more money. Another £50,000 I was told. The very thought made me feel weary and tired. For eighteen years I seem to have walked around with my hand out. It's a wonder people didn't turn tail and run when they saw me coming. We had applied to the Lottery for a grant but were turned down. It made me quite angry because I'd read of dance groups, play groups and boy bands, historical sites, theatres and opera houses, all being given huge amounts of money. Unfortunately, victims of crime are not a glamorous cause, there was obviously no publicity to be had from them. All I could do was sigh and wonder once again at the cock-eyed world we were living in.

*　　†　　*

After my husband retired, I would ring him every afternoon from one of the shelters to tell him where I was and how soon I would be on my way home. It was on the afternoon of 20 September 1994 that I made the phone call which changed my life forever. As soon as Tony answered the phone I knew something was wrong, and he said he had sent for the doctor because he was having very bad pains in his chest and thought it was a heart attack. It was half an hour since he'd rung and the doctor still hadn't come.

I just froze with fear. What was I doing here, twenty-five miles away from home, when my husband was having a heart attack? It would take me at least an hour to get there, I couldn't leave him on his own until then. So I rang my eldest sister, Edna, and she and her husband rushed round to find Tony doubled up with pain. Still the doctor hadn't come, so my sister rang for an ambulance. By the time I arrived, shaking with fright, Tony had been taken to hospital and my brother-in-law, Griff, had stayed until I got there to tell me what had happened. He said it didn't look very good because the paramedics had worked on Tony for twenty minutes in the ambulance before taking him to hospital. He said he would wait there to let Philip in, but that I should hurry to the hospital.

My nerves were shattered as I drove the short distance. To this day I don't remember parking the car and running to the Accident and Emergency Unit where Tony had been taken. I was met by a woman doctor who stopped me on the way in and explained that it had been a massive attack and they were giving Tony the strongest drugs possible. I could tell she was trying to warn me, to prepare me for the worst, but I pushed aside the warning because I couldn't live with it.

They wouldn't let me stay long that day, but I was back the next morning, and again in the afternoon. Tony was putting a brave face on and was very talkative, too talkative to be normal. Later that night I couldn't settle to get undressed for bed,

466

so I rang the hospital. The nurse who answered sounded breathless. She told me they were working on my husband now, and I should get down straight away. I rang my sister and her husband who said they would come with me, then I rang my son Paul. But when we got to the hospital we were too late, Tony had died. And part of me died with him.

* * *

It was a month before I could face going back to work. I rang Bernice first to ask if she would mention to the staff that I would be grateful if they wouldn't sympathize or mention Tony's name because the wound was still too new and I wouldn't be able to cope. All my friends and colleagues had been ringing constantly to encourage and support me, and I was grateful for that even though each call brought tears. My son Paul had taken time off work when Tony died, and it was he who filled in all the necessary forms and arranged the funeral, and also a buffet at a local hotel for friends and the men my husband had worked with for thirty years. I was numb with grief but knew I couldn't shut myself away for ever, so after a month away from the charity I returned to work. Lorna and Bernice had kept everything running smoothly and it wasn't long before I was back into my routine and as busy as ever.

Four months later I was just about coming to terms with the loss of my husband when I went to see my doctor for a routine examination and was told I had a breast tumour. I was knocked for six, and for the first time in my life felt vulnerable because Tony's shoulder wasn't there for me to cry

467

on. When Lady Butlin rang to see how I was, I told her I was feeling very apprehensive about the result of the biopsy.

'You've had too much worry about Mann Lodge,' she said. 'You could do without that right now.' When I didn't answer, she asked, 'How much do you need to raise to finish the job completely?'

I sighed. 'About forty thousand.'

'Well, I want you to forget about it—put it out of your mind. I'll raise the money for you, so that will be one worry less for you.'

'You can't do that!' I said. 'Our organization has had more than enough off you over the years.'

'Joan, I'll get it for you. I have someone I can ask for a donation towards it, just give me until the weekend.'

The following morning I received a letter asking me to go to the hospital that day to see the specialist. When I got there I was told they would like to admit me the following week for a mastectomy. The arrangements were made without me showing my true feelings, but they surfaced when I got home. Up until the day before Tony died, I had led a charmed life with wonderful, loving parents, two sisters and a brother, a warm happy life full of laughter and happiness. And when I met and married Tony, life continued to be wonderful. Now, it seemed, I was to get all my heartaches and troubles in quick succession. But crying wouldn't help, I should be grateful for all the good times. So I put a smile on my face and drove to McCarthy Lodge.

On the Friday morning I opened my post to find two cheques for £20,000 each, one from Lady Butlin's Trust, and one from her stepson Bobby

Butlin's Trust. For the first time in months I felt my spirits rise, and told myself I was very lucky to have such wonderful friends and should stop feeling sorry for myself. I handed the cheques over to Lorna who paid them into the bank before making a cheque out to the architect for £40,000. It was handed over with strict instructions that I wanted Mann Lodge completed by the time I came out of hospital.

*   *   *

When Mann Lodge opened in the summer of 1995, all the guests invited were amazed at how beautiful the place was. The Victorians knew how to build houses of distinction and elegance, and they built them to last. The exterior was striking and a fitting introduction to the fine rooms inside. It had been hard work for me and my colleagues, getting the furniture together and adding homely touches to the large rooms with their wide windows and high ceilings. As usual the people of Merseyside had played a huge part in making it all possible. There was praise for the project coming from left, right and centre, and I was so proud I felt I was walking on air.

But I knew the time had come to train someone to take over if, or when, I left. Someone needed to know how to approach victims and which avenues they must go down to find help for them. They had to get to know all my contacts in the media, in the shops, clubs and pubs, who had supported the charity from the start. And most of all they must be outgoing, willing to speak at meetings and raise funds, all with a smile on their face. But at least

469

they wouldn't be starting from scratch, like I did, because I'd make sure they knew my job inside out. I had enjoyed the last nineteen years, had met the most marvellous people and been lucky enough to have been able to help so many. Surely there must be someone, somewhere, who felt as I did?

I had made an appointment to meet a victim at Mann Lodge on the Monday morning, and I got there early so I could discuss with Lorna the need to find someone who would eventually take over from me.

'You'll never find anyone to take over from you, Joan, and everyone I've spoken to says the same thing. You *are* Victims of Violence, everyone associates you with it. For all these years it's you who have given the charity its high profile and kept it in the public eye. No one else will put in the hours and the work that you do, without a wage. And they'd want a good wage, too!' Lorna shook her head. 'You've been doing it for nearly twenty years, you know everyone and everyone on Merseyside knows you.'

'I still think we need someone else. It would be irresponsible not to think about it. I can't guarantee to be doing the job in ten years' time, and we could afford to pay someone a wage, even if it's not high. Are you agreeable to that?'

Lorna nodded, but her face told me she wasn't convinced.

We were beginning to get referrals from Police Domestic Violence Units who were eager to find a safe refuge for women who were victims of domestic violence and their children. This type of crime was one we had not really been involved with, but we couldn't refuse to take in women who

470

were being battered by violent husbands while their terrified children looked on. Within ten days we had five mothers and ten children in Mann Lodge. Some of the tales of violence were horrific, the most wicked to my mind being the case of a young mother being forced to lie flat on the floor while her husband pointed a gun between her legs and the children screamed in fear. What sort of effect would this have on a child's mind as it grew older?

I was well aware from speaking to someone who ran a women's refuge that a violent husband often found out where his wife and children were being sheltered, and would come around in a drunken rage and cause trouble. So it was important to have tight security, especially at night. A local businessman had kindly donated, and installed, an outside camera for us, so if there was a knock on the door, all the staff had to do was turn the television to a special station and they could see who was outside. However, we couldn't expect female staff to cope with drunken, violent men, so we took two men on to our staff. We could ill afford to pay their wages, which were the minimum allowed, as we were only getting housing benefit for the adult residents which barely covered the outgoings of the house. But we didn't really have any choice. We had to protect the women and children in our care. And the two men, Kevin and Paul, were a real bonus to the house. They had agreed to share the hours between them, and showed interest in their work, got on well with the residents and children, and did odd jobs in the house and gardens. It was heart-warming to see the change in the children after they'd been with us a few days. They'd been very withdrawn when they came, hiding behind their mother's skirts and afraid of the least sound. They had only known shouting and violence, and didn't trust people who were being kind to them. But after a short time in Mann Lodge we could see smiles on young faces who had never known peace, and it was a joy to hear them laughing. While Mann Lodge was catering for victims of domestic violence, McCarthy Lodge was reserved for the elderly. Both shelters were run by caring staff and were always warm and welcoming.

I was given a lovely surprise one day when I was told I'd been nominated as Lancashire Woman of the Year by Soroptimist International. It was a great honour and I was really proud when I was presented with a beautiful crystal bowl at the dinner held to mark the occasion. It was one of the highlights of my life. Close on the heels of that, I was chosen as one of Liverpool's Mersey Marvels for the second time, and over the years have twice been presented with certificates for Citizen of the Year by Chief Constable Kenneth Oxford. I am proud of all the recognition I've received, but I didn't start Victims of Violence for personal glory, I started it because I didn't like what was happening in our society—especially to the elderly and most vulnerable. And in my own small way I did what I could to make public the injustices suffered.

*　　*　　*

It was two weeks before Christmas and we had twenty-two children in Mann Lodge. The mothers had decorated the rooms and put up a Christmas tree, and I knew they would do their best to buy their children toys. But because these children were special, having suffered from their violent fathers, I wanted them to have a really good Christmas, like most other children in the country would be having. So once again I rang the *Echo* and asked if they would appeal to their readers. There was a full-page spread in the next night's edition and the response was immediate. My daughter-in-law and I made several calls, and even though I'm used to the generosity of Merseysiders, I was stunned by the number and the quality of the toys they donated. One club in Toxteth donated five hundred pounds-worth of new toys and I couldn't thank the manager enough. He loaded them into the boot of my car and filled the back seat with them. Driving back to Mann Lodge, we were so delighted we couldn't wipe the smiles off our faces. When we got to the Lodge it was to find people had been passing presents in at the door, and boxes of chocolates and biscuits. There was another call to make, so after a cup of tea we set off to a residential home where another load of beautiful new toys awaited us. Altogether there must have been well over twelve hundred pounds-worth of toys, and I was overwhelmed. I would have loved the readers of the *Echo*, who had been so generous, to have seen the happiness they'd put on the faces of those children.

*   *   *

Christmas was two weeks behind us when Lorna and I were sitting in the office and I once again brought up the subject of employing someone to take over from me. I also had Lorna in mind, because she'd started off fifteen years earlier as a volunteer working a couple of hours one evening a week. Now, she was still a volunteer but working practically a full week. The residents were changing constantly because some of the victims couldn't stay away from their husbands, even though they knew they were going back to violence. I had no pity for them, they were old enough to know what they were doing, but I did have for the poor children who were being pushed from pillar to post and would never know what a normal loving home was. The turnover of residents meant a lot of extra paperwork and form-filling, this on top of the new victims of crime we were seeing daily. Without Lorna and Bernice I would have been lost.

'I've been giving very serious thought to finding a replacement, Lorna, I really can't carry on much longer at the rate I've been going for the last twenty years, it's too much for me. And I'm sure you'd be glad to have less on your plate.'

She nodded. 'It has been getting increasingly busy with so many women and children here, and I would like a break. I'll stay on as long as you need me, but it would be nice if we both had less to do. So I'll wish you luck in trying to find a suitable replacement—you'll certainly need it.'

Over the next eighteen months Lorna's doubts proved to be well-founded, unfortunately, because the three people we hired for a trial period all turned out to be unsuitable. There wasn't the compassion, the commitment or the dedication in them which was so essential when dealing with victims. I could not see any of them putting their arm around an elderly victim and hugging them.

And, as a friend said to me, each one lacked that fire in the belly so necessary when fighting for the rights of a victim or fund-raising.

I lay in bed one night and went over everything in my head. It had taken me twenty-one years to acquire the respect the charity now had, and I would prefer to close it down completely than pass it over to someone who just wanted a job out of it. The caring face of Victims of Violence would be changed forever, and I couldn't bring myself to let that happen. I couldn't let someone pull down what my colleagues and I had built up. So next morning I told Lorna and Bernie that I wanted to wind the charity down. Mann Lodge would be no problem, we could stop taking in new victims and refer them to other shelters, just carry on until the residents there now were offered accommodation from the Council or went back to their husbands. McCarthy Lodge would stay as it was for the time being, but no new residents would be admitted on a permanent basis.

It was 2001 before the shelters were closed. McCarthy Lodge was returned to the McCarthy Foundation, and Mann Lodge was sold, fully furnished but in need of decoration. I was still visiting victims and giving out donations while Lorna dealt with the outstanding Criminal Injuries Compensation claims. I had rung the Charity Commission to say the charity was closing down and was told any money we had must go to a charity doing the same work as Victims of Violence. So we chose Victims of Crime Trust, who were very grateful to be told there would be a substantial donation coming their way. It was 2002 before all outstanding debts were paid and the

475

accounts cleared by the Charity Commission. The remaining money was sent to the Victims of Crime Trust who would use it as we would have used it, to help victims of crime.

Victims of Violence lasted twenty-six years, a long time and a large slice of my life. It was only with considerable sadness I let go, but I could not bring myself to pass the charity over to someone who would change it completely. I have been told I'm old-fashioned because charity is big business now, but I don't think it's a real charity if most of the money raised from the public goes out in high wages. When anyone tells me they are a charity worker, I always like to think they do things from the heart, not for money. I can promise those generous people who donated so willingly to Victims of Violence that all the money they donated went to helping people, which is what they wanted.

I wouldn't change any part of the last twenty-six years for anything because I have made some wonderful friends, and look back with affection on the first elderly victims I met, Ethel, Albert, Sally, Maggie, Bessie, Jimmy, Fred, Nellie, May and Dolly, and so many more who were courageous and lovable. Some of them made their home with us, and when they were ill were cared for as though they were part of one big family. When they died, they were buried with dignity and the tears shed by the staff were genuine. I can't remember all the victims I've met because there were about twelve thousand in all, but I was glad to be of help to them. In that time I raised over £2 million, which I could not have done without the kindness, compassion and generosity of ordinary people who

476

care about the society they live in. They have my gratitude and my respect.

I still feel the sadness, frustration and anger I felt all those years ago when I met the first victim. I thought then, and God knows I shouted it loud enough, that unless someone had the sense, and the guts, to punish anyone who broke the law we would eventually become a lawless society. In 2002 there were over 5.2 million reported crimes so, sadly, time has proved me right.